PRACTICAL LIBERATORS
———————

CIVIL WAR AMERICA

*Peter S. Carmichael, Caroline E. Janney,
and Aaron Sheehan-Dean, editors*

This landmark series interprets broadly the history and culture of the Civil War era through the long nineteenth century and beyond. Drawing on diverse approaches and methods, the series publishes historical works that explore all aspects of the war, biographies of leading commanders, and tactical and campaign studies, along with select editions of primary sources. Together, these books shed new light on an era that remains central to our understanding of American and world history.

PRACTICAL
LIBERATORS

Union Officers in the Western Theater
during the Civil War

KRISTOPHER A. TETERS

THE UNIVERSITY OF NORTH CAROLINA PRESS

Chapel Hill

This book was published with the assistance of the
Authors Fund of the University of North Carolina Press.

© 2018 The University of North Carolina Press

All rights reserved

Designed by Jamison Cockerham
Set in Arno, Cutright, and Trade Gothic Next
by codeMantra

The University of North Carolina Press has been a member
of the Green Press Initiative since 2003.

Cover illustrations: *top left,* William T. Sherman; *top right,* Ulysses S. Grant; *bottom,*
Contrabands accompanying the line of Sherman's march through Georgia (from *Frank
Leslie's Illustrated Newspaper,* March 18, 1865). All courtesy of the Library of Congress.

LIBRARY OF CONGRESS CATALOGING-IN-PUBLICATION DATA
Names: Teters, Kristopher A., author.
Title: Practical liberators : Union officers in the western
theater during the Civil War / Kristopher A. Teters.
Other titles: Civil War America (Series)
Description: Chapel Hill : University of North Carolina Press, [2018] |
Series: Civil War America | Includes bibliographical references and index.
Identifiers: LCCN 2017050242| ISBN 9781469638867 (cloth : alk. paper) |
ISBN 9781469668826 (pbk : alk. paper) | ISBN 9781469638874 (ebook)
Subjects: LCSH: United States. Army—History—Civil War, 1861–1865. | United
States. Army—Officers—Attitudes. | Slaves—Emancipation—Government
policy—Southwest, Old. | Southwest, Old—History—Civil War, 1861–1865—
Campaigns. | United States—History—Civil War, 1861–1865—Campaigns.
Classification: LCC E491 .T46 2018 | DDC 973.7/3—dc23 LC record
available at https://lccn.loc.gov/2017050242

To my parents, for all their love and support.

Without them none of this would have been possible.

———————————

CONTENTS

Introduction   Looking for Chamberlain 1

1   The Union Army's Struggle over the
     Limits of Confiscation in the West 8

2   An Emancipationist Turn of Policy 36

3   Union Officers and the Intense Debate over
     Emancipation and Black Troops 60

4   Officers, Servants, and Race 83

5   A Practical Army of Liberation: How the Union
     Army Carried Out Emancipation in the West 106

6   William T. Sherman and His Officers:
     The Reluctant Emancipators 133

Conclusion   How Transformative Was the Civil War? 153

     Acknowledgments 159

     Notes on Methodology 163

     Notes 167

     Bibliography 197

     Index 217

PRACTICAL LIBERATORS

INTRODUCTION

Looking for Chamberlain

My interest in the American Civil War dates back to a Sunday afternoon in the fall of 1993. On that day, I saw the movie *Gettysburg* and was hooked. Everything about the movie captivated me, from Brig. Gen. John Buford's gallant stand on the first day of the battle to Maj. Gen. George Pickett's famous charge on the last day. But like so many other fans of the movie, I was particularly fascinated with the character of Col. Joshua L. Chamberlain. For me, Chamberlain, who was portrayed by Jeff Daniels, embodied the heroism of Civil War soldiers. I was deeply moved by the famous scene where Chamberlain leads his Twentieth Maine in a desperate bayonet charge to save the Union army's flank on Little Round Top. The fact that Chamberlain had been a college professor before the war added to my fascination. After seeing the movie several times, I also came to admire Chamberlain's idealistic views about the Union war effort. There was one scene specifically that I watched repeatedly. It depicted Chamberlain giving a speech about the meaning of the Union's struggle to a group of recalcitrant soldiers from the Second Maine. During the speech Chamberlain waxed eloquent about the Union army's special purpose to free the slaves: "This is a different kind of army. If you look back through history, you will see men fighting for pay, for women, for some other kind of loot.... But we are here for something new. This has not happened much in the history of the world. We are an army out to set other men free. America should be free ground, all of it, not divided by a line between slave state and free." Chamberlain's words inspired me and shaped my first impressions of the attitudes of Union soldiers toward slavery.[1]

When I decided to look at the attitudes of western Union officers toward emancipation for this project, I understood that all of them would not be, like Chamberlain, idealistic and moralistic about ending slavery. In fact, I suspected that many of them would have expressed intense opposition to freeing the slaves. But I was hoping to find that at least a significant portion had embraced emancipation for primarily moral reasons. I really wanted to discover that Chamberlain's sentiments were fairly widespread in the army. What I actually found instead was that pragmatism, far more than morality, motivated western officers to support emancipation. They viewed it primarily as a necessary military measure that would help the Union, hurt the Confederacy, and end the war. There were a few officers who embraced emancipation for more moral reasons, but they were greatly outnumbered by their practical comrades.

Emancipation was very controversial among western theater officers. When the Preliminary Emancipation Proclamation was issued in September 1862, a significant number of officers vehemently opposed it, and this strong opposition continued at least through the first half of 1863. Emancipation produced intense divisions; only later in the war did some officers who at first opposed emancipation come around to support it. Their conversion grew out of practical considerations. Emancipation was accepted by many officers only because it would help them achieve their primary goal of saving the Union.

While officers came to accept emancipation as a useful instrument to win the war, their racial attitudes changed very little. From beginning to end, they expressed the deep racial prejudices of their era regarding black people as vastly inferior to white people. In fact, some of them went as far as to abuse and mistreat black people. Many of these officers were midwesterners who reflected their region's racial animus. Even at the end of the war, hardly any of them voiced support for racial equality or even black voting rights. In short, the war was not a revolutionary experience for these officers when it came to race. At times, they did express more favorable views of individual black men and women, such as their servants, but their overall perceptions of the black race remained decidedly negative.

In conjunction with attitudes, this study examines how western officers—both high-ranking and junior—carried out emancipation in the field. Rather than dwelling on the exceptions and anomalies, it focuses on the general patterns and characteristics of this policy. What emerges is a very complex story but one with definite patterns.

During the war's first fifteen months the army's policies toward fugitive slaves were inconsistent. While some officers barred slaves altogether from their lines, others took in significant numbers of "contrabands." At this early stage of the conflict, an officer's individual attitudes toward slavery, particularly if that officer was a commander, significantly influenced army policy. The administration in Washington offered very little definitive policy on this subject during this time, and thus commanders were largely left to their own devices on how to deal with slaves. This would not be the case as the war progressed. Differences in policy often caused intense conflict between officers, especially between high-ranking officers and their subordinates. These conflicts at times put great strains on the army chain of command. Recalcitrant junior officers drew the intense anger of their commanders, and some of these officers even found themselves under arrest. Certainly, these arguments over policy drained the time and energy of officers trying to win a war, but they also affected the morale of officers and their men. Officers who resigned or threatened to resign over slavery policy were clearly expressing severe disenchantment. Additionally, the looming or actual arrest of an officer, especially if that officer was the leader of a regiment, would affect both the officer's and his men's effectiveness as soldiers. While these conflicts never disrupted the overall Union war effort, or even significantly undermined a campaign, they did at times prove problematic for the discipline and cohesion of the army.

When the Second Confiscation Act, which allowed for the confiscation of slaves belonging to rebels, went into effect in July 1862, army policy became much more consistent and emancipationist. In all the major armies in the western theater, officers confiscated slaves and employed them in the service in such capacities as teamsters, laborers, or cooks. The conflict among officers largely vanished except in the politically sensitive border states of Kentucky and Missouri, where there were large populations of slaveholding Unionists. There, the conflicts approached the brink of violence as army units fought between themselves and with Southern civilians over slavery. In both states, Union officers and soldiers used weapons to threaten and intimidate each other. Kentucky was especially problematic as Union soldiers found themselves defending slaves at the point of the bayonet against angry citizens, and Union officers were sued over slaves they had confiscated. These conflicts were very prominent, and damaging at times, in the Union Army of Kentucky. But regardless of all this bitter fighting in the Border South, the Union army had started to become a powerful agent of liberation in the latter half of 1862.

When the final Emancipation Proclamation was issued on January 1, 1863, the army became a full-fledged liberator. During the second half of the war western armies advanced deep into the Confederacy and freed thousands and thousands of slaves. Officers, however, carried out emancipation primarily for the army's benefit. Their top priority was to free slaves so they could help the army as pioneers, laborers, servants, and soldiers. This would free up white soldiers for what was deemed more important work. With these very practical goals in mind, the army focused on liberating able-bodied male slaves.

The women, children, and elderly who came into Union lines were viewed as a military burden and disposed of as quickly as possible, generally in contraband camps or on plantations working for wages. More than anything else, then, the army proved to be practical liberators. Emancipation policy thus reflected the pragmatic attitudes of many Union officers. If they endorsed emancipation as a necessary and useful measure to win the war, then that was how they implemented it in the field. But as much as hard-nosed military considerations guided emancipation, the army was still freeing huge numbers of slaves and thoroughly wrecking the institution wherever it went. Slaves understood this fact well and consistently greeted Federal soldiers as their deliverers and helped the army in any way possible.

In examining both the policies and attitudes of western officers toward emancipation, this study challenges much of the current historical literature. Some historians stress that the Union army viewed emancipation as a moral issue and that the war from its outset was a struggle to abolish slavery. This book demonstrates that this was far from the truth. Union officers were committed to winning the war and saving the Union, and emancipation proved a practical policy to accomplish these goals. At the war's beginning, Union officers by and large did not yet embrace emancipation because its military necessity was not evident. Many supported the policy only after its necessity became an inescapable conclusion for them.

The practical bent of the Union army becomes even clearer when looking at the process of emancipation on the ground. For the most part, historians have ignored how the army carried out emancipation in the West. There are only a few works that deal with the subject in any depth, and much of that scholarship focuses on the army's plantation-labor policies and does not extensively address how different commanders and their subordinates handled emancipation questions during active campaigns. It was during these campaigns that western Union officers proved willing to use slaves in any way that could help win the war. Emancipation thus came about in the crucible of war in which practical military considerations always trumped moral prerogatives. Failing to look at how emancipation happened in the field, some historians have reached dubious conclusions about the beliefs of the Union army and how emancipation actually unfolded.[2]

This project stresses the Union army's importance in the emancipation process. This is not in any way to slight the efforts made by slaves to gain their own freedom. Certainly, slaves fled plantations and farms and sometimes traveled long distances to reach Union lines. But there was a reason they were fleeing to the army. They understood that if they reached Federal lines they would find freedom. The army was the primary instrument by which emancipation became a reality on the ground. As the army moved south, freedom advanced along with it, and more and more slaves found a refuge. This makes the army's emancipation policies particularly important for understanding how and why slavery came to an end.[3]

And the massive western theater is the ideal location for examining emancipation policy. As a whole, the western theater primarily consisted of the region between the Appalachian Mountains and the Mississippi River. It included the states of Alabama, Mississippi, Georgia, Tennessee, and Kentucky. Additionally, it contained parts of Louisiana and Florida along the Gulf coast. When the western armies of Maj. Gen. William T. Sherman marched into the Carolinas in 1865, North and South Carolina became part of the theater too. This work also contains a brief discussion of the occupation of Helena, Arkansas, which was right on the edge of the western theater and important for emancipation policy. Moreover, the study extensively deals with the state of Missouri, which is usually classified as part of the trans-Mississippi theater. There are good reasons for the inclusion of Missouri as part of the western theater here. First, Missouri was where many of the western armies that invaded Tennessee and eventually penetrated deeper south began their campaigns. More important, what happened in Missouri was critical in the formation of early army policy regarding slavery in the West. Both Maj. Gen. John C. Fremont's proclamation of emancipation and Maj. Gen. Henry Halleck's very influential General Orders No. 3, which banned slaves from Union lines, were issued in Missouri. The huge western theater contrasted markedly with the eastern theater, which was dominated by just the state of Virginia. The western theater can be separated into multiple subregions, among them the Upper South and the Lower South. These two regions were distinct in their relationship to slavery and their political attitudes.[4]

Tennessee, Arkansas, North Carolina, Kentucky, and Missouri, for the purposes of this study, make up the Upper South. In this region, there were far fewer slaves than in the Lower South. In 1860, these states collectively contained a little over 1 million slaves, but this only accounted for about 33 percent of the total number of slaves in the whole theater of operations. Kentucky and Missouri between them only had 340,414 slaves, which was close to 11 percent of the total. To further put these numbers in perspective, the whole South had almost 4 million slaves at the outbreak of war. With fewer slaves, these Upper South states were not eager to secede like the Lower South. Tennessee, Arkansas, and North Carolina seceded only after the firing on Fort Sumter and Lincoln's call for troops, and Kentucky and Missouri never did. Unionism in Kentucky and Missouri remained strong for many reasons, including their economic ties to the North, less dependence on slavery, and more moderate politics, which still featured a robust two-party system. But most citizens in these loyal border states did not want the emancipation of the slaves, and the president could absolutely not afford to alienate the border state Unionists. As a result, Lincoln and Union army officers had to be very careful when dealing with slaves there. It was in Kentucky and Missouri, more than any other place in the western theater, that geography mattered when it came to the development and evolution of slavery policy.[5]

Far different from the Upper South, particularly the border states, was the Lower South. The Lower South was where slavery was concentrated and where cotton was king. By 1860, the major cotton belt of the South ran through Georgia, Alabama, Mississippi, and Louisiana, and slavery was dominant across this very fertile region. Indeed, the Lower South states comprised about 67 percent of the slaves in the western theater. Just the states of Alabama, Mississippi, and Georgia together contained significantly more slaves than the entire Upper South in the West, about 275,000 more. Any one of these states had many more slaves than the border states of Kentucky and Missouri combined. With their larger numbers of slaves, Lower South states were quick to leave the Union, seceding shortly after Lincoln's election. In the end, the Lower South was the area where the Union army would free the most slaves and smash the heart of the South's slave-based economy.[6]

This is the primary reason why looking at the western theater is so important for telling the emancipation story. Put simply, most of the South's slaves resided there. Virginia, which was the primary state in the eastern theater, contained only 490,865 slaves in 1860. This number represented about 15 percent of the number of slaves in the West. So truly understanding the process of emancipation on the ground requires a systematic look at policies in the western theater. The theater is ideal for examining emancipation policy for several additional reasons. First, examining the West allows for the comparison of policies across various armies. Unlike the eastern theater, which was dominated by the Union Army of the Potomac's campaigns in Virginia, the western theater encompassed several different armies operating across a vast territory. Moreover, since the West comprised such a huge geographic expanse, Union armies were constantly entering areas where slavery had not yet been touched. This affords the opportunity to see how much the army's presence mattered in the destruction of slavery. Finally, certain campaigns in the West, such as Maj. Gen. Ulysses S. Grant's Vicksburg campaign and Maj. Gen. William T. Sherman's marches through Georgia and the Carolinas, were notable for their length and deep penetration into slave country. Thus the diversity and extent of the western theater permits a thorough examination of how officers balanced the demands of military operations and emancipation.[7]

The story that emerges in the following pages is one of primarily practical officers carrying out a practical emancipation policy. These officers were very different from the idealistic Col. Joshua L. Chamberlain, who had inspired me in my youth. At times, it disappointed me that they did not view emancipation as more of a moral prerogative. But, in the end, we cannot make history into what we desire.

CHAPTER ONE

The Union Army's Struggle over the Limits of Confiscation in the West

When the Civil War began, Union armies did not set out to liberate slaves, and President Abraham Lincoln had made it clear that he did not intend to interfere with the South's slave property. But almost the instant Union armies went into the field, they were confronted with slaves seeking refuge in their lines. This was particularly true in the war's western theater, where armies very quickly made significant advances into Confederate territory. From the beginning of the war to the summer of 1862, officers in the West adopted policies toward fugitive slaves that ranged from barring them altogether from their lines to aggressively liberating them. These policies could be labeled as follows: very conservative, moderately conservative, not conservative, and radical.

Officers who were very conservative prohibited all slaves from entering Union camps with no exceptions. Those that were moderately conservative allowed a very limited number of slaves into camp. These slaves had typically been employed by the Confederacy or had helped the Union army in some way. By contrast, commanders who were not conservative were willing to confiscate and harbor any slaves that belonged to rebels. Radical officers went even further than this by liberating all slaves, whether they were the property of a Unionist or rebel.

These diverse policies caused enormous conflict among officers. Top commanders in the West adopted generally very conservative or moderately conservative approaches in dealing with fugitive slaves. In August 1861, Congress offered some guidance on the issue with the First Confiscation Act, which allowed Union armies to confiscate any slaves the Confederacy used in the service of the rebellion. Not surprisingly, the act's limited scope led to minimal confiscation or none at all by top officers. During their movements into Kentucky and Tennessee, Generals Henry Halleck and Don Carlos Buell cared little about emancipation and sought for the most part to keep slaves out of their camps. In Louisiana, Maj. Gen. Benjamin Butler went beyond this approach by employing slaves seized from rebels even as he sought to protect the property of Louisiana Unionists. Although some of the subordinate officers under these commanders maintained this generally conservative approach toward slavery, others challenged them with more emancipationist policies. Sometimes, these challenges came from general officers, but at other times, colonels, or even company officers, pushed the issue. So the policy that evolved on the ground during this initial phase of the war was at once uneven, contested, and inconsistent. Officers' motives for these policies were diverse and oftentimes overlapped. They acted out of personal beliefs, military necessity, and obedience to the law and the orders of their superiors. When it came to shaping policy, during this early phase of the war, officers' opinions on slavery mattered more than they would later.

A major exception to the conservative tendencies of army commanders regarding slavery was Maj. Gen. John C. Fremont. Fremont—head of the Western Department—was best known as a western adventurer and as the 1856 Republican nominee for president but had significant military experience with the army topographical engineers and helped conquer California during the Mexican War. Nevertheless, he proved inept as a Civil War general. Losing large amounts of territory to Confederate forces in Missouri and facing strong guerrilla activity in the state, Fremont issued what proved to be a politically explosive proclamation. On August 30, 1861, he declared martial law in Missouri, implemented harsh measures to deal with guerrilla activity, and declared free any slaves belonging to rebels. This last provision drew the ire of Lincoln, who eventually ordered him to change it to conform to the provisions of the First Confiscation Act. Keenly sensitive to the sentiments of the border states, Lincoln was not yet ready to push for emancipation.[1]

Lincoln had every reason to be cautious when dealing with Missouri and slavery. With its strong Unionist sentiment, the state had not seceded from the Union, but in 1861, a heavy majority of white Missourians wanted slavery preserved. Most Missourians identified with the Democratic Party before the war, particularly embracing its stances on limited government and personal liberty. As sectional tensions deepened, many Missouri residents were eager to avoid war, disavowing the extremists, as they saw them, in both the North and the South. In 1860, the state narrowly awarded its electoral votes to Northern Democrat Stephen Douglas with Constitutional Unionist John Bell finishing a close second. Together the two men garnered about 71 percent of Missouri's total vote. The candidates with more sectional views did not fare near as well. While Southern Democrat John C. Breckinridge, who captured much of the South, only received a little less than 19 percent of the vote, Republican Abraham Lincoln got a little over 10 percent of the vote, mostly coming from St. Louis. Missouri voters had clearly voiced their strong sentiment against sectionalism and secession. They would do so again in February 1861 when they overwhelmingly chose Unionist delegates for a convention to consider secession. But as much as white Missourians cherished the Union, they did not want to be coerced or interfered with by the federal government and the army. Once the war started and Federal forces invaded the state, Missourians were confronted with a hard choice about their allegiance. Many would have preferred to just remain neutral and stay out of the conflict, but this became virtually impossible. While some Missourians aligned themselves with the Confederacy, many more stayed loyal to the Union.[2]

Much of Missouri's Unionism was inextricably linked to protecting the institution of slavery. Slavery was not near as prominent in Missouri as it was in states further south. In 1860, slaves made up 9.7 percent of the state's total population and numbered 114,931. Far from being evenly distributed throughout Missouri, slaves were concentrated in the central region of the state along the Missouri River, where they were used to particularly raise tobacco and hemp. For the most part, Missouri's slaveholders owned a small number of slaves. In the central counties, where slavery was the most present, slaveholders owned on average 5.7 slaves. But despite the smaller number of slaves in the state, slavery profoundly shaped the politics and culture of Missouri. Critically, Missouri slaveholders and their interests exerted a dominant influence over the direction of state politics. Additionally, slavery produced an economic system and racial ideology that affected nearly all Missourians and gained the approbation of most. The last thing most white Missourians wanted was their social order undermined. This fact made Lincoln and many of his later commanders cautious when dealing with slavery in Missouri and in the rest of the border states. They absolutely did not want to drive these crucial Unionists into the arms of the Confederacy.[3]

At times, however, officers still pushed against slavery in the Border South. The president had squashed Fremont's bold move to attack slavery in Missouri, but officers there still carried out the First Confiscation Act and even in some cases moved beyond it. Brig. Gen. Justus McKinstry, provost marshal in St. Louis, delivered to Capt. Gordon Granger runaway slaves who had been put in the military prison. McKinstry told Granger to employ them "at police duty and such other labor as you may choose until they are reclaimed by their masters." But in order to reclaim them, their masters had to prove both their ownership and loyalty to the Union. Col. Grenville Dodge ordered Col. Nicholas Greusel of the Thirty-Sixth Illinois to seize the slaves of men who were fighting in the Confederate army. "I simply treated them [the slaves] as other property," Dodge recalled after the war. The order "was written innocently, but made a sensation I never dreamed of, and I have often since been quoted as one of the first to liberate and utilize the negro," he added.[4] In effect, Dodge was reaching beyond the limitations of the First Confiscation Act. Instead of just confiscating slaves that were somehow aiding Confederate armies, he was more generally seizing slaves owned by rebels, or at least from families with men in the army. His measures anticipated the Second Confiscation Act, which would allow for the seizure of all slaves belonging to rebels.

Officers did not confiscate slaves in Missouri just for the sake of it. Sometimes there were quite specific reasons. Capt. Robert Carnahan of the Third Illinois Cavalry took a "contraband" as a servant and even asked his wife if she wanted him to send one home. The use of former slaves as servants soon became a common practice among Union officers. But George Gordon of the Fourth Ohio Cavalry reported an even more compelling reason to confiscate a slave. A black man owned by a Confederate colonel was crossing the lines, giving the rebels information about the approach of Union forces. Gordon said he "was sent to Cairo, Ills., as his own man." But much depended on the dispositions and political views of the officers. Some were not willing to confiscate. According to Lt. Col. A. W. Gilbert of the Thirty-Ninth Ohio, Col. John Groesbeck had two black men who were trying to run off removed from a train. Gilbert suspected that the men's "ideas of the *abolitionists of the North* were somewhat modified upon learning we would not take them."[5]

As confiscation occurred in Missouri, Brig. Gen. William T. Sherman tried to prevent the practice from spreading to Kentucky. Sherman had been born in Ohio and raised to maturity by Thomas and Maria Ewing. Thomas Ewing was a U.S. senator with pronounced proslavery views, and Sherman would adopt the views of his foster father. With Ewing's influence, Sherman was able to attend West Point and acquire a first-rate military education. He went on to serve at various army posts in the South and in California during the Mexican War. By the time the nation was moving toward civil war in 1860–61, Sherman was the superintendent of the Louisiana Military Seminary in Alexandria. When Southern states began leaving the Union and Louisiana began preparing for war, Sherman resigned his position there and bid his Southern colleagues and friends a tearful goodbye. He left the South, but his attitudes toward slavery remained quintessentially Southern, reinforced and nurtured by the extensive time he had spent in the region.[6]

At the war's outset then, Sherman wanted to preserve the Union but not free the slaves. Less than two weeks before South Carolina seceded from the Union, Sherman made his views on slavery clear: "I think it would be folly to liberate or materially modify the condition of the Slaves. Their labor & its fruits are necessary to the civilized world, and American slavery is the most modified form of compulsory labor. Any tampering with it is unkind to the negros, and causes the very natural outburst of passion of the whites." In April 1861, Sherman was still describing Southern slavery as "the mildest and best regulated system of slavery in the world now or heretofore." He favored Lincoln using all necessary powers to save the Union but believed the issues of the Union and slavery would be best kept separate, "for otherwise it will gradually become a war of extermination."[7]

Given these views, it was hardly surprising that Sherman attempted to keep slaves from entering his lines. In October 1861, Sherman wrote to Col. John Basil Turchin of the Nineteenth Illinois about slaves being sheltered in his camp and said that by state and federal law they should be returned to their rightful owners. Sherman sent the same message to Brig. Gen. Alexander McCook a few weeks later. McCook told Sherman how the runaway slaves coming into his lines "have already become a source of annoyance," and allowing them to stay would hurt the Union cause in Kentucky. Sherman agreed that the slaves should be returned to their masters and reiterated his opinion that all slaves should be kept out of Union camps. Interestingly, Sherman's reply to McCook, on November 8, 1861, came only four days after Colonel Dodge had ordered Colonel Greusel to seize the slaves of rebels in Missouri. Unlike Fremont or Dodge, Sherman had no desire to interfere with slavery or carry out confiscation in any form. He was not just personally against emancipation, but he also thought he had no legal right to tamper with slavery.[8]

Sherman's very conservative policies became prevalent among top commanders in the western theater. The Union high command in the West underwent major changes in November 1861, and slavery policy, at least as it was given direction from the top, would largely follow Sherman's policies. Fremont had made political and military missteps in Missouri. For his part, Sherman was buckling under the pressure of command in Kentucky and exhibiting signs of intense exhaustion and anxiety. So it seemed that both had to be replaced. Maj. Gen. Henry Halleck took over Fremont's command in

Missouri, and Brig. Gen. Don Carlos Buell assumed Sherman's position in Kentucky. Both Halleck and Buell had very conservative political attitudes, which were reflected in their policies toward fugitive slaves. They were both determined to avoid the issue as much as possible and ensure that the war remain a struggle to restore the old Union. Indeed, Halleck, reacting to the opening salvos at Fort Sumter, hoped that Maryland would not leave the Union because "if no slave States remain in the Union, the North will become ultra anti-slavery" and "in the course of the war will declare for emancipation and thus add the horrors of a servile to that of a civil war."[9]

By the time Henry Halleck assumed this important command, he already had a distinguished career in the army. After compiling a stellar record at West Point, Halleck worked on and studied army fortifications. He established himself as a top scholar of military strategy, tactics, organization, and a host of other issues involving the conduct of war. Like Sherman, Halleck was stationed in California during the war with Mexico and helped frame the state's constitution. During this process Halleck revealed his strong prejudice toward black people when he made it clear that he wanted all of them, free and slave, to be excluded from the state. With his scholarly achievements and military training and service, Halleck was an obvious choice for a major command position in the Union army. He had thought deeply about questions of war and now could put theory into practice, but as he demonstrated, he had no desire to make emancipation a goal of the war.[10]

Arriving in Missouri, Halleck quickly spelled out his policy regarding slavery in General Orders No. 3, stating that "important information respecting the numbers and condition of our forces is conveyed to the enemy by means of fugitive slaves who are admitted within our lines." Thus, slaves should not be allowed to enter Union lines and those already in Union camps should be expelled. It is not clear what evidence Halleck possessed to suggest that slaves were providing intelligence to Confederate forces. Nevertheless, it was apparent that he intended not to confiscate slaves, even those eligible to be seized under the First Confiscation Act. Understanding the trouble Fremont had gotten himself into with the president and slaveholding Unionists with his strike against slavery, Halleck wanted to stay completely clear of the issue. Halleck's policy became a guiding principle for Union officers in the West during the first part of the war.[11]

Halleck's most important subordinate, Brig. Gen. Ulysses S. Grant, was willing to carry out these very conservative policies. This willingness stemmed in part from Grant's own views on slavery. He did think that the war would eventually destroy slavery but was not ready to push the issue.

Grant would rather save the Union above all else, and only if the rebellion "cannot be whipped in any other way than through a war against slavery" would emancipation become necessary. However, in November 1861, Grant was far from envisioning such a necessity. "That portion of the press that advocates the beginning of such a war [for emancipation] now, are as great enemies to their country as if they were open and avowed secessionists," the general informed his father. Indeed, Grant was very much a dutiful soldier who obeyed the orders of his superiors. This keen sense of military obligation probably more than his personal attitudes accounted for Grant's policies.[12]

Grant had a strong sense of military duty ingrained in him. A graduate of the West Point class of 1843, Grant had served with heroism in the Mexican War, earning two brevet promotions. With his martial background, Grant purposefully stayed away from politics. In fact, he did not vote for president until 1856, and during the critical election of 1860 he asserted, "I don't know anything of party politics, and I don't want to." Grant had proven himself a very capable and brave soldier, and these were the qualities he would bring to the Civil War, not any partisan agenda. In this early phase of the war, Grant left politics to the politicians and concerned himself with achieving military success and executing the orders of his commanders.[13]

Yet Grant soon discovered difficulties in carrying out Halleck's General Orders No. 3. He had to tell Col. Richard Oglesby to put a slave captured by a Union major on a government steamer, to be dropped off at Commerce, Missouri, "with permission to go to his Mistress she being reported a staunch Unionist." Grant also had trouble with one of his brigade commanders, Col. John Cook, who was stationed at Fort Holt, Kentucky. Grant permitted a man to search Cook's camp for his slaves. Cook claimed he approved the search but acknowledged that he had been confined to bed at the time. It was reported to Grant that the man's slaves "were found concealed in one of the huts at Fort Holt and that the owner was forcibly prevented from recovering his property." Grant was furious. "If true this is treating law, the orders of the commander of the Department and my orders with contempt," Grant fumed. Personal opinions aside, Grant told Cook, the orders of the department must be obeyed: "I do not want the Army used as negro-catchers, but still less do I want to see it used as a cloak to cover their escape." Colonel Cook denied that the man was obstructed in his search for his slaves but admitted that he was initially prohibited from looking under one of the beds. There was a good possibility that slaves were taking refuge in Cook's camp, whether Cook was responsible for their presence or not.[14]

About a month later, in January 1862, Grant was alerted to another violation of Halleck's policies. A soldier named James Holmes reported that while the Tenth Illinois was on reconnaissance in Kentucky, two officers in that regiment were "guilty of abducting slaves." One of the owners of these slaves, who was loyal, came to the regiment in search of his property. His slave was hidden, and he was arrested until he furnished "evidence that he was a good union man." When the regiment left Kentucky, the slave "was wrapped in a tent cloth and put on a wagon." Holmes suggested that "these Negro thieves ... be dealt with in a proper manner," and Grant referred the matter to Brig. Gen. John McClernand. Not only were these officers flouting Halleck's restrictions on harboring slaves, but they were also taking slaves from Union men—far in advance of official policy.[15]

Like Grant, Col. Grenville Dodge tried to carry out Halleck's fugitive slave policy. He had been willing earlier to issue confiscation orders but now sought to keep slaves out of his lines. Echoing Halleck, Dodge ordered all fugitives delivered to headquarters and prohibited any slaves from coming into Union lines. Lt. Col. John Phelps complied with this order and was ready to expel four slaves from his camp. One of the slaves, named Kelly, had been the personal servant of John M. Richardson, who was a captain in the Missouri Home Guard. Richardson appealed directly to the secretary of war, Simon Cameron, to have Kelly returned to him. After all, Kelly had belonged to a man who was openly disloyal. Reflecting on the army's policy, Richardson thought it "strange" that the Union army "is engaged [in] hunting up & guarding the slaves of traitors while the secessionists are robbing & plundering loyal men in the western part of the state." Returning slaves only strengthened the rebel cause in Missouri, and Richardson "hope[d] the policy will be abandoned." The only clue about what ended up happening to Kelly was a notation on Richardson's letter that said he should be held "until his status is determined."[16] Obviously, Halleck's policies caused confusion and conflict on the ground.

Halleck intended his order to prevent the Union army from having to determine the rightful owner of a slave. He did not want his army to become "negro-stealers" or "negro-catchers." Nevertheless, as demonstrated by both Phelps and Grant, commanders trying to carry out Halleck's policies sometimes thought they should return slaves to their masters. Halleck had to clarify this point for several officers. When Maj. George Waring of the Fremont Hussars turned over a female cook to a Captain Holland because she allegedly belonged to his family, Halleck told Waring's commander that it violated "the intent of General Orders, No. 3." Halleck warned that "the relation between the slave and his master is not a matter to be determined by military officers." Forbidding slaves from coming into Union lines should keep the army out of such a sticky situation. Halleck reiterated these instructions to Col. William Carlin who had ordered Col. Robert Murphy of the Eighth Wisconsin to return a slave to his master. The rebuke was pointed: "I think you mistook your duty as a military officer in this matter. I do not consider it any part of the duty of the military to decide upon the rights of master and slave. It is our duty to leave that question for the action of the loyal civil authorities of the State." These points became a constant refrain in Halleck's communications with his officers as he saw his orders abused on both ends; officers and soldiers took slaves into camp and some tried to return these slaves. As hard as he tried, Halleck could not avoid entanglement with the slavery question.[17]

Despite all the problems, Halleck persisted in having General Orders No. 3 carried out, and some of the officers under his command kept trying to accommodate him. Grant instructed Brig. Gen. E. A. Paine to send the goodly number of contrabands in his camp back to their masters. Yet he cautioned Paine that "some discretion will have to be used in forcing these people out of camp." Brig. Gen. John Pope was more direct when he told one of his colonels to inspect the companies under his charge, "and if any runaway negro slave be found there . . . put the commanding officer of the company having such negro in arrest and prefer charges against him."[18]

It is important to note that Halleck did pay some heed to the First Confiscation Act during his first months of command. He sometimes made an exception to his strict prohibition against slaves entering Union lines if they were seized according to the provisions of the First Confiscation Act. He might have been reacting to political pressure. After all, Congressman Owen Lovejoy of Illinois introduced a resolution in the House of Representatives in December 1861 calling for Lincoln to instruct Halleck to recall General Orders No. 3 or modify it to conform to the policies of other commanders. This resolution claimed that Halleck's order was "cruel and inhuman." Lovejoy was "opposed to the Army of the United States being turned into slave catchers" and thought freeing the slaves was the best way to put down the rebellion. Whatever motivated him, Halleck would still confiscate only what the law demanded. Barring slaves from his army was always his preference.[19]

When Union forces moved into Tennessee in February 1862, this proved a formidable challenge. Even though Tennessee had far fewer slaves than states in the Deep South, there were still over 275,000 slaves in the state in 1860. Slaves accounted for 25 percent of Tennessee's total population and were concentrated in the central and western regions of the state. These were the very regions that the Union army would first attack and occupy. So early in the war, invading Federal forces had to deal with significant numbers of slaves even if they would rather have avoided them. Just looking at some of the principal counties that the Union army operated in during the first part of 1862 reveals that Union soldiers were in relatively close proximity to perhaps over 70,000 slaves. This figure does not include the many slave-rich counties that were adjacent to those the army moved through in the state, and slaves often traveled many miles to seek refuge in Union camps.[20]

Along with slavery, the Union army confronted a largely hostile white population with pockets of Unionists in certain areas, particularly in the Tennessee River valley. Tennessee had not seceded from the Union during the first wave of secession in the winter of 1860–61. A competitive two-party system and a smaller number of slaves than in the Deep South were two key factors that kept Tennessee in the Union during the secession winter. In early 1861, Tennessee Unionists sought to secure Southern rights within the Union. But after the firing on Fort Sumter and Lincoln's subsequent call for troops, the state was pushed in a decidedly secessionist direction. Forced to choose between North and South, Tennesseans chose to cast their lot with their Southern compatriots. Secessionist sentiment was particularly strong in Middle and West Tennessee. In June 1861, the people in these regions endorsed secession by huge margins, which was unsurprising given the high concentration of slaves in those areas. Almost all the counties in West Tennessee that did not go along with secession were in or near the Tennessee River valley, where there were generally fewer slaves. As a whole, though, slavery was central to the economy and wealth of central and western Tennessee. For example, in the Tennessee heartland, consisting of thirteen counties in the middle of the state, 40 percent of the population was slaves. Moreover, slaves made up 55 percent of the value of personal property in the region. The desire to protect this valuable slave property eventually made many West and Middle Tennesseans embrace the Confederacy. As the Union army invaded Tennessee, however, its top commanders tried their best not to interfere with slavery.[21]

Proving this point, when Halleck's soldiers were advancing into Tennessee in early 1862, the general again called for excluding black people from Union camps and directed commanders at all levels to search their respective commands for fugitive slaves. If they were found, the officer who let them in would "be arrested and tried for neglect of duty and disobedience of orders." A little over a week later, Halleck sought "to impress upon all officers" how vital it was to maintain discipline in their ranks—and this meant keeping fugitive slaves at arm's length. The army simply had no business interfering with the master-slave relationship. From Fort Donelson, Grant declared that General Orders No. 3 was "still in force and must be observed." He claimed that the very fact that so many people were trying to obtain passes to look for their slaves in Union lines "proves the necessity of the order and its faithful observance." These passes could not be given, so the slaves must be kept out in the first place. However, Grant did allow slaves who were in Confederate lines or constructing rebel fortifications at the time of Fort Donelson's capitulation to "be employed in the quartermaster's department for the benefit of Government."[22] Hence, Grant was enforcing the First Confiscation Act while still adhering to Halleck's policy.

Though Grant and Halleck tried to keep slaves away from Union lines during the 1862 campaign into western Tennessee, they faced challenges from below. Grant had to tell Col. Marcellus Crocker of the Thirteenth Iowa to get rid of two reported slaves who were with his regiment on a steamer. Whoever "induced them aboard," Grant said, should be reported to headquarters. The chaplain of this regiment, John Steele, noted that the fugitives had actually "been concealed for a time" before they were made to depart. When Grant learned that a captain in the Fifth Iowa Cavalry had taken two female slaves and a boy from Fort Henry, he instructed the regiment's colonel to return the slaves to the fort and put them outside Union lines. Citizens in or near Savannah, Tennessee, complained that Maj. Gen. John McClernand's troops had seized some of their slaves. Grant told McClernand that "this is in violation of orders from Head Quarters of the Dept, and of my orders," and the guilty parties should be arrested. McClernand claimed to have no knowledge of any such violations but promised to investigate and punish any offenders.[23]

In March 1862, Grant faced even more problems from Col. C. J. Wright of the Thirteenth Missouri who was operating in Clarksville, Tennessee. According to Col. Philip Fouke, citizens of Clarksville had lost many slaves to Union forces and therefore decided to join the Confederate army. In particular, Fouke referred to two slaves belonging to a Mrs. R. W. Thomas whom Wright's forces had seized. A former U.S. congressman, James M. Quarles, lobbied for the return of Thomas's slaves, claiming that they had never been used for work by the Confederate government. Grant thought the slaves should be returned and asked Halleck's permission to do so. While it is unclear from the record whether these slaves were actually returned, what was evident was that Colonel Wright had violated Grant's orders. This placed Grant in the difficult position of having to ask permission to return slaves. In fact, Grant's request went against a recent congressional article of war that prohibited "all officers or persons in the military or naval service of the United States ... from employing any of the forces under their respective commands for the purpose of returning" slaves to their owners. If an officer was found guilty of returning slaves to anyone, Unionist or rebel, they would be dismissed from the military.[24]

Not every officer in the Thirteenth Missouri was so insubordinate when it came to carrying out orders concerning slaves. The regiment's provost marshal in Clarksville, Channing Richards, closely adhered to Halleck's and Grant's policies. On his first day as provost, Richards had a young slave come in who claimed to have worked on Confederate fortifications. Consistent with the First Confiscation Act, Richards allowed the slave to stay in his lines. A female slave who sought protection from Richards was not so lucky. She arrived with an iron shackle around her ankle, which her master had used to chain her to a tree. Richards denied her asylum because "the order was imperative—fugitives must not be harbored in the Camps." Before she left, though, a few officers spent an hour filing and hammering the chain off. Only the slave of a rebel and not actively employed aiding the Confederate army, she was not subject to confiscation. So Richards sent her away as his superiors would have wanted, but with considerable regret. "Poor Woman! she had been deceived—having been informed that we were battling for human rights and universal freedom she had not learned until then that our humanity was limited by color, and that the poor wretch who had sought shelter was beyond the pale," lamented Richards. The examples of Richards and Wright illustrate how confiscation policy could play out differently even within a single regiment.[25]

Many officers proved to be much less circumspect than Richards. This was particularly true in the Army of the Mississippi under Maj. Gen. John Pope (like Grant's army under the overall direction of Halleck). As Grant campaigned in western Tennessee, Pope led his army on an expedition that would eventually result in the capture of Island Number Ten on the Mississippi River. Some of Pope's officers largely ignored Halleck's very conservative policies respecting slavery and confiscation. Col. Hans Christian Heg of the Fifteenth Wisconsin had protected the slaves of a plantation owner, but as soon as he verified the man's rebel sympathies, that came to an end. Lt. William Stevens of the Third Michigan Cavalry reported that rebels were quickly losing their slave property to the Union army. "I am confident that when our army leaves here," Stevens informed his father, "there will not be in the county of New Madrid one tenth part the number of slaves that were here when we came." The battalion adjutant of the Seventh Illinois Calvary, Charles Wills, estimated that the army seized 500 slaves from the area around New Madrid. He contended that army generals assured the slave owners that the slaves would not be permitted to leave with the army. Slaves, however, were clearly being welcomed into Union lines by Pope's army. Lt. Col. A. W. Gilbert affirmed this when he asserted, "The slavery question is assuming new phases as we get into Dixie & contrabands are no longer driven out of Camp, but are used by all the officers wherever needed."[26]

Officers in Pope's army found the confiscated slaves very useful. A captain in the Sixty-Third Ohio, Oscar Jackson, received valuable information about rebel fortifications from a slave who had come on board his boat. Soon Jackson found a servant from among the contrabands. Another black man who became a servant to a Wisconsin captain remembered years later his liberation by Pope's soldiers: "After the capture of all the forts [at Island Number Ten] the Yankees came on our plantation and told us we were all as free as they were and could go where we pleased. It seemed too good to be true." Useful or not, Pope's army did not confiscate every slave in its path. Jackson empathetically told of a slave who tried desperately to get a Union boat to stop for him on the Tennessee River but to no avail: "How I pitied this son of Africa, striving for that which we all love so well, 'liberty,' and thus far unsuccessfully. God grant him success yet." Nevertheless, many officers in Pope's army were aggressively carrying out confiscation and pushing beyond the limits of Halleck's policies.[27]

Commanding the Army of the Ohio, Maj. Gen. Don Carlos Buell proved to be very conservative in his policies, even slightly more so than Halleck. Buell grew up in the Midwest and was a West Point graduate. He staunchly believed in the professionalism of the army. Like so many Civil War commanders, Buell's first major battlefield experiences came during the Mexican War, in which he proved himself a gallant and able officer. Buell married a native Southerner, Margaret Hunter Mason, and acquired eight slaves through marriage. He had no objections to the institution of slavery and was comfortable being a slave owner. Though the record on his racial views is slim, Buell believed that the Constitution protected an individual's right to own slaves. As an army commander, he did everything in his power to uphold that right. Buell excluded slaves from his lines and, unlike Halleck, had few qualms about returning them to their masters.[28]

Occupying Nashville in February 1862 in the wake of Grant's victory at Fort Donelson, Buell enforced this very conservative policy vigorously. He wrote to J. R. Underwood, the head of the Military Committee in Kentucky's state house: "Several applications have been made to me by persons whose servants have been found in our camps and in every instance that I know of the master has recovered his servant and taken him away." When Brig. Gen. Ormsby Mitchel's division allowed slaves to enter its lines, Buell harshly repudiated the practice. He instructed Mitchel to arrest any slaves still in his camp and allow their masters to reclaim them. In any case, the slaves would be driven out of Union lines and no more would be permitted to come into the camps. This policy greatly dismayed Col. L. A. Harris of the Second Ohio, who tendered his resignation because such an order was "repugnant to my feelings as a man." Ormsby Mitchel was a West Point graduate with diverse intellectual interests, particularly in the field of astronomy. He had a powerful mind and was soon to prove an effective Union commander who would try to undermine the rebellion in any way possible. Buell would continue to have problems with Mitchel and his troops on matters involving slavery.[29]

Officers in other commands were also moving beyond Buell's policies regarding slaves. A major in the Forty-Second Indiana, James Shanklin, allowed confiscation: "We have not had many negroes come to us for protection—but occasionally they do, and I for my part never intend to force them to go back." One owner was able to retrieve his slaves from the regiment's lines. While it was the job of the regiment's colonel to prevent this, Shanklin still "felt ashamed" of himself for not doing something. As he watched the slaves being driven off with their hands bound, he reflected, "[I] do not think I shall ever see any person of the human family treated that brutally again without interfering a little."[30]

Mitchel's division remained the most difficult for Buell to rein in on confiscation. This was especially true when Mitchel led his command into north Alabama in April 1862. Mitchel primarily occupied the counties in the Tennessee Valley, which contained a significant slave population. According to the 1860 census, slaves made up about 42.6 percent of the population in this area and numbered 51,789. Mitchel established his headquarters in Huntsville, a strategically important city along the Memphis and Charleston Railroad in the very heart of slave country. Huntsville was located in a county in which 55.5 percent of the population was slaves. Among this sizable slave population, Mitchel found many allies who were willing to risk everything for the Union cause.[31]

Mitchel, however, did not locate many allies among white people in the region. North Alabama had sent cooperationist delegates to the secession convention to argue against leaving the Union immediately. The region's inhabitants were concerned that severing their ties with the Union would lead to Federal invasion and hurt their economy, which was dependent on markets outside the state. But the immediate secessionists in the state outvoted the cooperationists decisively, and Alabama seceded in January 1861 with much of the Deep South. Even though north Alabamians generally counseled patience during the debate over secession in Alabama, once the state left the Union, they quickly became ardent Confederate nationalists. Mitchel's men came to understand how true this was when they faced numerous acts of defiance by the civilians in the region. These acts included attacking Union supply lines and ambushing Union soldiers. The more intransigent and rebellious the people of north Alabama were, the more Mitchel saw the necessity of adopting harsher policies to deal with them. And nothing would strike at the heart of Southern resistance more than undermining the institution of slavery. This was exactly what Mitchel began to do at a very early point in the war.[32]

Mitchel and his soldiers pursued policies that were not conservative regarding slavery. Col. John Beatty of the Third Ohio at first reported driving slaves away. "It seems cruel to turn our backs on these, our only friends," he lamented. However, by May 1862, Beatty's regiment had abandoned this policy. Indeed, there was "a superabundance of negroes" almost "too numerous to mention" in his camp. Lt. George Landrum's Second Ohio was even quicker to confiscate. As early as the end of March, Landrum reported having slaves in his lines and readily justified the practice: "They belong to Sesesh masters so we are doing good in taking them away." In April, the Second Ohio employed another slave in the regiment.[33]

If Mitchel's soldiers were busy confiscating slaves, Mitchel himself was pushing the issue directly with Washington. "I had supposed that the slaves of masters in arms against the Government were confiscated," he suggested to Secretary of the Treasury Salmon P. Chase. To Mitchel, slaves seemed an important potential asset to the Union army. "The negroes are our only friends," he informed Secretary of War Edwin Stanton, "and in two instances I owe my own safety to their faithfulness. I shall very soon have watchful guards among the slaves on the plantations bordering the river from Bridgeport to Florence." Mitchel solicited Stanton's approval for protecting slaves who provided the army with information. Without their support, Mitchel felt he could not maintain his current position in northern Alabama. Stanton readily assented, asserting that the rebels were already using the slaves, and if the Union did not, it "would be a failure to employ means to suppress the rebellion and restore the authority of the Government." Mitchel grasped that confiscating slaves was a military necessity before most other generals. His policies foreshadowed, in limited form, the Second Confiscation Act and the approach many commanders would adopt during the summer of 1862.[34]

Unquestionably, Mitchel's division was growing more emancipationist in its approach to slavery. Lt. George Landrum of the Second Ohio declared, "Our Division is fast becoming Abolitionist, both men and officers who a few months ago were intensely pro-slavery, are just as much the other way now." This was fine with Landrum, for his observations confirmed "all that [Charles] Sumner ever said of the 'Barbarism of Slavery.'" Lt. Alfred Pirtle of the Tenth Ohio agreed that the "Abolition element" was becoming stronger in the entire command. In contrast to Landrum, Pirtle was not happy with this development. The abolitionist-leaning soldiers were a "set of thieves, robbers and scoundrels generally and having so far escaped punishment." He and his fellow soldiers had been "deceived" into "fighting the battles of a party and not of a great people."[35]

When Buell and the rest of his army arrived in north Alabama in June 1862, the commanding general tried to clamp down on confiscation in Mitchel's division and throughout the army. For example, Buell ordered Brig. Gen. Alexander McCook to turn all slaves out of his lines and prevent them from crossing the Tennessee River with the division. Such policies heightened tension and even provoked resistance from some officers. When Brig. Gen. Thomas Wood told Brig. Gen. James Garfield to search his lines for a slave, Garfield adamantly refused, insisting that nobody under his direction would participate in disobeying congressional legislation. Unhappy about the very conservative policies of the Union army, the abolitionist Garfield despaired: "My heart sinks down very low when I see the mode in which the war is conducted.... Everything they [the rebels] have is protected with the most scrupulous care, especially their property in human flesh." Garfield referred to an incident that dramatically illustrated the Union army's protection of slave property. As Union soldiers passed a plantation, slaves greeted them with elation and begged to go with the army, offering to help in any way possible. The colonel was unmoved and "drew his pistol and with terrible oaths said to the leading slave who spoke for the rest, 'Go back to your work or I will put a bullet through your blue heart.'" Garfield thought it "hardly possible that God will let us succeed while such enormities are practiced."[36]

The conscientious and deeply religious Garfield was not alone. The Tenth Wisconsin refused to expel officers' servants from its camp. Capt. William Moore of Company G noted, "This order being opposed to the known laws of Congress, it was decided at a meeting of our officers not to execute it, or to aid in executing it." Moore reported that this same order had caused the officers in the Twenty-Fourth Illinois to resign. Moore's superior, Maj. John McMynn, detested Buell's policy toward slaves. McMynn had a servant, referred to as "Uncle John," who had provided the army with valuable information, and McMynn vowed to protect him. Casting his servant, or any slave for that matter, out of camp to be reclaimed by his or her master was simply unconscionable. "If my life is needed to defend the Constitution it will be offered but I cannot be made a slave catcher by any power on earth," McMynn declared. "My soul shall be unstained by any such crime when it goes to judgment and my manhood shall be free from such a reproach while I live on earth."[37]

The dilemma of another Wisconsin officer who refused to be a slave catcher made it all the way to the president. In a letter to his wife, this officer related how, in his absence, a slave owner was permitted to seize a slave under an order from Brig. Gen. Lovell Rousseau. Upon his return, the officer forbade "a notorious rebel lawyer" from searching the camp. The lawyer said he had been "assured" that he would be permitted to recover his slaves. The officer held firm and risked being arrested himself. This letter was sent to Lincoln by Senator James Doolittle of Wisconsin, who recommended that since "the order No 3 of Genl Halleck has been subject to a construction by some Generals under him, which makes it equivalent to the surrender of fugitives by our soldiers . . . a general order to all the Generals in command from Washington would be wise & proper." Doolittle never specified what such a general order should contain, and it is unclear what actions, if any, Lincoln took upon learning of this incident.[38] What was quite apparent though was that the tension and conflict in Buell's army over slavery was significant enough to get the attention of officials in Washington and even reach the desk of the commander in chief.

Even if they did not disobey orders explicitly, by the summer of 1862 some officers were expressing their increasing frustration with Buell's conservatism on the slavery issue and caution in dealing with the rebellion generally. John Beatty harshly characterized Buell's policy as "that of the amiable idiot." Beatty supported an approach that would "not fear to hurt the feelings of traitors" or worry about "that traitor's negroes run[ning] away." William Brown observed, "Gen. Buell is so badly affected with the *loving* policy that he is in bad odor in some Divisions of the army (particularly Mitchells) and a rebel can get anything, do anything, or go anyplace, if he only says there is a 'nigger' got loose." A lieutenant in the Twenty-First Ohio, John Bolton, thought that the army was "playing war in this department" by "guarding our enemies' property" and giving back "thousands of slaves" to their owners. But he had hope for the future, provided the policy was changed. "If that accursed human scourge is once wholy abolished," Bolton wrote, "then the root of this evil is taken away and if once that curse is abolished and the rebellion effectively crushed I feel that we then can have a lasting peace."[39]

As Buell was facing challenges from his army on policies involving slavery, Halleck was still trying to implement his orders regarding fugitive slaves in western Tennessee and northern Mississippi. He was in fact softening his stance a bit, becoming moderately conservative in his policies. As early as late April 1862, he had issued orders that provided for the army to take in slaves who could be seized under the First Confiscation Act or had supplied information to the army. Halleck, however, set down strict guidelines to ensure that only slaves who fell into these categories would be allowed to stay with the army. Any officer who employed a slave as a servant who had been confiscated legitimately was required to "give a certificate of the facts, stating where the negro was captured or how and when he was made free," and any slave who had aided the army in some way also had to have a certificate with the approbation of the commanding general of the appropriate army. Certain categories of slaves could remain with the army, but General Orders No. 3 was still in effect. Slaves that were not in these categories, Halleck advised one officer, must be turned out of Union lines "as any other vagrant."[40]

An important reason why many in the Union high command, as well as many officers throughout the army, were so reluctant to let huge numbers of slaves into their lines might have had to do with the very success that Union armies enjoyed in the western theater. As will be shown later, military necessity was the driving reason behind most Union officers' eventual support for emancipation, and at this point in the war, emancipation did not appear to be necessary for victory in the West. In the first half of 1862, Union armies were on the advance seemingly everywhere, from Tennessee to Mississippi to Louisiana. The Union was smashing the Confederacy without emancipation. It would be only later, as the war dragged on, that emancipation would appear more of a military necessity to many officers. Additionally, western Union armies were consistently on the move during this period, which made it difficult to liberate large numbers of slaves. To be sure, not all officers were trying to keep slaves out of their lines during this period, but many were, particularly those at the top levels of command.

Undoubtedly, Sherman was one of those commanders. "The well-settled policy of the whole army now," Sherman explained in orders to the Fifth Division in June 1862, "is to have nothing to do with the negro.... We cannot have our trains encumbered by them, nor can we afford to feed them, and it is deceiving the poor fellow to allow him to start and have him forcibly driven away afterward." Accordingly, Sherman directed officers at all levels to force fugitives out of Union camps and stop any additional ones from coming in. He did, however, make an exception for slaves that fell under the provisions of the First Confiscation Act. Their labor could be used by the army, but their actual freedom would have to be granted through a civil tribunal. Unlike Halleck, Sherman never mentioned protecting slaves who had rendered valuable service to the army. In pursuing this policy, Sherman was clearly thinking at this point about the demands of military necessity. This contrasts directly with General Mitchel's posture in north Alabama. While Mitchel thought it was necessary to let slaves in his lines, Sherman felt it was just as vital to keep them out of his camps. Military necessity could cut both ways, depending on the predilections of a commander.[41]

Maj. Gen. Lew Wallace also willingly carried out Halleck's exclusionary policies but not without some misgivings. While marching in West Tennessee, Wallace thought black people "were sights to see." They filled barrels with water for parched Union soldiers. The general remembered how his soldiers greeted the slaves "with jokes, and cheers, and such hearty goodwill that the sullen gentry on the verandahs ought to have been ashamed of their prejudices." This goodwill would be left. The slaves were not welcomed into Wallace's column, though he hinted at some regret in not liberating them: "With a word I could have had at my heels an army the most pied, trusting, and helpless ever seen. Never before, never since, have I had such an opportunity to become a Moses."[42]

Some officers would not pass up assuming the role of a Moses even if it brought them into conflict with their superiors. Lt. Col. Daniel Anthony of the Seventh Kansas Cavalry had been entrusted by his brigade commander, Brig. Gen. Robert Mitchell, with reading recent orders reiterating Halleck's exclusionary policies before the entire brigade. Anthony delivered the order "and then another of his own, threatening punishment to any officer or soldier who should dare" carry it out. Anthony was arrested on charges that included allowing slaves into Union camps against orders and portraying "the purpose of the troops to be the freeing of Slaves and taking of all private property." Kansas senator James H. Lane, a giant in Kansas politics known for his militant abolitionism and energetic oratory, took an interest in Anthony's predicament, and all of a sudden, Anthony was freed. Anthony was not the only officer of the Seventh Kansas arrested after clashing with his superiors on slavery policy. When Brig. Gen. Grenville Dodge expelled all slaves from the regiment's lines that "were not clearly contraband," a Captain Rafferty put up enough opposition to land him under arrest. In a Union army that had a significant amount of tension over confiscation questions, these Kansans stood out in their radical policies and willingness to defy their superiors.[43]

If officers in Union armies operating in parts of Tennessee, Mississippi, and Alabama tested the limits of confiscation during the first half of 1862, they were far from alone. Similar disputes broke out in the Department of the Gulf under Maj. Gen. Benjamin Butler. Butler was not a professionally trained army officer before the war. He was a lawyer, militia commander, and, most prominently, a Democratic politician. Serving in the state government of Massachusetts, Butler battled the Republican Party on economic issues and questions concerning slavery's extension into the territories. Significantly, Butler ardently opposed enrolling black men in the state militia. During the critical election year of 1860, Butler pushed hard for the nomination of Jefferson Davis for president at the Democratic convention. Yet despite his past political allegiances, Butler strongly backed Lincoln and his administration at the outbreak of war. Eager to win the approval of Democrats, Lincoln made Butler a major general early on in the conflict. As a commander, Butler was involved in several military campaigns, but he earned the most fame or infamy for his role as army commander in New Orleans.[44]

Butler's forces occupied New Orleans after a combined army and navy expedition caused the city's capitulation in April 1862. Almost immediately, Butler confronted problems with fugitive slaves. He had dealt with them before at Fort Monroe, Virginia, almost a year earlier, establishing the "contraband of war" idea that involved welcoming any slaves into his lines who had served the Confederacy. Butler's policy became embodied in the First Confiscation Act, yet in New Orleans, Butler adopted a more conservative approach to confiscation. This shift in policy resulted from the different situation Butler faced in Louisiana.[45]

New Orleans was the largest and most diverse city in the Confederacy. Its population was well over four times the population of the Confederate capital city of Richmond, Virginia. The Crescent City's inhabitants represented many different cultures and nationalities and had significant numbers of Irish, Germans, and French, just to name a few. A bustling and prosperous metropolis, New Orleans primarily grew because of its extremely lucrative export and import trade. Because of its commercial interests, New Orleans had supported the Whig Party in national elections before the war. In the crucial election of 1860, the city gave the edge to Constitutional Union candidate

John Bell, who was a former Whig and ran on a platform to preserve the Union. The city had thus never been a hotbed of secessionist sentiment. But when Lincoln won the presidential contest, many people in New Orleans embraced secession and became committed to the rebellion.[46]

Some of the city's citizens, however, did not support the idea of a new Southern nation. Although determining the number of people in New Orleans who could be classified as Unionists at the beginning of the war or at the time of Federal occupation is impossible, there was a significant group of them, albeit a distinct minority of the city's population. Unionism was particularly strong among the free black people and German and Irish immigrants in the city, some of whom would enlist in the Union army. Benjamin Butler was very eager to cultivate this Unionism in New Orleans and did not want to undermine this objective by taking the property of people who were already friendly or might be made friendly to the Union. The general observed, with some hyperbole, that "a large majority" of the city's residents were compliant and trying to live in peace under the law. So, unlike in Virginia, Butler confronted a significant Unionist population in New Orleans. This population made him more restrained in attacking slavery.[47]

Butler was also very concerned about the effects of confiscation on the area's economy. The general was in control of a more expansive region in Louisiana than he had been in Virginia and was very aware of the importance of slavery to the area. The slaves "till the soil, raise the sugar, corn, and cotton, load and unload the ships; they perform every domestic office, and are permeated through every branch of industry and peaceful calling," Butler wrote. With the occupation of New Orleans, and eventually much of southern Louisiana, Federal forces found themselves in the heart of this slave economy. Indeed, they controlled parishes where over 90,000 slaves resided, according to the 1860 census. In Orleans Parish alone, where the city of New Orleans was located, there were over 14,000 slaves. The sugar plantations of southern Louisiana were some of the most prosperous in the entire South. Butler was not eager to witness the erosion of this plantation system. He pointed out that it was "manifestly unjust" to seize just the slave property of planters because it was the same thing as seizing all their property, since without slaves they could no longer run their plantations.[48]

Butler's newfound conservatism on slavery placed him at odds with one of his chief subordinates, Brig. Gen. John Phelps, who pushed radical confiscation policies. A strong abolitionist, Phelps had already issued a decree against slavery from Ship Island, Mississippi, in December 1861 before Butler's arrival.

In his proclamation, Phelps had waxed eloquent about slavery's incompatibility with free labor. He considered slavery "a universally recognized social and moral evil" and "free labor ... the granite basis on which free institutions must rest." By February 1862, Phelps informed Adj. Gen. Lorenzo Thomas that he was employing twenty-four rebel slaves who "appear to be intelligent, and far more dignified and manly than many of their masters." After recounting the travails some of these slaves went through to reach Union lines, Phelps revealingly declared, "They are ripe for manumission, and any measure to avert it may put off, but cannot long prevent, a revolution—a revolution of that kind where men are restored to their original rights." Ironically, just as Phelps was accepting these slaves into his lines and talking of an inevitable "revolution," Grant and Halleck were pressing upon their troops the absolute necessity of not interfering with slavery.[49]

Nor was Butler eager for a revolution. At the end of May 1862, the general outlined his confiscation policies to the secretary of war. He would not interfere with the property of loyal Louisianans—most notably in New Orleans—who were "attending to their usual avocations and endeavoring in good faith to live quietly under the laws of the Union." Butler, however, would take slaves of rebels if he had use for them. If not, he would rather not have them in his lines. It would be "a physical impossibility to take all," Butler maintained. The general preferred a limited form of confiscation based on the requirements of military necessity. Butler's policies could be classified as moderately conservative, more proconfiscation than Buell's but less than those of someone like Mitchel.

Butler's reluctance to open up his lines to more slaves might have stemmed partly from his racial attitudes. Upon receiving word of Maj. Gen. David Hunter's efforts in the Department of the South to emancipate slaves and recruit them into the Union army, Butler remarked that arming black men was not yet a "military necessity" in his department. Besides, the general maintained, black men had "acquired a great horror of fire-arms, sometimes ludicrous in the extreme when the weapon is in his own hand." It had been wise for John Brown in his aborted raid on Harpers Ferry to bring along pikes and spears rather than guns to arm the slaves, Butler remarked. If this was not enough to demonstrate why black men should not be soldiers, Butler then reached further back into history and argued that a major factor in the British debacle at New Orleans in 1815 was the British army's decision to use a black regiment to carry the fascines. Butler ended this discussion by talking more generally about slavery. He thought the institution was "a curse to a nation ... from its baleful effects upon the master." Not seeing slaves as equal to the test of soldiering or even handling a firearm, Butler was not ready to move forward on emancipation.[50]

Disagreeing with these sentiments, Phelps pushed his own emancipation program at Camp Parapet near New Orleans. Ignoring the limitations Butler placed on confiscation, he turned his camp into a refuge for slaves. Butler quickly tried to rein in his wayward subordinate. After learning that a slave belonging to a Mr. J. B. G. Armand was at Camp Parapet, he reiterated his policy to Phelps: if the slave could be of value to the army, employ him, but if not, let him go. Butler thought that a slave of no use was "like any other vagrant about the camp." When levees needed to be fixed near New Orleans, Butler found himself again discussing fugitive slaves with Phelps. "You will see the need of giving them [planters] every aid in your power to save and protect the levee," Butler wrote Phelps, "even to returning their own negroes and adding others if need be to their forces." Even more directly, on May 23, Butler ordered Phelps to turn out of his camp anyone who was not employed. Anyone coming into Phelps's camp must have a pass from headquarters except if "brought in under guard as captured persons with information." Four days later, the commanding general sent one of his aides to Camp Parapet to ensure this order was being carried out. "Report to me the number of negroes in that camp," Butler instructed, and "cause all women and children," with the exception of those who already had their homes there, "to be excluded therefrom." Less than a year earlier, Butler had recommended Phelps be made a brigadier general because it "would be of infinite value to the service." Ironically, at that time, Butler observed that Phelps's abolitionist views did "not unfit him to fight the battles of the North." Now, he did not even trust his lieutenant.[51]

Butler had good reason to believe that Phelps was not driving out idle slaves or preventing new ones from entering Camp Parapet. The very day that he sent his aide to Phelps's camp, another aide, Capt. Edward Page of the Thirty-First Massachusetts, presented a disturbing report. Page claimed that Phelps's men were "allowed to range the country, insult the planters, and entice negroes away from their plantations." More than that, if they learned any slaves were being punished by their masters, they quickly went to the plantation and freed them. Page cited four slaves liberated under such circumstances. One slave, guilty of barn burning, was released from the stocks despite belonging to a lady that had "a safeguard" for her property from Butler. As a result, slaves would not labor diligently for their owners. Shortly thereafter, Polycarpe Fortier confirmed this when he told Butler,

"Our negroes, heretofore quiet, now feeling under no restraint commit burglary and depredations, and then seek a refuge in camp where they are received and protected." Fortier had been trying in vain for about a month to extract seven of his slaves from Phelps's lines.[52]

The controversy between Phelps and Butler would eventually reach Washington. When Maj. Frank Peck of the Twelfth Connecticut informed Phelps of the large numbers of destitute fugitive slaves gathering outside the lines, Phelps was ready for a showdown over policy. He apprised Butler of the situation, offered his own detailed views of slavery, and asked that Butler pass his letter along to the president. Clearly, Phelps was hoping for a change of policy. In the letter, his abolitionism shone through from the start. He recounted how the slaves lacked basic rights and received little justice. Then, Phelps pointed out the obvious contradiction between slavery and the nation's founding credo. "It is nearly a hundred years since our people first declared to the nations of the world that all men are born free," Phelps noted, "and still we have not made our declaration good." Warning of a slave revolution if nothing was done, he insisted slavery must be abolished by the president. Phelps hoped that his arguments on behalf of emancipation might help prod the government in that direction so that he could more effectively deal with the slaves suffering outside of his lines and not worry about Butler's moderately conservative policies.[53]

Tired of his troublesome lieutenant, Butler sent the letter to Stanton but held firm on his policies. He asserted that as far as he understood, he was executing the government's policy regarding fugitive slaves and was not free to adopt any other course. Nevertheless, Butler admitted that his and Phelps's difference over policy was "a source of trouble." Butler maintained that the destitute slaves waiting outside of Phelps's pickets were there because of an order forbidding them to come into Union lines. Many of these slaves belonged to a Mr. Lablanche, who "claims to be loyal and to have taken no part in the war, but to have been quietly on his plantation." These slaves, according to Butler, were enticed away by promises of freedom from Phelps's command. Phelps argued that Lablanche had sent them to the Union army with threats of punishment if they returned. How the government decided to resolve this controversy mattered a great deal to Butler. He candidly remarked that if Washington sided with him, Phelps was "worse than useless here," but if they went with Phelps, he was "invaluable," for "his [Phelps's] whole soul is in it, and he is a good soldier, of large experience, and no braver man lives."[54]

Butler received no definitive reply from Washington. Neither Stanton nor Lincoln was eager to wade into the controversy. Indeed, Stanton wrote Butler,

"It has not yet . . . been deemed necessary or wise to fetter your judgment by any specific instructions in this regard." Washington was not going to recall Phelps and wanted Butler to work with him as well as possible. While giving no official instructions, Chase around the same time pressed upon Butler that slavery had to go in order to save the country. The secretary, however, admitted that until the government decided on a firm policy on slavery, "the commanding General will be greatly embarrassed by it." Thus, the conflict between the two men remained unresolved. It would not go away though, for Butler and Phelps had irreconcilable differences that had to be dealt with sooner rather than later. Butler's pragmatism would continue to clash with Phelps's moral beliefs.[55]

Problems with fugitive slaves dogged lower-ranking officers as well. Leading a brigade in Butler's army, Brig. Gen. Thomas Williams was a professional military man who had attended West Point, fought the Seminoles, and served on Gen. Winfield Scott's staff through the Mexican War. He came into conflict on the slavery issue with a couple of his colonels, particularly Halbert Paine of the Fourth Wisconsin. During operations around Vicksburg, Paine's regiment had allowed some fugitive slaves, who had provided the army with information about the enemy, to accompany his soldiers on a steamer. When the steamer reached Baton Rouge, Williams gave two masters permission to reclaim their slaves. According to the regiment's chaplain, A. C. Barry, the slaves hid on the steamer, and sentries informed the slave owners that there were no black people there. Not believing this, the owners appealed to one of Williams's aides, who authorized a search. "The engineer was ordered to turn his steam into the hold, which he did, and actually steamed them [the slaves] out," Barry recounted. Then, the owners took the slaves just beyond Union lines and whipped them each with 150 lashes, after which they were marched away in spiked-iron collars. The same slaves ran back to the Fourth Wisconsin five days later, still wearing their gruesome collars. Paine had his men remove the collars, one of which was kept "as a memento of the barbarism of slavery." Despite orders from Williams, Paine would not turn the slaves over to their owners again. For this insubordination, Paine found himself under arrest, marching at the rear of his column but cheered by his men. Barry exclaimed, "Never was I so proud of my Colonel, as at that moment!"[56]

Paine's arrest stemmed from more than just his disobedience in this instance. Indeed, around the time Paine was unwilling to give up the two slaves, he refused to return any slaves to their masters or drive any out of his lines. On June 5, echoing the very conservative policies of Halleck and Buell, Williams ordered fugitive slaves to be turned out of Union camps. Williams reasoned that keeping fugitives had a "demoralizing and disorganizing" effect on his men. Paine disagreed and thought Williams's orders were tantamount to delivering up slaves to their masters. This not only violated an act of Congress, but, Paine believed, "it would also in its moral aspects be obnoxious to the gravest objections." Paine was thus willing to jeopardize his military career to protect slaves and ensure they were not reclaimed by their owners.[57]

This controversy reached the floor of the U.S. Senate, where Williams's policy of turning slaves out of his lines received little sympathy. Senator Timothy Howe of Wisconsin read the communications between Williams and Paine and then harshly attacked Williams's actions and character. "[He] has no more appreciation of the duties of this Service, in which he is employed," Howe said of Williams, "than he has of the duties of an apostle in the Christian church. He is no more fit for the one than for the other." After asserting that Union forces should offer protection in their lines for slaves owned by rebels, Howe said that he would gladly trade generals of Williams's type for any slave. "He is worth more to the service; he is worth more to the government; he is worth more to mankind," Howe averred. Even Senator Jacob Howard from Williams's home state of Michigan did not defend the general's actions. He claimed Williams's very conservative policies were a result of his staunch proslavery attitudes, which were not shared by the people of Michigan. Howard applauded Paine's disobedience of Williams's "illegal ... harsh, unfeeling and cruel order" and hoped the general would be investigated.[58]

Howard had an additional reason to be angry with Williams. At around the same time Paine was arrested, Col. Frederick Curtenius of the Sixth Michigan was also arrested for refusing to drive slaves out of his camp. Other officers of this regiment faced similar charges. "Not one of our Officers," Harrison Soule wrote his father, "have the least respect for Genl Williams and he says he has none for Volunteers so you see the condition in which we stand in our Brigade." According to Soule, every officer in three regiments of Williams's brigade signed a petition to have their units removed from the general's command. This was fine by Soule, for he thought Williams was "only fit to be in command of Hogs and fools."[59]

The Sixth Michigan would keep confiscating slaves despite Williams's mandates. Lt. William White thought the slaves were of great practical value. "We find the contrabands to be great institutions they do all of the police work and help us about the quarters," he asserted. But not everyone in the Sixth Michigan agreed. Before the regiment even left for the Gulf, Charles Henry Moulton mentioned his dislike for soldiers in the unit who stole and hid slaves. This was because, as he bluntly put it, "I hate a *damn nigger* more every day." His opinions had not changed six months later. If confiscation continued, he thought, "our army Will not bee Worth a cent they will mutinize for all the men Swear they did not come to fight for niggers."[60]

Whatever the opinions of individuals, serious policy differences remained between Williams and his officers. The situation reached a climax at the end of July and beginning of August 1862. Williams sent to department headquarters his charges against Colonel Paine and a number of officers from the Sixth Michigan. Their disobedience of his orders seemed "intended for abolition capital stock at home." In Paine's case, it was working, as Wisconsin abolitionist newspapers had already commented favorably on the colonel's defiant actions. Williams had "no use" for these officers and believed they had already demoralized their men. He suggested that the Michigan officers be replaced and that Paine be suspended or relieved from command. This latter recommendation was "an act of high justice and high necessity." Interestingly, Williams felt it necessary to reassert his patriotism at the end of the letter: "Twenty-five years in the military service of my country in the days of her success have not lessened my devotion to flag and Constitution in the days of her travail."[61]

With the official charges filed, Paine and the others made their way to New Orleans to report to Butler. According to Paine, Butler told him to resolve his differences with Williams (Paine had earlier filed his own charges against Williams). Paine agreed to reconcile, provided he did not have to admit that he had been wrong in refusing to abide by Williams's orders or comply with any such orders in the future. Butler and Paine then proceeded to quarrel over the meaning of the congressional act that forbade the Union army from returning slaves to their masters. All of this became moot when news arrived that Williams had been killed in battle at Baton Rouge. Butler soon released Paine and the Michiganders from arrest and ordered them to Baton Rouge.[62]

The bitter, protracted conflict between Williams and his officers offers a fitting conclusion to the story of how Union armies in the West handled confiscation in the war's first fifteen months. In armies from Tennessee to Alabama to Louisiana, there was tension and conflict over this issue. Officers struggled with one another over how far the army should go in confiscating slaves. Generally, top-level commanders adopted conservative policies toward slavery. Their subordinates, confronting actual slaves desperately fleeing bondage, sometimes chose to push beyond the orders of their superiors. What emerged during this first phase of the war was an army divided in some respects over the meaning and purpose of its struggle. Undoubtedly, part of this division stemmed from the ambiguity of Washington's slavery policy.

After all, Congress had passed only a relatively weak First Confiscation Act and a measure that prohibited the Union army from returning slaves to their masters. All this would soon change when Congress adopted the much stronger Second Confiscation Act in July 1862. Nevertheless, divisions over slavery policy in the army would not disappear. If this first part of the war proved anything, it was that officers had very different ideas about how to handle fugitive slaves, and they were willing to pursue them even if it meant conflict with their superiors or Washington.

CHAPTER TWO

An Emancipationist Turn of Policy

During the second half of 1862 most Union officers in the West adopted more emancipationist policies. They routinely confiscated the slaves of rebels and employed many of them as laborers, teamsters, servants, cooks, etc. This became the predominant policy across the several armies operating in the West. Official policy not only authorized confiscation but also made the practice more uniform. This shift was partly the result of new legislation in Washington. In July, Congress passed the Second Confiscation Act, which allowed for the seizure of any slaves belonging to rebels. At the same time, army commanders began to realize how slaves could serve the Union army and the military necessity of taking them away from rebels. Carrying out these emancipationist policies, army commanders such as Grant and Buell faced far fewer challenges from subordinate officers. Any remaining conflicts over confiscation policy were mainly confined to the border states. Officers operating in Kentucky and Missouri sometimes quarreled bitterly over fugitive slaves. Nevertheless, as summer turned into fall and Lincoln issued his Preliminary Emancipation Proclamation, Union armies were much more consistent and emancipationist in their policies.

The Second Confiscation Act was the key to this change in policy. By allowing the army to confiscate any slave owned by a rebel, the act dramatically increased the number of slaves subject to seizure. Previously, the army could only take slaves that were directly aiding the rebellion. The measure, however, was cumbersome and ambiguous. Most important, it was not clear whether a slave could be "freed" by the army or only through the courts. In order to safeguard the property of Unionists, moderate Republicans and Democrats in Congress purposely made it necessary to convict someone of treason in court before they could lose their property. The separate slavery section of the bill did not make it entirely apparent whether court action was required to technically free a rebel's slaves. Union commanders interpreted this provision differently, and in fact, historians have come to varying conclusions on the subject.[1] Nevertheless, no matter how particular Union officers interpreted their authority, they still allowed huge numbers of slaves to enter Union lines. Thus the Second Confiscation Act marked a radical change in army policies.

One commander who did not need the Second Confiscation Act to aggressively seize slaves was Maj. Gen. Samuel Curtis, commander of Union forces in Arkansas and Missouri. A West Point graduate and Mexican War veteran, Curtis had quickly risen to army command in the West and almost as quickly tasted military success. In March 1862, he led his Army of the Southwest to a decisive victory in Arkansas at the battle of Pea Ridge. For Curtis, the war was primarily a struggle to save the Union, and he was no abolitionist. But he came to realize before many other high-ranking officers that slavery had to be eliminated to put down the rebellion. As he wrote to Brig. Gen. Eugene Carr, "The rebellion must be shaken to its foundation, which is slavery, and the idea of saving rebels from the inevitable consequences of their rebellion is no part of our business while they persist." Military necessity and the desire to win the war drove Curtis to adopt very pro-emancipationist policies.[2]

This first became apparent during the summer of 1862 as Curtis marched his army through eastern Arkansas. Curtis's men confiscated rebel slaves in great numbers and gave them "free papers," certificates guaranteeing freedom. Curtis became a liberator largely out of military necessity. The slaves "were mustered by their rebel masters to blockade my way to my supplies," he commented to Henry Halleck. "These negro prisoners were the most efficient foes I had to encounter." Once they were offered their freedom, however, the slaves no longer posed a significant obstacle to the Union advance. "They are now throwing down their axes and rushing in for free papers. It is creating a general stampede in this region of cotton," reported Curtis. By the time the army reached Helena, Arkansas, several thousand slaves had joined Curtis's ranks. The free papers that Curtis was handing out were most likely beyond the scope of either the First or Second Confiscation Acts. Indeed, no other commander in the West went as far at this time.[3]

Following this somewhat overzealous approach, lower-level officers under Curtis carried out confiscation effectively. Capt. Nathan Paine of the First Wisconsin Cavalry noted how forty contrabands joined his unit in one night: "The privates almost all have one for [a] waiter. If we all live to come back we shall be 2400 *strong and* . . . half of them will be niggers." Maj. Henry Eggleston of the same unit claimed to have over 200 fugitive slaves with his battalion. Eggleston worried that this was "irritating the people [of Arkansas] wonderfully" and wished his colonel would just keep them out. Regardless of Eggleston's or anyone else's feelings on the issue, confiscation continued aggressively in Curtis's command.[4]

This was particularly true when the army occupied Helena. There Curtis made his position on enforcing the Second Confiscation Act quite clear: "The spirit of the recent law of congress, confiscating property will, in the absence of civil officers, be executed by the military authority of this command, as a military right, to weaken the enemy and strengthen the Federal power." Slaves brought into Union lines helped the army in a variety of ways by serving as scouts, spies, and laborers. Halleck directed Curtis to use the slaves to build a fort, compensating them with wages, rations, and clothing. This project was likely undertaken at least partly out of a desire to provide the slaves with employment. Reportedly, the chief engineer of the fort thought it "will be of no service."[5]

In truth, there were more slaves than Curtis could use, not to mention many women, children, and old men. Curtis developed a creative solution for this problem: he allowed them to sell the cotton of rebels, who had left their plantations at the approach of the Union army, and use the proceeds to acquire food and clothing. "By this means," Curtis wrote to Lincoln, "a thousand poor negroes, whose masters had run away, got means to which they were justly entitled, and have been saved from starvation." The general helped black people sell their cotton by pointing them to merchants he knew would treat them fairly. Sometimes he handled the transactions or paid for the cotton directly to guarantee just treatment. For example, Curtis gave a slave, David Haywood, an above-average price of fifty dollars each for twenty bales of cotton. In some instances, Curtis simply doled out money to slaves or put them on government steamers heading north.[6]

All this changed dramatically at the end of August 1862 when Brig. Gen. Frederick Steele replaced Curtis as head of the Army of the Southwest. Curtis had been elevated to direct the entire Department of Missouri. Steele seemed to be a logical choice for this command. He was a career military officer who had proved himself on the battlefields in Mexico. Moreover, he had been a division commander in Curtis's army. But coming from a staunch Democratic background, Steele disagreed with Curtis's policies toward slaves and adopted a much more conservative approach. To begin with, Steele did not recognize the legitimacy of the "free papers" Curtis had issued nor did he continue Curtis's program of permitting slaves to sell cotton to support themselves. Far less eager to confiscate, Steele only allowed those slaves who could be employed by the army to remain in his lines. And he imposed additional restrictions. For instance, officers were prohibited from having black servants because Steele thought they would somehow undermine an officer's character. Unemployed slaves, particularly women and children, were cast out of army camps and, in some cases, even returned to their masters. "This business of returning fugitives was the chief occupation of Steele and his subordinates," Chap. J. G. Forman of the Third Missouri complained. Steele's policies proved out of step with most other top commanders in the West. Forcing slaves of rebels out of Union lines, or returning them to their masters, was no longer a common practice. Most generals tried to find employment for slaves with the army. While there was still deep concern over what to do with slave women and children (indeed, this concern would persist until the end of the war), they were not usually forcibly removed from Union camps and were often sent to specially established contraband camps.[7]

Steele's policies soon got the general himself in trouble. The most notable incident involved the slaves of a Mr. Craig, a reputed rebel living close to Helena. Steele allowed Craig to reclaim several of his slaves who had been working in a Union hospital and take them in a wagon back to his plantation. A surgeon protested, showing the slaves' "free papers" from General Curtis, but was ignored. Craig actually had the aid of a Union guard in recovering his "property." This was in direct violation of a March 1862 congressional act and the Second Confiscation Act, which both forbade using soldiers for this purpose. The fact was not lost on Chaplain Forman, who thought that General Steele was breaking the law "without any real excuse, except his desire to oblige his slaveholding friend, Mr. Craig."[8]

Forman called Lincoln's attention to the matter, and the president refused to nominate Steele for a promotion to major general until he received an explanation of what happened regarding Craig's slaves. Steele informed Lincoln that the slaves had been employed in a brothel, not a hospital, and that Craig was a Unionist. Defending his policies in terms of military necessity, Steele asserted that "our camps and ... Helena were overrun with fugitive Slaves of both sexes. ... Vice, immorality and distress ... followed [and] I considered it my imperative duty to use every proper means ... to abate these evils." Grant quickly came to Steele's defense: "Gen. Steele is one of our very best soldiers as well as one of the most able. He is in every sense a soldier, one who believes, as such, his first duty is obedience to law and the orders of his superiors." With this strong endorsement from Grant, Lincoln was prepared to let the matter rest.[9]

This was not the only controversy over fugitive slaves in Curtis's department. On the day before Steele assumed command of the army in

Helena, Col. John Edwards of the Eighteenth Iowa wrote angrily to the governor of Iowa, Samuel Kirkwood, from Missouri that his regiment had been ordered to force fugitive slaves out of his camp "without discrimination between loyalty and disloyalty in their owners." This order came from Missouri militia officers. It was particularly grating to Edwards because it would compel his soldiers "to do camp drudgery" when the work could be done by contrabands instead. Edwards hoped the governor could get his command reassigned. Governor Kirkwood pressed the issue directly with the secretary of war. "The State troops in Missouri under whom officers and soldiers from this State are placed not only hold opinions," he told Edwin Stanton, "but act with reference to the . . . contraband question directly in opposition to the convictions of our officers and men." As a result of this and other problems, Kirkwood asked that the Iowa men be placed under officers from their own state. Washington was not willing to accommodate this request, and it is unclear if or when the Missouri officers stopped excluding slaves or how the controversy was resolved. What was apparent was that there was significant conflict over confiscation among some of Curtis's soldiers.[10]

Such conflicts even threatened to become violent. At the end of November 1862, the Twelfth Kansas crossed the Kansas-Missouri border in pursuit of reported Confederate guerrillas, allowing slaves to seek refuge in their lines as they advanced. While the regiment was encamped at Pink Hill, Missouri, it was confronted by the Enrolled Missouri Militia under Brig. Gen. Richard Vaughan. Vaughan ordered the Kansans to expel all slaves from their lines, turn over all property confiscated from Missourians, and leave the state. Both Col. Charles Adams and Lt. Col. Josiah Hayes of the Kansas regiment refused to carry out these orders and were arrested. Faced with this intransigence, Vaughan placed his artillery within range of the Kansans and virtually surrounded them with his cavalry. He then used a detachment of his troops to remove the slaves from the Union camp. The Missourians then escorted the Kansas soldiers out of the state. Maj. Thomas Kennedy reported that when the Twelfth got to Kansas, several of the slaves who had escaped Vaughan's soldiers rejoined the regiment. In his defense, Vaughan claimed that the Kansas men were in Missouri without orders and were plundering from the citizens of the state. The Kansans denied these charges. But whatever the truth of the matter, it is easy to see how Missouri officers would be keenly sensitive to soldiers from other states confiscating slaves in their state. After all, Missouri's civilian population was deeply divided in its loyalties and any interference with slavery could possibly alienate Missouri Unionists.[11]

Despite these conflicts, Curtis persisted in carrying out confiscation but was careful to confine it to slaves belonging to rebels. Curtis told one of his brigadiers, Ben Loan, that while rebels' slaves were "free," the slaves of Unionists "should be encouraged to stay at home and mind their business." At the end of December 1862, Curtis outlined the specific procedures to be followed. Provost marshals were to determine through "evidence as to the facts" whether a slave was the property of a rebel and thus eligible to be confiscated and freed under the law. If the slave was, the provost marshal would give him or her a paper that included the slave's name, color, size, and age. This document guaranteed the slave freedom under the Second Confiscation Act. Once slaves were liberated, it was the duty of provost marshals to protect them and arrest anyone who violated their freedom. No other commander in the West was as specific when it came to confiscation policy as Curtis. These "free papers" may not have been exactly legal, but Curtis could have been anticipating the Emancipation Proclamation going into effect the very next month.[12]

While Curtis was ordering confiscation in his Department of Missouri, Maj. Gen. Benjamin Butler was becoming more emancipationist in the Gulf. During the second half of 1862, Butler no longer tried to protect slavery. He inaugurated a system of "free labor," under which former slaves were compensated for their work, and confiscated more and more rebel slaves. This change undoubtedly resulted partly from the Second Confiscation Act. "By the act of Congress," Butler claimed, slaves "having come from rebel masters into our lines in occupation of rebel territory" were free. But the general's attitudes toward slavery were also shifting. Butler began to realize that slavery had to be abolished. "Certain it is I speak the almost universal sentiment and opinion of my Officers that Slavery is doomed," he informed Lincoln. "I have no doubt of it, and with every prejudice and early teaching against the result to which my mind had been irresistibly brought by my experience here." Butler became convinced that white people could perform labor "more economically" than black people and that black people could be employed just as profitably free as they could enslaved. Besides these economic considerations, Butler emphasized the military necessity of emancipation. "Months of experience and of observation," Butler reported to the people of New Orleans, "have forced the conviction that the existence of slavery is incompatible with the safety either of yourselves or of the Union." While he would have preferred gradual emancipation, it was better that slavery be eliminated immediately than continue to divide the country. Butler's emancipationist attitudes ultimately sprang from practical considerations rather than any moral principles or humanitarian concern for the slaves.[13]

Despite Butler's new attitudes and policies, he remained at odds with his abolitionist subordinate, Brig. Gen. John Phelps. In the wake of the Second Confiscation Act, Phelps became even more radical, wanting not only to welcome slaves into his lines but to enlist them as soldiers. This caused a new round of clashes with Butler. When Phelps asked Butler for arms and military supplies for his new black regiments, Butler ordered him to simply use the contrabands to chop down trees. "I am not willing to become the mere slave-driver which you propose," Phelps sputtered and then submitted his resignation. Butler refused to accept it and questioned Phelps's patriotism for resigning "in the face of an enemy." He pointed out that clearing the trees was a military necessity, and it was vital that black men perform this labor. In Butler's opinion, neither the government nor the president permitted arming black men. Phelps was unmoved and pressed to have his resignation sent to the president, so he could be freed "from that sense of suffocation, from that darkling sense of bondage and enthrallment," which he felt serving under Butler. Privately, Butler more bluntly deplored Phelps's radicalism. "He [Phelps] is mad as a March Hare on the 'nigger question,'" Butler wrote his wife. Both men were relieved from having to serve with each other when Lincoln accepted Phelps's resignation.[14]

Unlike Butler, other officers were not so happy to see Phelps go. Although Frank Wells, an officer in the Thirteenth Connecticut, thought all the slaves coming into Phelps's lines were lazy thieves, adding "I know I shall not fight very long to free any such lot of thievish dirty negroes as present themselves here," he still admired Phelps. "He [Phelps] is a trump . . . for Prest Lincoln to play as soon as he comes to the conclusion to abolish slavery," Wells noted savvily. Another Connecticut officer deemed Phelps "a terrible abolitionist— just a little cracked on that point, but he's one of the finest men that ever lived . . . ye can't help takin' to him." Nor did officers necessarily disagree with Phelps's policies. After stating his affection for Phelps, an officer in the Twelfth Connecticut contended that "the negroes ought to be liberated, and ought to be armed. If Gen. Phelps had had full sway here from the time of our coming. . . . We should have taken Mobile instead of merely holding on to New Orleans." In the middle of 1862, Butler was on solid ground in trying to constrain his zealous subordinate, but he would soon adopt policies himself that were little different than those of Phelps.[15]

Butler began to move in a more emancipationist direction in the summer of 1862. In August, he instructed the superintendent of the state prison not to enslave any children of female convicts. The children were to be treated as "other destitute children." A few months later, Butler ordered all slaves not belonging to Unionists released from prison and said that no slaves should be arrested unless it was known they were the property of a loyal citizen.

All the while, slaves poured into Butler's lines, and the army set up a contraband camp in Algiers, Louisiana, southeast of New Orleans, to handle the influx. Rufus Kinsley of the Eighth Vermont was put in charge of taking care of the contrabands, whose numbers, he noted, had swelled to 6,000 by the end of September. An abolitionist like Phelps, Kinsley not only provided for the contrabands but energetically tried to educate them. "In the education of the black," believed Kinsley, "is centered my hope for the redemption of the race, and the salvation of my country." So Butler was no longer just turning away any slave that was of no military value, and the army instead became a refuge for many slaves. Indeed, in November, Butler informed Lincoln that "we have some ten thousand negroes to feed . . . principally women & children."[16]

Some of these slaves filled vital roles in Butler's army. When Butler feared that Confederates were preparing for an attack on New Orleans near the end of August, he ordered the organization of black men into Union regiments. In theory, these regiments were supposed to consist only of men drawn from the large free black population of Louisiana, which numbered around 18,000. But in fact, significant numbers of slaves seized under the Second Confiscation Act were mustered into service. Butler organized three regiments of Louisiana Native Guards; most likely, the second and third regiments came largely from slaves confiscated by Butler's forces. It is impossible to know the exact composition of these units, but their very existence testifies to the remarkable changes in Butler's attitudes toward black soldiers in just a few months. At the end of May, Butler did not think black men were even capable of bearing firearms, and now he was relying on them as a crucial component of his military force. Undoubtedly, this change was driven by the demands of military necessity. As Butler wrote his wife, "I shall arm the 'free Blacks,' I think, for I must have more troops, and I see no way of getting them save by arming the black brigade that the rebels had." In making this decision, Butler was in fact approaching the policy of General Phelps, whom he had so harshly reprimanded for similar action. Yet the two generals had very different motives for turning to black soldiers. While Phelps was on a mission to eliminate slavery and uplift the downtrodden slave, Butler was a hard-nosed realist who realized that slaves could fill his critical manpower needs.[17]

Not everyone under Butler's command, however, was convinced of the wisdom of seizing slaves and making them soldiers. Brig. Gen. Godfrey Weitzel refused to assume command of fertile lands west of New Orleans in Lafourche Parish because it would force him to lead black troops. These black troops were reportedly causing slaves to show "symptoms of servile insurrection" in the area. "I have no confidence in the organization" of black regiments, Weitzel wrote Butler. "Its moral effect in this community, which is stripped of nearly all its able-bodied men and will be stripped of a great many of its arms, is terrible. Women and children, and even men, are in terror. It is heart-rending, and I cannot make myself responsible for it." Butler did not buy such arguments, reminding his subordinate that Gen. Andrew Jackson had confidence in black troops. More pointedly, Butler took issue with the claim that black soldiers were causing rebelliousness among the slaves. Instead, it seemed that the presence of the army, "carrying, by the act of Congress, freedom to this servile race," was the cause. Even if there was a slave insurrection, Butler argued that it was not the Union's fault. It was the responsibility of the Southerners who started the war and "who have stopped at no barbarity, no act of outrage, upon the citizens and troops of the United States." Butler asked Weitzel to consider the fact that one of those white families for whom he was so solicitous was that of Gen. Braxton Bragg. As a result of this protection, Bragg was "at liberty to ravage the homes of our brethren of Kentucky." Butler ordered Weitzel to command the black troops.[18]

Butler's army found other ways to use confiscated slaves. Col. Halbert Paine of the Fourth Wisconsin confiscated around 500 slaves to work on entrenchments near Baton Rouge. Paine did not want his soldiers to seize any slaves "who have families of children," but he allowed them to take the wives of able-bodied men if they wanted to work on the entrenchments. When the army left Baton Rouge, Paine told the black population that they could either stay in the city or go with his soldiers. Many went with Paine's troops and later enlisted in the Union army. Paine noted that the entrenchments they left behind proved "useful" to the army the next year. A few weeks earlier in Baton Rouge, Capt. Eli Griffin had reported that the Sixth Michigan had 200 contrabands constructing a fort "so that in case we are attacked we can hold our own." Contrabands were fast becoming an essential part of the labor force in Butler's army.[19]

That fall, Brig. Gen. Thomas W. Sherman made extensive use of contrabands in fortifying Manchac Pass north of New Orleans. Sherman provided the contrabands with clothes and food and paid them wages. One staff officer, Wickham Hoffman, remarked that his commander "was no professed friend of the negro, but ... did more practically for their welfare to make them useful, and save them from vagabondage, than Phelps or any other violent abolitionist." The abolitionists would supposedly let the slaves stay "in idleness," and

Hoffman observed that the work gave the contrabands satisfaction: "They were proud of being paid like white men." Capt. Joseph Bailey, chief engineer of New Orleans, was able to get the contrabands to labor hard, but he did not like them. He derisively described the 700 or 800 contrabands he was leading as "sweet scented sons of Ham," and "*lazy, lying, thieving, dirty, black gluttens.*" An ardent Unionist, Bailey minced no words when he asserted, "I had rather see every Negro in the United States burned at a stake, than to see this once peacefull, powerfull, and glorious nation destroyed."[20]

These examples demonstrate that officers held diverse attitudes toward black people and confiscation. But regardless of their attitudes, they were generally willing to carry out emancipationist policies. This was because of changes in the law. In the West, government policy, more than any other factor, drove officers to change their practices toward slaves. It certainly was no coincidence that army policy across the entire western theater changed in mid to late summer 1862, right when the Second Confiscation Act became law. Although officers' attitudes certainly played a role in the development of these emancipationist policies and influenced how far officers were willing to go in confiscating slaves and implementing programs to provide for the fugitives, the shape and substance of policy came from Washington. Officers, however, were left with the problem of how best to implement the policies, which was no easy task, considering the influx of slaves into their lines.

This was what led Butler to a creative solution. While the general allowed many slaves into his lines and employed them, he could not provide for the large numbers of slaves that would be confiscated under the Second Confiscation Act. He therefore implemented a system of labor. Black people would work for wages on the plantations of loyal men who agreed to abide by certain terms spelled out by the army. Planters had to provide these laborers with food and health care. In return, the farmers had to work ten-hour days, twenty-six days a month. While black people were protected from corporal punishment by planters, they could be punished by provost marshals, usually by "imprisonment in darkness on bread and water." Butler's troops would guard the plantations to preserve order. Butler's system helped preserve the valuable sugar crop in Louisiana and began the process of transforming slaves into free laborers. The general himself trumpeted the successes of his labor project. He informed Secretary of War Stanton that the experiment was "succeeding admirably" and told the president the same thing, adding that at least on one sugar plantation free labor was outproducing slave labor. Such an optimistic assessment was based on a very short trial and belied the more repressive features that later developed. Whatever the long-term merits of the system, it represented Butler's attempt to compromise between the demands of confiscation, military necessity, and preserving the economy of the region. Once again, Butler was playing the role of pragmatist. On his departure from New Orleans, Butler lauded his soldiers' success. "You have now the confidence of the 'oppressed race' and the slave," Butler assured his men. "Hailing you as deliverers, they are ready to aid you as willing servants, faithful laborers, or, using the tactics taught them by your enemies, to fight with you in the field."[21]

Ulysses S. Grant proved equally pragmatic. When Henry Halleck was promoted to general-in-chief in July 1862, Grant took command of troops in western Tennessee and northern Mississippi. In this capacity, he abandoned Halleck's General Orders No. 3 and permitted the employment of slaves as nurses, cooks, teamsters, servants, and laborers throughout the army. Thus, Grant was willing to energetically carry out the Second Confiscation Act.[22]

Grant's decision to open up his lines to fugitive slaves resulted mainly from his desire to carry out government policy. If Congress passed the Second Confiscation Act, he would enforce it. Grant made it clear that this act was vitally important in his change in policies. In early August 1862, he spelled out the specific procedures for confiscating and using slaves in his army because "recent Acts of Congress prohibit the Army from returning fugitives from labor to their claimants, and authorize the employment of such persons in the service of the Government." Grant would always defer to his civilian superiors on this matter. As he revealingly informed his father: "I have no hobby of my own with regard to the negro, either to effect his freedom or to continue his bondage. If Congress pass any law and the President approves, I am willing to execute it." Grant's soldierly instincts meant it was foolish even to discuss "the propriety of laws and official orders by the army." Yet aside from legality, he also started to see the benefits and indeed the inevitability of such a policy. The "*institution* are beginning to have ideas of their own and every time an expedition goes out more or less of them [slaves] follow in the wake of the army and come into camp," he wrote his sister. After putting the former slaves to good use in a variety of jobs, Grant reflected, "I dont know what is to become of these poor people in the end but it [is] weakning the enemy to take them from them."[23]

Grant's understanding of the importance of confiscating the slaves of rebels was most likely influenced by his close friend, Elihu B. Washburne, a congressman from Grant's hometown of Galena, Illinois. Washburne had been instrumental in Grant's rise to prominence and remained his staunchest defender in Congress. Washburne told Grant that protecting the property of rebels was "'played out' in public estimation. . . . The negroes must now be made our auxiliaries in every possible way they can be, whether by working or fighting." Washburne prodded Grant to take the lead in this: "That General who takes the most decided step in this respect will be held in the highest estimation by the loyal and true men in the country." Washburne's advice mattered, for just a little over two weeks later Grant moved to extensively confiscate and employ the slaves of rebels. Grant's command, like that of Butler's and Curtis's, became an important haven on the road to freedom for slaves in the late summer and fall of 1862.[24]

Even before Grant laid out his policies, Maj. Gen. William T. Sherman was implementing his own program for using slave labor in Memphis, Tennessee, because of the "law of Congress recently enacted." He employed able-bodied black men to work on the fortifications at Fort Pickering and to unload steamboats and coal boats at the levee. Moreover, Sherman permitted regiments to use slaves as teamsters and cooks. While the army provided these slaves with rations, clothing, and tobacco, slaves were prohibited from receiving wages, bearing arms, or wearing uniforms. Slaves could voluntarily return to their owners, but Sherman forbade masters or mistresses from recovering their slave property through "force or undue persuasion." Soon Sherman claimed to have 2,000 slaves with his command, and he was troubled about what to do with all the women and children. He did not force them out but would not provide them with provisions either. Less than two months after Sherman had affirmed that army policy was "to have nothing to do with the negro," he was allowing significant numbers of fugitive slaves to take refuge in his camp and work for the army.[25]

Yet he was still not liberating the slaves who came under his control. Sherman believed it was up to the courts to grant a slave freedom. He summarized his policy as follows: "We permit negroes to take refuge in our lines. . . . If good able bodied hands, we employ them as laborers, teamsters &c. and feed them, but donot say they are free. This is as far as I go." While Sherman anticipated that the courts would liberate the rebels' slaves and return the slaves of Unionists, he had no power to decide a slave's status. He would not follow Curtis's policy of granting slaves "free papers." Although Sherman might have been technically correct in arguing that freedom for the slaves had to come from the judiciary, the Second Confiscation Act was ambiguous and open to interpretation. Some generals, such as Curtis and Butler, chose to interpret the law expansively and did not recognize the need for the courts to grant legal freedom to the slaves, especially since courts were not functioning in many of the occupied areas of the South. Indeed, Sherman was the only major commander in the West to so thoroughly discuss the legal requirements of the act.[26]

If Sherman examined the act closely and understood some of its apparent weaknesses and limitations, he still supported confiscation. Sherman told Grant: "Your orders about property and mine about 'Niggers' make them feel that they [the rebels] can be hurt, and they are about as sensitive about their property as Yankees. I believe in universal Confiscation." Sherman thought the Confederates opened themselves up to confiscation when they rebelled and that the Union forces had the right to seize Southern property, including slaves, to weaken their enemy. As much as Sherman saw some of the benefits of confiscation, he most likely supported it just as much out of a desire to adhere to the law and the wishes of his government. "I reached Memphis at a time, when for the first time were let loose two great causes of solid disorder viz. the nigger & confiscation acts. Of course my duty is to obey the law, and orders of my superiors," the general conceded. Sherman believed in order above all, and abiding by the law was an important principle for creating an orderly society.[27]

At the same time, Sherman's approval of confiscation did not translate into support for emancipation. He was deeply concerned about the practical side of carrying out any sweeping emancipation program. Declaring slaves free was one thing, but Sherman wondered how the army could provide them all with food, clothing, and shelter. Even a "radical" like Gen. John C. Fremont would have trouble with these issues, Sherman thought. Yet such practical concerns were undoubtedly reinforced by his racial attitudes. Sherman worried that black people and white people could not live peacefully together. "When Negros are liberated either they or [their] masters must perish," Sherman believed. "They cannot exist together except in their present relation, and to expect negros to change from Slaves to masters without one of those horrible convulsions which at times Startle the world is absurd." Besides, Sherman still thought slavery a valuable system, and "not one nigger in ten wants to run off" anyway. So as much as Sherman came to appreciate the value of confiscation for the Union war effort and altered his policies with the changing law, he hardly stood ready to embrace emancipation. Indeed, Sherman seemed to be wrestling with the contradictions of his personal beliefs and a war that promised to upset many of his assumptions about politics and society.[28]

This emancipationist character of the war could be seen in the policies of officers at all levels in Grant's army, not just the upper echelon. Lower-level officers proved just as eager to confiscate slaves as the generals.

Col. A. W. Gilbert of the Thirty-Ninth Ohio reported slaves coming in by the trainload to Union camps in Iuka, Mississippi. Gilbert found himself a "young and spry" male slave to attend to the horses in the regiment. He anticipated that black men would soon be driving all the teams, freeing up nineteen of his soldiers. "This is the right way to employ the contrabands," Gilbert thought. Commanding the guard of all the Union forces at Iuka, Capt. Oscar Jackson of the Sixty-Third Ohio confiscated ninety-four slaves "of all sizes, ages, and sexes" in one night. At around the same time, Lt. George Palmer of the Eighty-Third Illinois was permitting hundreds of slaves to enter his post at Fort Donelson. Some of them became cooks and servants, while others were given passes to travel north. Grant had virtually no problems in getting junior officers to carry out his proconfiscation policies and to find suitable employment for fugitive slaves.[29]

One of the reasons these junior officers so readily confiscated was that many, like Gilbert, realized that slaves were a practical benefit to the Union war effort. Capt. William Britton of the Eighth Wisconsin pointed out how hundreds of former slaves in his regiment alone were loading and unloading all the trains and serving as cooks and teamsters. For Britton, this was a positive development since it allowed more soldiers to serve in the front lines. It also boosted troop morale. "There appears to be a new life in the army," Britton observed, "since the government has decided to use the black folks to help put down the rebellion. The men are anxious to have them to do their work for them." Another captain, James Lawrence of the Sixty-First Illinois, agreed that confiscating slaves was of value to the army. As he put it, "I think the *War* is about to take a new phase the niger is in the way and I think he will be put whare he can do some *good*." Capt. Channing Richards of the Twenty-Second Ohio noted how black laborers would allow thirty to fifty men in each regiment to take up their muskets again and added that future events would prove the "wisdom" of vigorous confiscation.[30]

It was clear that black people were finding Grant's army to be a refuge from the shackles of slavery, out of the reach of their masters' grasp, but as their numbers increased, Grant had to figure out what to do with them all. Initially, learning that Northerners desired black servants, he sent many of the women and children to Cairo, Illinois. But the White House stopped this practice quickly, fearing that a flood of black people into the North would undermine Republican chances in the midterm elections that November. Grant then turned to putting former slaves to work on deserted plantations, where they would be paid wages for raising cotton. From these wages, former slaves would be provided with clothing and other necessities. Grant detailed soldiers from his army to protect the working parties. This plan obviously grew out of military considerations; Grant could not possibly care for so many fugitive slaves and still carry out effective operations in the field. Indeed, just as he was initiating this program, he was about to embark on his first attempt to capture Vicksburg. But Grant was motivated by more than just hard-nosed military considerations. The slaves who escaped to Union lines often came without the bare necessities of life and suffered greatly from disease. Grant certainly had some humanitarian impulses and did not want to see the slaves die. In fact, he was legitimately concerned about black people and their future. The general reportedly told Chap. John Eaton, who was placed in charge of the program, that when a black man demonstrated that he could be an effective laborer, "it would be very easy to put a musket in his hands and make a soldier of him, and if he fought well, eventually to put the ballot in his hand and make him a citizen." So Grant saw his program as a way to fight white racial prejudices and, not coincidentally, to smooth the path to black military service and even citizenship. Clearly, Grant himself was developing greater faith in the capacity of black people and was aiding their movement from slavery to freedom. This was a very different Grant than the one who had entered the war.[31]

The commander of the Army of the Ohio, Maj. Gen. Don Carlos Buell, proved far less willing than Grant to change his views on slavery. Buell never came around to embrace emancipation, even as a strictly military measure. He always believed that the war could be won without touching Southern property and slaves. Secretary of the Treasury Salmon P. Chase described Buell as "proslavery to the last degree" and thought this explained his slowness as a general. Buell himself, while not directly mentioning emancipation, believed that the government's harsher policies toward Southerners were "discreditable to the nation, and a stain upon civilization." They would not lead to the preservation of the Union, and "their tendency was to subvert the institutions under which the country had realized unexampled prosperity—and happiness."[32]

But while he never approved of the war taking on an emancipationist purpose, in the late summer of 1862 Buell began to grudgingly adopt more proconfiscation policies. This was largely an outgrowth of the Second Confiscation Act. Buell agreed with one of his division commanders, Brig. Gen. Thomas Wood, that "the passage of the confiscation act" made it improper to allow rebels to reclaim fugitive slaves from Union lines. When Wood suggested that slaves be used as teamsters in the army, Buell approved, but he added that slaves should be expelled from Union camps "when they cannot be made useful to the Government and become a nuisance." So Buell permitted the confiscation of slaves belonging to rebels, but only those slaves that could be employed by the army. He later explained his reasons for this limited confiscation: "I considered that the presence of large numbers of negroes, as for that matter any other hangers-on about the camps to be injurious to the discipline and efficiency of the army." Some commanders probably would have agreed with Buell, at least with regard to those slaves that were of no practical military use, but commanders usually did not drive slaves away. So compared to other top generals in the West, Buell took in far fewer fugitives. Nevertheless, any confiscation marked a significant change in Buell's policies.[33]

Another change, alluded to above, was that Buell and his officers were less likely to return slaves directly to their owners. Slaves excluded from Buell's lines might be eventually recaptured by their masters, but the army would no longer assist in this process. There were exceptions, especially when slaves owned by Kentuckians were involved, but instances of officers abetting slave owners in the recovery of their property were few and far between. A controversy between Maj. Gen. Ormsby Mitchel and the high command of Buell's army in August 1862 illustrates this change in policy. Mitchel defined the war as "a death struggle between the north + the south—between the enemies and the friends of slavery. That is just it and nothing more." It was therefore hardly surprising that Mitchel was alarmed when he learned from a newspaper article that some of the slaves he had promised to protect had possibly been returned to their masters. As Mitchel was no longer with the army due to his frustration with Buell's cautious military strategy and leniency toward Southern civilians, he begged Stanton to intervene. Stanton initiated an investigation, directing Buell to ascertain the facts of the case. Through the reports of both Brig. Gen. W. S. Smith and Brig. Gen. Lovell Rousseau, Buell demonstrated that none of Mitchel's "protected" slaves had been returned. Indeed, Rousseau testified that a slave belonging to a Unionist had not been given back to his master. The War Department was satisfied with this, telling Mitchel that his newspaper source was unreliable. Buell was pleased that none of these slaves were returned because "it would be contrary to my feelings and orders if such should have been the case." Buell would no longer primarily play the role of slave catcher; the law and the war had made such a role almost untenable for Union officers.[34]

As a testament to his new policies, Buell extensively used slaves as laborers across Tennessee and northern Alabama during the summer of 1862 as his army sluggishly advanced toward Chattanooga, Tennessee. Officers were instructed to employ slaves to build stockades and erect fortifications. But interestingly, Buell worried about the effect this would have on slave owners. He cautioned Col. Charles Harker, when seizing slaves to dig entrenchments, to "try, if possible, to leave enough with the owner to do the ordinary and indispensable work about an establishment." Then, Buell ordered Harker to return one slave to a Mr. Harris for necessary labor. Most of the slaves taken, however, were never given back to their masters. They moved with the army when Buell fell back to deal with the Confederate thrusts into Tennessee and Kentucky that fall. Capt. Francis Darr, the army's chief commissary officer, stated that the slaves "received every facility for being sent northward with the troops" and traveled by train and wagon. Darr added, "There was a great sympathy felt for them by officers and soldiers and a general desire to help them along." [35] This was understandable considering the important services they had just rendered the army.

Junior officers in Buell's army understood all this and were willing to implement aggressive confiscation on the ground, even more so than Buell. Noting that two companies of his regiment were sent into the country to confiscate slaves, William Kemper of the Seventeenth Indiana remarked, "As a confiscation bill has been passed by Congress, we thought we would see how it would work down here." His men found twenty slaves, who came in happily in ranks with one of their own pretending to be captain. Just a few days earlier, Lt. Ephraim Holloway of the Forty-First Ohio informed his wife that the soldiers no longer protected rebel property and used slaves whenever they needed work done. A month later, he reported that fifteen to thirty slaves were coming in each day and remaining with the regiment. Among them, Holloway found a servant named "Uncle Ned," whom he wanted to send north.[36]

A surgeon in the Fifty-Eighth Indiana, William Blair, found an especially valuable servant. After a fight near McMinnville, Tennessee, Blair's regiment captured Confederate brigadier general Nathan Bedford Forrest's horse and servant. Describing the slave as "the finest looking negro man I ever saw" and "very intelligent," Blair also welcomed information about the strength of Confederate forces and the true rebel sympathies of the citizens in that part of the state. Upon learning that some declared Union men had served as guides for Forrest, Blair seized their slaves. Deeply impressed with his new servant, Blair assured the slave that if he remained with him until the conflict ended, "he 'should have a sight at the North Star.'" In addition to the servant, Blair's regiment confiscated a number of other slaves, who were put to work driving the division's teams.[37] The lower-level officers in Buell's army thus proved more than willing to seize the enemy's slaves after the Second Confiscation Act was passed. This is unsurprising, considering the fact that many junior officers in the Army of the Ohio had pushed for confiscation earlier in the war.

Brig. Gen. Lovell Rousseau's division, however, was an exception to this pattern of vigorous confiscation on the ground. Rousseau was a Kentucky politician who had no sympathy for emancipation. "The negroes have been annoying us and we have driven a great many of them off but they follow at a distance and come up at night ... [and] most of them still hang on our skirts," a Buckeye lieutenant commented. Nor was the Second Ohio seizing slaves to dig trenches, though Lt. George Landrum wished they would. After his first night of work, Landrum complained, "I blistered my hands handling the spade, and could not help thinking how much better we could be employed, and how much better it would be to use the negroes for that kind of work than the free white men of the north." The time when brigades of black men would be working for every division could not come soon enough for Landrum. The fact that it was Rousseau's division that was, at the very least, slow with confiscation was all the more ironic, considering this division had once been under the command of General Mitchel, one of the most aggressive and earliest confiscators in the Union army.[38]

Rousseau even returned fugitive slaves to Kentucky masters. At Bloomfield, in October 1862, Rousseau got into a bitter dispute with the Twenty-First Wisconsin over this. The regiment had allowed two slaves into their camp. When their owners tried to recover this property, the soldiers drove them out of their lines, hurling corncobs and threatening to shoot. The owners then returned with General Rousseau, who ordered the other regiments of the brigade to surround the Twenty-First Wisconsin with their guns loaded. Rousseau asked the regiment if they would now reveal where the slaves were and obey his orders. In response, one soldier boldly declared, "Yes General, if consistent with our duty and Concience, but no slave catching." Enraged, Rousseau arrested the line officers and confined the rest of the regiment to camp. Although it is unclear why, the next day Rousseau changed his mind and released them all. Marching out that day, the Wisconsinites passed a sour-faced Rousseau and his staff with their slaves hidden in an ambulance. The slaves eventually became officers' servants. The night of the regiment's arrest, someone had actually torched the slave owners' plantation buildings. It was evident that these men did not like being asked to return slaves. Indeed, Rousseau himself apparently avoided such a practice unless the slaves belonged to Kentuckians.[39]

Significantly, this was far from the only incident of controversy over the confiscation of fugitive slaves in Kentucky, and despite this, junior officers remained willing to confiscate. Col. Leander Stem of the 101st Ohio noted how slaves along the road would offer their services to Union troops and be taken as servants. Other times, soldiers reportedly "accosted" the slaves and tried to forcibly persuade them to go with the army. While still in Kentucky, Stem planned to end the bad cooking in the regiment by confiscating a rebel's slave. An officer in the Seventy-Ninth Ohio, Thomas E. Smith, had two slaves cooking for him and another soldier. These slaves, along with others serving the regiment, had to be hidden from slave masters, who would stop at nothing to recover their property. Smith observed that "owners of slaves could be seen constantly riding along the lines looking for negroes. Evry day they come round through the camp spying about." In fact, Smith almost lost his prized cook, whose master came searching through the camp, but the men prevented him from finding his slave.[40]

There were important reasons that Kentucky became the site of continuing conflict in the Union army over the confiscation of slaves. Kentucky was loyal and was immeasurably important to the Union war effort. But the state had a significant slave population that many of its citizens did not want to give up. In 1860, nearly 20 percent of its population was slaves, and they numbered 225,483. In fact, more people were in bondage in Kentucky than in the rest of the border states put together. Most Kentuckians who owned slaves owned a small number of them and engaged in more diversified agriculture than much of the deeper South, which was dominated by the growing of valuable cash crops. As was the case in Missouri, Kentucky's slaves were unevenly distributed throughout the state. While the mountainous region of eastern Kentucky and much of the northern part of the state had few slaves, the Bluegrass region around Lexington had the most significant concentration of slaves in the state. Indeed, Lexington was the most prominent Kentucky slave market for the sale of slaves to the Deep South. Union troops were constantly marching through the slave-rich area of the Bluegrass and dealing with slaves seeking refuge and angry citizens seeking their return to bondage. The last thing many white Kentuckians wanted to see was the war for the Union turn into a war for emancipation.[41]

If emancipation was a thorny issue for Kentuckians, a strong sense of Unionism pervaded much of the state. Coming from a rich tradition that included Henry Clay, the venerated "Great Compromiser," many Kentuckians felt a powerful commitment to the Union, refusing to allow sectional differences to tear it apart. Clay had been a leader of the Whig Party, which had dominated Kentucky's politics for much of the antebellum period. But that party had collapsed in the 1850s due to intensifying sectional tensions. In the election of 1860, John Bell won the state of Kentucky. As noted previously, Bell had been a lifelong Whig, and in 1860, he was the nominee of the Constitutional Union Party, which had become a haven for many old Whigs who stood firmly for the Union. As Southern states left the Union in 1860–61 and the nation went to war, Kentuckians at first declared neutrality. This, however, was an untenable long-term position, and Kentucky's powerful Unionist sentiment soon became apparent. In the summer of 1861, Kentuckians gave Unionists huge political victories in both the congressional elections and in the elections for the new state legislature. Indeed, the Unionists won every congressional seat except one. When Confederates invaded the state in September 1861, followed soon after by Union forces, Kentucky officially went with the Union side. Certainly, divisions among civilians and soldiers would plague Kentucky society throughout the war, but the state remained loyal during this time of intense crisis.[42]

Given Kentucky's large Unionist population that was, for the most part, committed to the institution of slavery, it is not surprising that some Union officers were very cautious in attacking slavery in the state. Any tampering with the institution could potentially alienate these valuable Bluegrass supporters from the Union cause. Additionally, it was much more likely that slaves in the state were the property of Unionists and not rebels, making them ineligible to be confiscated in the first place. Thus political and legal considerations made army officers, especially those in the upper echelons of command, more hesitant to confiscate slaves in Kentucky than elsewhere. But, at the same time, other officers showed no such hesitancy. This inconsistency created great tension in the army and the state.

The conflict was most pronounced in the Army of Kentucky during the fall of 1862. The brass wanted nothing to do with slaves and confiscation. The army commander, Maj. Gen. Gordon Granger, ordered that "no citizen nor non-combatant" be allowed in the army's lines. One of Granger's division commanders, Brig. Gen. Quincy Gillmore, was even more explicit, instructing his men "to refuse admission" into Union camps "to that class of people known as 'contrabands.'" Gillmore thought it was "demoralizing" for his soldiers to be burdened with noncombatants. The fact that Kentucky was a loyal state also influenced Gillmore's actions. When the general was harshly criticized in the Ohio press, he replied, "We are not in the enemy's country... martial law does not exist here... [and] the civil authorities are in the full exercise and enjoyment of their legitimate functions." Gillmore explained how Grant's troops operated in states that were "in persistent rebellion," while Kentucky was "true to her allegiance." Both Granger and Gillmore were West Point–trained professional military men who would have had a keen sense of the delicate military situation in Kentucky. They would not have wanted to cause any turmoil for their superiors in Washington by moving on the slavery issue. Brig. Gen. Stephen Burbridge, a native Kentuckian, was similarly determined to prevent his soldiers from taking slave property. He gave his brigade three hours to drive out all fugitive slaves and returned some to their masters. Burbridge went as far as to invite his uncle to recover any slaves that belonged to him or friends of the family. "I can get them without any trouble," the general promised. In order to carry out these policies, Burbridge was compelled to place several officers under arrest.[43]

While the high command of the Army of Kentucky made clear their policies on slaves, lower-level officers did not always obey their superiors' orders. In fact, many overtly defied them and aggressively seized and harbored slaves as they operated in the state. The Seventy-Seventh Illinois gathered "quite a regiment" of slaves during its movement from Richmond to Louisville. They confiscated so extensively that Burbridge reportedly claimed they "would steal all the niggers in Kentucky if they had a chance to do so." As they marched through Louisville, slave catchers confronted the Illinoisans with revolvers drawn, swearing "dire vengeance on the ... yankey abolition niger thieves." In response, the soldiers drew their own weapons, and the slave catchers quickly retreated. Such activities by the Eighteenth Michigan drew the ire of Col. Marc Mundy of the Twenty-Third Kentucky, who appealed directly to Lincoln. Mundy claimed that the Michigan soldiers had taken at least twenty-five slaves of Unionists, including one that belonged to him personally. There is no evidence that Washington did anything about this, but the colonel of the Eighteenth Michigan was arrested for not excluding slaves or turning them out of his lines. Many junior officers were more willing than their commanders to seize slaves in Kentucky. Perhaps those at the top were more sensitive to the political costs of confiscating slaves in a loyal state. Plus, it was not even legal to seize the slaves of Kentucky Unionists. Because it was difficult to determine whether a particular slave's owner had Union or Confederate sympathies, it was easier to not confiscate any. This way the law would never be violated. Whatever the case may be, some confiscation in the state was consistent with the Second Confiscation Act, and lower-level officers did not shy away from aggressively carrying it out.[44]

The Ninety-Second Illinois was a case in point. While at Mt. Sterling, Kentucky, in November 1862, the regiment's commander, Col. Smith

D. Atkins, refused a direct order from his brigade commander, Col. J. C. Cochran, to return slaves to their masters. "I cannot conscientiously force my boys to become the slavehounds of Kentuckians," Atkins explained to his friend. Significantly, these slaves apparently belonged to rebels; Atkins would not take the slaves of loyal men. In fact, Thomas Winston, an assistant surgeon in the regiment, witnessed Atkins turn away one Union man's slave, and Winston did the same thing, hardly able to hold back tears in the process. Even though he confiscated only rebels' slaves, Atkins still had to fight to keep them. When the regiment was ordered away from the area in hopes of defusing the crisis, it ran into more conflict. At Winchester, Kentucky, Atkins's men marched through town "with bayonets fixed and guns loaded" to protect the slaves from hostile citizens and the Fourteenth Kentucky Union Infantry, which tried to physically remove the fugitives. In Lexington, they drove a mob away at the point of the bayonet, with Atkins reportedly threatening that "he would fire a volley into them, so help him God."

After these confrontations, Atkins faced more problems over the fugitive slaves. He was sued several times in Kentucky for seizing slaves and was summoned to appear in court. "We have no right to resist the execution of any civil process," General Gillmore informed him. Luckily for Atkins, he was not directly under Gillmore's command and thus did not have to comply with this advice. Atkins described himself as "too busy with a terrible rebellion and bloody war, to be fooling away my time in writing answers to bills in chancery filed by secession sympathizers." After all, he was only following the law in confiscating these slaves. Atkins wrote his congressman, Owen Lovejoy, and the secretary of war to complain about these lawsuits. Apparently, Atkins successfully weathered this storm in Kentucky, which pitted him against his commanders, citizens of the state, and the courts.[45]

Similar actions by Col. William Utley of the Twenty-Second Wisconsin forced the president to intervene. Utley, fervently antislavery in principle, made his camp a safe haven for slaves and remained steadfast in his determination to not give them up. In October 1862, despite being threatened with arrest, Utley declined to obey several directives from General Gillmore to turn slaves out of his lines and return them to their owners. He defended this insubordination by invoking the congressional law that outlawed using soldiers to return slaves. Gillmore chose not to arrest his wayward subordinate, who was supported by his men. After successfully standing up to his division commander, Utley had to confront the threats of citizens in Georgetown, Kentucky, who had taken slaves from the ranks of the Twenty-Second Michigan at gunpoint as the soldiers marched through town and threatened to do the same to Utley's men. Pvt. Benjamin F. Heuston thought that if they attempted to seize the slaves, "may God have mercy on their doomed village!" Utley directed his men to move through Georgetown with loaded guns and fixed bayonets. A citizen watching the column march by believed "it was almost dangerous for a man to try to get his negro out of their ranks." Indeed, it remained almost impossible to get any slaves from the Wisconsin men.[46]

The Twenty-Second Wisconsin went to extraordinary lengths to protect fugitive slaves. When a teenage female slave came into Utley's camp asserting that her master was going to make her a prostitute, Utley was moved to help her. With two soldiers from the regiment as an escort, she was sent to Cincinnati to meet the abolitionist Levi Coffin. Dressed as a Union soldier, hiding in the back of an army wagon, the woman made it to Cincinnati with her soldier companions before being sent farther northward to Wisconsin. The soldiers even had a picture made with her. All of this would never have been approved by Utley's superiors. Nor did they approve of him seizing a slave named Adam, who was the property of George Robertson, a Unionist, a former chief justice of the Kentucky Supreme Court, and an acquaintance of Lincoln's. Robertson showed up at Utley's camp and demanded his slave. The slave was not willing to leave and informed the colonel that the judge had hired him out to a brutal man who beat him badly. With this information, the colonel adamantly refused to turn the slave over to the judge. In a heated exchange, Utley berated Robertson, reportedly declaring, "If Kentucky's loyalty and unionism depends upon my willingness to be converted into a negro hunter for her bloated, aristocratic Union hypocrites, she may go to hell, with all the nations that forget God." Faced with such a rebuke, Robertson appealed to both Utley's superiors and the state courts, though neither could pry the slave away from Utley. Then, the judge turned to the president, but Lincoln would not force Utley to return the slave; instead, he offered Robertson $500 for him. Robertson refused Lincoln's extraordinary offer, and Adam, with the rest of the regiment's slaves, accompanied the Wisconsin men into Tennessee.[47]

Despite all the drama, the intense conflict over slavery in Union armies in Kentucky was an anomaly during the latter half of 1862. Elsewhere in the West, both upper-level and junior officers consistently carried out emancipationist policies at the ground level. They not only confiscated and employed rebel slaves extensively but started contraband camps and labor programs. This marked an important shift away from the policies of the war's first fifteen months, when slaves had been routinely sent away from Union lines or permitted to enter in very limited numbers. The Second Confiscation Act was instrumental in this change. Despite limitations, it transformed army policy. While many Union officers felt duty bound to carry out the new legislation, they also recognized its wisdom. As the war dragged on into its second year and the Union had failed to subdue the rebellion, many officers believed that harsher policies were necessary. The sweeping confiscation of slaves, which before now had seemed out of the question, now appeared prudent—in fact essential. Military necessity became the dominant reason these officers embraced confiscation, and only overwhelming political considerations could dictate otherwise. This helps explain why the border states, especially Kentucky, were the only areas in the West during this period where officers were still willing to exclude all slaves from Union lines, return them to their masters, and even forcibly remove them from Union camps. Yet on the whole, by the end of 1862, Union forces had struck an irrecoverable blow to slavery and were on their way to becoming a full-fledged army of liberation.

CHAPTER THREE

Union Officers and the Intense Debate over Emancipation and Black Troops

---

As Washington officials moved toward an emancipationist policy during the second half of 1862 and the beginning of 1863, the attitudes of many Union officers in the West lagged behind. The Second Confiscation Act along with the Preliminary and final Emancipation Proclamations produced deep divisions in the army. Significant numbers of officers opposed these measures out of political, practical, and racial concerns. Other officers just as fervently approved these policies, with many believing that freeing the slaves was necessary to save the Union. These intense divisions over emancipation lasted roughly through the first half of 1863. By that time, many officers who had initially opposed emancipation had changed their minds. There were some who never came around, but on the whole by the latter stages of the war, officers were unified in their commitment to emancipation on some level. This pattern did not hold when it came to enrolling black troops. Many officers supported this policy, but there was also considerable opposition that lasted through the end of the conflict.[1]

One of the major reasons for this lagging support for the government's policies toward emancipation and black troops was the fact that few officers had enlisted primarily to liberate the slaves. In their view, the war's primary objective was to save the Union and preserve a free and democratic government. As he was organizing the Eleventh Illinois in Springfield, W. H. L. Wallace commented, "The feeling here is tremendous and almost unanimous in sustaining the Government." Another Illinoisan, Capt. David Sparks of the Third Illinois Cavalry, loved his family so much that he would risk his life so "that they may have a free government." George Avery, who would soon serve as an officer in the Third Missouri Cavalry, explained to his skeptical future wife the importance of fighting for the Union less than a month after he left home: "Is it not reasonable to suppose that if we make one division without resenting it at the peril of our lives, we would soon be called upon to sanction another upon the same terms.... I will fight till I die before I will see this once glorious Union rent in twain." At the same time, Avery deplored any move toward emancipation. Not wanting black people in the North or anywhere close to him, Avery "would not sleep one night in the 'Tented Field' to free every slave in America." Indeed, he went as far as to claim that "when President Lincoln declares the slaves emancipated I will declare myself no longer an American citizen." Even though such extreme anti-emancipation sentiments were rare during the first year of the war (probably due to the fact that emancipation had not yet become policy), most Union officers believed that Union—not emancipation—was their cause.[2]

Given this motivation, it is not surprising that officers expressed a variety of opinions when the war began to assume an emancipationist character in the summer of 1862. Some officers wholeheartedly supported the Second Confiscation Act largely for its practical benefits. At the head of the Third Ohio, Col. John Beatty lamented recent military setbacks, particularly the failure to capture Richmond, but trusted the confiscation act would "have good effect." This was because "slavery is the enemy's weak point, the key to his position. If we can tear down this institution, the rebels will lose all interest in the Confederacy." Another colonel, leading the Fifth Minnesota, agreed: "It certainly makes the rebels wince to see their 'niggers' taken off which is a source of private satisfaction to me.... Crippling the institution of slavery is ... striking a blow at the heart of the rebellion." James Madison Bowler, also from Minnesota, considered the Second Confiscation Act "glorious" and was happy that the war was being prosecuted more vigorously. "'Governing by love' is played out," he observed.[3]

At the same time, some officers were going much further and becoming downright abolitionists. For some, this stemmed from witnessing slavery firsthand. Capt. William Moore of the Tenth Wisconsin was utterly appalled to see female slaves working in the fields. Whoever was responsible, Moore fumed, "deserves not the *name of man*. He should have inhabited some lonely Isle where the Female form should never greet his sight, and where pondering upon this curious freak of nature, he might hate himself to death." For Moore, this all raised an additional question: "Is there a Just God and will he always see his creatures thus oppressed, and not send retributive justice with a sword of vengence to teach Traitors their duty, and punish them for passed offences?" Charles Brackett, an assistant surgeon in the Ninth Illinois

Cavalry, ran into a black boy who was to be sold away from his mother when he was old enough to pick cotton. This was so shocking that Brackett decided that perhaps the slaves should be free. Lt. George Landrum in the Second Ohio was equally horrified over what he saw of slavery: "There is more barbarism in one little place like this in the south, than there is in the state of Ohio. Uncle Tom's Cabin should be enlarged upon." Even more significant, he commented, though obviously with considerable exaggeration, "We are all becoming Abolitionists here."[4]

Landrum referred to an aspect of slavery that was particularly galling to officers: light-skinned slaves. "The 'nigger' is mixed up too much with the whites," complained the Buckeye lieutenant. "I am thoroughly disgusted with them and their society." The Illinois captain David Sparks was certain that some of his friends would criticize him for becoming an abolitionist: "But let them leave their homes . . . and witness the blighting influences of the 'institution' where persons with not more than one-quarter African blood in them are held in bondage, bought and sold like brutes—and then tell me if you think such practices consistent with Democracy." William Kemper of the Seventeenth Indiana was horrified when two enslaved children that appeared "white" to him came into camp. They "had flaxen hair and blue eyes," and one had been whipped "unmercifully." Seeing these sights, Kemper was not surprised that a "Just God" would "scourge" their country. Such encounters were "fast abolitionizing" the army. When one considers the prevalent racial attitudes of the day, it is hardly surprising that running into these "white" slaves would have such an impact. Most Northerners saw white people as superior, entitled to certain political rights and economic privileges, and were repulsed by any racial amalgamation. These officers could not fathom how anyone who looked so "white" could ever be enslaved. If the system of slavery produced such results, it had to go.[5]

But more often, officers embraced emancipation for a quite practical reason: ending slavery would help end the war. By the end of May 1862, Capt. Emerson Opdycke of the Forty-First Ohio was ready "to make all needed sacrifices" to destroy slavery. "*Slavery must go out*" if the South was ever to be conquered, he concluded. A little over two months later, an Ohio surgeon, John Rice, struck a similar chord: "No power on earth can subdue the South, without freeing and arming the only loyal southerners, the slaves." Rice was so certain that the war needed to be prosecuted more vigorously and proceed in an emancipationist direction that he "never would shoulder a musket" until it did. In a very pragmatic way, some officers came to realize that emancipation was a powerful weapon against the rebellion that they so despised.[6]

The course of the war itself encouraged such beliefs. At the end of June 1862, Gen. Robert E. Lee's Confederate forces drove back Gen. George McClellan's Union army from the very gates of Richmond, Virginia, in a series of engagements known as the Seven Days' Battles. This critical military setback for the Union, coming during a lull in western campaigning, shaped attitudes toward slavery and emancipation. The Fifteenth Wisconsin's Col. Hans Christian Heg sadly commented on the bad news from Richmond and elsewhere. "It can not be otherwise," he claimed. "When the Government learn[s] to put in Generals ... that are not afraid to hurt slavery or the Rebels, then we will begin to see the end of this war." The colonel of the Thirteenth Wisconsin hoped the defeat at Richmond would lead to "a more vigorous and more severe prosecution of the war. The time has come, or will soon come to march through this nest of vipers with fire and sword, to liberate every slave. I would like to help do that." Shortly after learning of the battles around Richmond, a doctor in the Seventy-Second Ohio, William Caldwell, seethed, "The very works against which our brave troops dashed themselves and from which they were repulsed so disastrously were built by the omnipresent nigger." During a recent campaign against Corinth, Mississippi, slaves had constructed fifty miles of breastworks. To Caldwell the conclusion seemed obvious: "Let us confiscate-emancipate any thing to weaken the power of the traitorous villains whose hands are already reeking with the best blood of the land."[7]

This shift in attitudes toward emancipation appeared quite remarkable. "This war is making a great revolution in the opinion of the intelligent men in the army," Lucius Hinkley of the Tenth Wisconsin commented at the end of July 1862. At the war's outset, Hinkley estimated that "three quarters of the officers & men in the western army" were opposed to abolition, but by midsummer 1862, he "heard some of these same conservative officers declare that they were in favor of emancipation, confiscation, or any thing else." Near the end of the summer, the colonel of the Thirty-Ninth Ohio detected a similar shift in attitudes that meant "vast strides towards crushing the rebellion."[8]

Hinkley had said "intelligent men" were embracing emancipation, hinting that these emancipationist views were by no means shared by all or perhaps even most of his comrades. From the available evidence, it appears that nearly as many officers still opposed taking the war in an emancipationist direction. A few even voiced their displeasure when slavery was abolished in the District of Columbia. Capt. John Ziegler of the Eleventh Illinois Cavalry noted that there was "considerable" opposition among officers to this legislation. "Perhaps it will caus[e] some Resignations," he speculated, and "if so you may Look for me with the Rest." A lieutenant in the Tenth Ohio, Alfred Pirtle, observed that the act eliminating slavery in the nation's capital "had a bad effect" on parts of the army and further incensed the Confederates against the Lincoln administration. He asked, "How can the Southern people ever be expected to come willingly, back to the Union, when they see such decisive action taken to overthrow the institution which is the main stay of the South?" In the spring of 1862, many officers still believed that they could conciliate the South, and so even small steps against slavery still generated opposition in the army.[9]

The Second Confiscation Act caused further discontent and division. Just after an extensive debate on confiscation in Congress, Lieutenant Pirtle bluntly told his mother that he did not see the war ending anytime soon unless "Congress will adjourn and let the niggers alone." Later, Pirtle mentioned that several officers in a Kentucky regiment tendered their resignations because of their unhappiness with the Second Confiscation Act. This alarmed Pirtle, for such disaffection buoyed the spirits of the rebels, and he was pleased that the resignations were not accepted. Perhaps such dramatic gestures reflected momentary pique more than anything else, but a captain in the Sixth Michigan worried about the military consequences of meddling with slavery. "If our Members in Congress will keep their mouths shut on the everlasting Slavery question until we get off the field what we have in hand," he wrote in mid-June, "we will then vacate the Ground and they then can take up the musket." He would not follow "the dictates of political Demagogues."[10]

Without explicitly mentioning Congress or confiscation, a number of officers made it clear that they remained opposed to turning the war into any type of crusade against slavery. Racial considerations and a desire not to have black people in the North exerted a powerful influence here. Charles Wills, an adjutant in the Seventh Illinois Cavalry, saw slaves working in the fields and "thanked God" that none of them were in Illinois. "Candidly, I'd rather see them and a whole crop of grindstones dumped into the Gulf," he admitted, "than have so many of them in our State, as there are even here." He would rather have the South hold onto its slaves than have the North "degraded by them." Lt. William McDowell of the Sixty-Fourth Ohio was certain that if freed, many slaves would go north, and he wanted no part of that. He worried that black people would not be able to find jobs and then would have to "be supported at the expense of the hard-working class of white people." But there were broader political considerations in play as well in McDowell's opposition to emancipation. The lieutenant feared that emancipation would alienate the border states and Southern Unionists, which would only make it that much harder to defeat the rebellion. McDowell summed up his feelings on the issue as follows: "I shall not be a target for a black prize." In November 1862, McDowell resigned his commission, quite possibly because of his strong objections to emancipation.[11]

Such officers especially despised abolitionism. An assistant surgeon in the Forty-First Ohio overheard a fellow surgeon claim that "the rebellion grew out of the rabid abolitionism of such men as [Joshua R.] Giddings + [Benjman F.] Wade, and they ought to be hung." The surgeon believed "that slavery was the just + right condition of the colored race ... [and] the union *as it was* should be restored." That phrase, of course, would soon become a favorite with the Peace (or Copperhead) faction of the Democratic Party, whose animus against abolitionists was equally fervent. Maj. Frederick Boardman of the Fourth Wisconsin would never attend the services of the supposedly abolitionist regimental chaplain. When the man resigned, Boardman appealed to a Democratic politician back home to "try to have one sent with as little abolition about him as can be helped." A Democratic lieutenant in the Fourteenth Michigan wanted "the abolition priesthood of the northern states" to have to suffer the hardships of military service. "No set of men have more to account for than they," contended Lt. William Ferry, and they should be "the mule drivers for this army."[12]

The spring and summer of 1862 saw officers in the West increasingly polarized over the questions of confiscation and emancipation. Policy on the ground was decisively turning emancipationist with thousands of slaves finding refuge in Union camps, yet many officers were far from committed to any such purpose. When Lincoln issued the Preliminary Emancipation Proclamation on September 22, 1862, freeing all slaves in areas still in rebellion on January 1, 1863, the divisions in the officer ranks intensified. This was undoubtedly because the proclamation more clearly than any previous statement defined the war as a crusade to liberate the slaves with no turning back. Indeed, the proclamation went beyond the Second Confiscation Act in several ways. It left no doubt that slaves coming into Union lines were "free," removing much of the ambiguity about their status. It also freed "all" slaves in rebellious areas, not just those owned by rebels. In the wake of the Preliminary Emancipation Proclamation and continuing after Lincoln issued the final Emancipation Proclamation (from late September 1862 through the spring of 1863), there occurred continuous and often acrimonious debate over emancipation as officers appeared divided on the very meaning and purpose of the war.

Capt. Oscar Jackson of the Sixty-Third Ohio was an ardent Republican who had campaigned vigorously for Lincoln in 1860 but was no abolitionist.

Yet, as a result of his wartime service, he had come to sympathize with black people and appreciate how they could help the army. After Jackson was shot in the face at the battle of Corinth, a black servant steadfastly cared for him in the hospital. In January 1863, shortly before returning to the ranks, Jackson gave a speech in Hocking County, Ohio. Despite death threats from Copperheads in the area, with a revolver on the stand, Jackson declared that he was "an unconditional abolitionist."[13]

While few officers embraced emancipation under such dramatic circumstances, many had come around to this position, and it was pragmatism more than principle that had gotten them there. And unlike Jackson, most shied away from the label "abolitionist." An assistant surgeon with the Thirteenth Iowa, Seneca Thrall, reported in November 1862 that "a *very large* majority [of this portion of the army] endorse the President's Proclamation on emancipation. They regard it as a military expedient and necessity to crush out the rebellion." They supported it "not because they favor [the] abolition of slavery, or the freedom of the negro, but because the Rebels use them as essential aids to their cause, because it is their vulnerable point." Channing Richards of the Twenty-Second Ohio favored the proclamation because it struck at the foundation of the rebellion, "the Slave Power," and was therefore "the most effectual way to end the War." Richards later remarked, "I never should take up arms to free the slaves," but they have to be freed because "they assist them [the Confederates] and are the cause of their being in rebellion, and when taken away they can be used to assist us."[14]

As the proclamation went into effect, many officers continued to express approval of its practical benefits. Ohio lieutenant George Landrum thought the proclamation was "doing us great good, as it requires a large number of the [Confederate] white men to stay at home to look after the 'niggers.'" He added: "We are in for any measure that will put down this rebellion, *constitutional or not*. . . . 'Military necessity,' that's the cry that suits me." Another lieutenant, from the Third Michigan Cavalry, was in all probability referring to the proclamation when in February 1863 he advocated "the course pursued by the President" because it was "the only course that is left us, and in this rests our only hope for the restoration of our government." He thought the South had forfeited "all right of protection" and that the war needed to be prosecuted "with the utmost vigor." Leading the 106th Illinois, Col. Robert Latham summed up his support for the proclamation briefly: "I believe it to be *the* way to put down the rebellion, and end the war, and that is what I am for."[15]

Latham, among others, angrily discussed how the Confederates were receiving comfort and support from the Peace Democrats, or Copperheads, in the North, who adamantly opposed emancipation and sought a negotiated peace. Union officers, like enlisted men, absolutely despised the Copperheads, believing they were undermining the war effort. In late 1862 and the early part of 1863, the Peace Democrats grew in strength, especially in the Midwest. The lower houses in both the Indiana and Illinois legislatures called for an end to hostilities and the withdrawal of the Emancipation Proclamation. Knowing these hated foes in their rear were against emancipation made some officers—many midwesterners themselves—embrace it.[16]

Officers often combined a hatred of Copperheads with practical arguments in their support of the proclamation. Lt. Henry Hole of the Seventeenth Illinois railed against Copperheads, who kept harping on the proclamation, "which is acknowledged by every General in the Union to be a military necessity necessary for the preservation of our armies, for the safety of our nation, necessary to prevent the unnecessary effusion of blood, to prevent interminable difficulties growing out of the negro question, to forestall the Confederate government in doing the very same thing, necessary to prevent foreign intervention." Hole was "for the President's Proclamation teeth and toe nails... because [Copperhead] C. L. Vanlanigham [sic] ... and a host of others are against it." Another Illinois officer, Maj. Luther Cowan of the Forty-Fifth, felt the "Secesh of the north" deserved to have "some of their infamous necks... stretched by a rope." If they believed the army was going to quit over emancipation, Cowan contended, the "infamous, sacrilegious, brawling devils" were "badly mistaken." The men in the field realized why emancipation was necessary and were for anything that would help save the Union. A lieutenant in the Seventy-Fourth Indiana, Orville Chamberlain, observed in January 1863 that everyone was "almost all '*down*'" on the proclamation, but by the end of May, "the labor of the copperheads" had "*abolitionize[d]*" the army. By then, even the Democratic officers of Chamberlain's company were sounding like "black hearted abolitionists." The Copperhead invective actually made some officers see how vital the measure was for winning the war.[17]

Although not as quickly as many junior-level officers, some top-level commanders in the West also saw emancipation's importance in achieving victory. In August 1863, Ulysses S. Grant admitted that he had never been "an Abolitionest" or "anti slavery," but he believed slavery needed to go if there was ever going to be a lasting peace between the North and South. Grant did not want to see the war end "until this question is forever settled." Grant had made his feelings plain to the president when he argued that using black troops and "the emancipation of the negro, is the heavyest blow yet given the Confederacy." The South "with the negro under subjection could spare their entire white population for the field," Grant reasoned. "Now they complain that nothing can be got out of their negroes." By June 1863, Maj. Gen. John M. Schofield—who like Grant had been no abolitionist before the war—"regard[ed] universal emancipation as one of the necessary consequences of the rebellion, or rather as one of the means absolutely necessary to a complete restoration of the Union—and this because slavery was the great cause of the rebellion, and the only obstacle in the way of a perfect union." One of Maj. Gen. William S. Rosecrans's staff officers noted that his chief usually avoided politics, but regarding slavery, "he was quite clear that there had grown up a necessity to emasculate that element of military power." The idea that emancipation was vital for defeating the Confederates and preserving the Union was a very convincing argument for officers at all levels in the West. Significantly, lower-level officers were generally a little quicker than their superiors to endorse full-scale emancipation. Perhaps this was because their experiences on the ground made it clearer why emancipation was so necessary. Regardless, practical considerations remained the most powerful reason for officer support of emancipation.[18]

Such pragmatic endorsements lent additional force to the views of officers who supported emancipation for moral reasons. When the Preliminary Emancipation Proclamation was issued, Brig. Gen. James Garfield "rejoiced" because "it give[s] us light in the midst of the darkness and shows us the beginning of the end." Whatever the proclamation's uncertain effects in Kentucky and Tennessee, Garfield believed, they would be "a thousand times overbalanced by the great moral force and significance which the measure will add to the war." The day after the final proclamation was issued, the idealistic brigadier reflected: "Strange that a second rate Illinois lawyer should be the instrument through whom one of the sublimest works of any age is accomplished." In January 1863, Lt. John Crawford of the Second Michigan Cavalry asked his cousin, "Can you not give thanks that we elected a man for President who had the courage to strike the bonds from off four millions of human beings and remove forever the stain and reproach upon our banner and stop forever the howlings of other Nations?" Col. Daniel Gilmer of the Thirty-Eighth Illinois reportedly commented that the Lord "will give us peace in good time, and that time will be when the institution of slavery has been rooted up and destroyed."[19]

These officers often found themselves far in advance of public opinion back home. A doctor turned captain in the Thirty-Sixth Iowa, William Vermilion, described himself as an "abolitionist full blooded" and wanted the president to "give every negro who is willing to fight a good gun and let him slay his thousands if he can. Let him assist in making every brook in the South run red with treasonable blood.... The Day of redemption will come." Sharing these sentiments, Vermilion's wife, Mary, angrily explained to her husband the powerful feelings against the war and emancipation in the Midwest. Such feelings were shared by the captain's own family, who would not even write to him. "Neither Thom, John or father has ever written me a line," Vermilion lamented, "since I came into the Service. They don't want to correspond with an Abolitionist I suppose." Commanding the Eighty-Eighth Illinois, Col. Francis T. Sherman also faced a skeptical family. When his father, Francis C. Sherman, was narrowly reelected as mayor of Chicago, Colonel Sherman congratulated him but criticized his platform—"The 'government as it was, and the Constitution as it is.'" This was no longer a possibility, thought Sherman. The rebellion would be suppressed, but "in doing so the blot of slavery on our free institutions will be wiped out, and the stain upon the 'Declaration of the Rights of Man' will be no longer the mark of Cain upon our nation and country."[20]

As moralistic as some officers could sound, many still emphasized the practical side of emancipation. John Quincy Adams Campbell, a soon-to-be lieutenant in the Fifth Iowa, believed January 1, 1863, was "to be the day of our nation's second birth. God bless and help Abraham Lincoln—help him to 'break every yoke and let the oppressed go free.'" But the twenty-three-year-old soldier also understood the more tangible benefits of emancipation: "The President has placed the Union pry under the corner stone of the Confederacy and the structure *will* fall." A German immigrant, Karl Adolph Frick, who served as an officer in Missouri, hated slavery for the way it exploited black people, especially through the slave trade, and wanted it to end. "After all," he wrote his sister in February 1863, "all men are born equal." Even with this perspective on slavery, Frick felt emancipation "will certainly deal the deathblow to these [the rebellious] states, since they [the slaves] were the backbone of the rebels, doing their work at home and raising their crops while their owners went off to war." The same officer then could express both moral and practical reasons for emancipation; they could in fact be mutually reinforcing. But it was more common for an officer motivated by moral reasons to express practical ones than vice versa. In other words, there were more officers who embraced emancipation out of practical necessity alone than those who just saw it as a moral imperative.[21]

On such a complex and troublesome issue there were bound to be officers who were simply lukewarm or even uncertain. "The proclamation is a thing I never asked for," wrote an assistant surgeon in the 117th Illinois.

Nevertheless, he was glad the president had acted after making the promise. Capt. Thomas Stevens of the Twenty-Eighth Wisconsin was hardly enthusiastic about emancipation when he assured his wife: "I am not risking my life here merely for freedom for the Negro, though that may be one of the fruits of the war, but for the preservation of our constitutional liberties." Alexander Varian, a soon-to-be lieutenant in the First Ohio, was simply indecisive. "I scarcely know what to think of the *President's late 'Emancipation Proclamation,'*" he told his sister. "Regarding it strictly as a War measure it may do, but it seems to me that if they would let the niggers alone + go to *hanging* every *traitor* they catch the war would be the sooner ended."[22]

Far more troubling for the Union cause and for the government was the large group of officers who vigorously opposed emancipation. In late 1862 and the first part of 1863, the voices of opposition almost equaled those of support. So powerful was this opposition to emancipation that a significant amount of dissatisfaction spread throughout the Union army. George Burmeister, a captain in the Thirty-Fifth Iowa, pointed out that the proclamation was "the topic of universal discussion" and "vehemently opposed by the anti-administration democrats." Burmeister's own lieutenants in Company C were not in favor of emancipation and "work[ed] to extend the spirit of dissatisfaction that is brooding over our troops." Some in John Robert Dow's Thirty-First Ohio were perhaps even more contentious. "We have officers in our Regt," Dow maintained, "that care no more for their Country than they do for a dog."[23]

Dow told how a Captain Putnam of his regiment had resigned over the proclamation and more than a few officers tried to follow suit. In March 1863, Capt. John McDermott of the Ninety-First New York noted that though few were accepted, there were "a great many Resignations" in the army in Louisiana. The amount of discontent there was "astonishing" as the proclamation was "alarmingly unpopular." McDermott declared: "It is my honest conviction that if the door was open [?] for Resignation that seven tenths of the line officers here would go home within a muster [?]. This I believe not on slight evidence either." General Grant received several resignations and recommended in every case that the officer be dismissed from the army with a dishonorable discharge. Not surprisingly, Kentuckians were especially disgusted with emancipation, and many Bluegrass officers tried to leave the service. The brother of a Confederate colonel, Lt. W. S. Johnson of the Seventeenth Kentucky, resigned over the issue only to be sent to prison. Once released, he resigned again and this time was dismissed. Another Kentucky officer, Maj. Henry Kalfus, sent in his resignation three times until he was finally arrested and escorted out of Union lines with a dishonorable discharge.[24]

Stopping well short of resigning their commissions, other officers simply expressed intense opposition to emancipation. One of these was William Ferry of the Fourteenth Michigan, who served nearly the entire war, at the end of which he was given a brevet lieutenant colonelcy for distinguished service. Motivated mainly by racial concerns, Ferry passionately denounced emancipation and abolitionists. "Oh infamous it seems from here to see the North still lending ear + heart + votes to a set of contemptible bigots" who "cause[d] the murder of thousands of White men, made widows and orphans of thousands upon thousands . . . to give What they call Freedom to a race of beings who only can be governed by the system adopted by the Saxon race . . . for the good of all," Ferry lamented at the end of October 1862. He added, "No one here in the army cares two straws for the negro. . . . Nothing cures men of abolitionism like this Experience." According to Ferry, freedom was a condition that black people were not capable of enjoying, a plain truth that the Founding Fathers themselves had understood.[25]

For some officers like Ferry, racial considerations appeared to dominate all others in their view of emancipation. On Christmas of 1862, Capt. Oliver Spaulding of the Twenty-Third Michigan recorded in his diary, "On the whole I think a system of servitude or serfdom better for both whites + blacks than immediate emancipation." This was because the masses of black people were "lazy and shiftless + would become worthless vagabonds if free. . . . They have been for generations dependant + treated like children + mentally they are nothing else." A sergeant and future lieutenant in the Twenty-First Wisconsin, Henry Clay Taylor, had no desire to see slaves liberated. "I think the place for them is south," he argued, "and that they need a *master* for they are a lazy indolent set and those that get in to the army will run away." Taylor fumed, "I am sure I dont want one in sight when I get home" to Fond du Lac, Wisconsin. Feeling that black men and women were "little more inteligent than the next link in the animal chain Viz [?] the monkey," the New York captain John McDermott questioned why "we whites are *exterminating* each other . . . for the settlement of the Slave question."[26]

If the vehemently racist McDermott believed that former slaves lacked the capability for freedom, he also observed that in Union lines they experienced "greater sufferings than they ever endured in a state of slavery." For some officers, the harsh conditions faced by liberated slaves only reinforced anti-emancipation views. By the end of November 1862, Lt. Col. John McMynn of the Tenth Wisconsin, who dismissed emancipation as "impracticable" and was losing faith in the administration, had witnessed hundreds of slaves in Union camps "left without food, clothing or anybody to look after them." He feared that "a government, that by its delusive promises and cruel neglect inflicts such outrages upon a poor and despised race, must call down the vengeance of God upon it, if he is a God of justice and mercy." Lt. Col. Marcus Spiegel of the 120th Ohio told his family that it would seem difficult "to deny a privilege to *be free*" to the slaves. However, when "you see thousands of the Contrabands pulled away in the same manner from their masters, in a miserable and starving and filthy condition, then in a spirit of philanthropy you will say, better be in slavery than such freedom as I can give you." These sights reinforced Spiegel's already ardent opposition to emancipation. Thus, experience on the ground could cut both ways for officers when it came to the slavery question. While some supported emancipation after seeing the horrors of slavery firsthand, others turned against it, or at least found additional reasons to oppose it, when they saw the conditions of slaves under the control of the Union army.[27]

The slaves were indeed suffering behind Union lines and particularly prone to illness. Sometimes, in getting to Union camps, slaves were forced to endure severe privations away from their families and kin. If they made it to the army without contracting some type of disease, they often got sick in the hellish contraband camps in which they were compelled to live. In these camps they often had insufficient food, clothing, and housing. Once sick, many slaves received poor or no medical attention and lacked the resources to combat the illness. So McDermott, McMynn, and Spiegel witnessed a tragic reality of the war and used it as just another justification for not freeing the slaves.[28]

But a more compelling reason for Union officers to oppose emancipation grew out of a conviction that the policy was hurting the Union and helping the Confederates. Spiegel believed that emancipation was a great error by the administration because it "strengthened the enemy." A Michigan cavalry officer, Lt. William Van Antwerp, agreed, contending that "if it wasn't for the President's Proclamation, I believe that thousands of Tennessee Rebel troops would, long before this, have deserted; but that proclamation has fired them up, and they will fight desperately." Van Antwerp also lamented how the prominence of the "'nigger' question" had divided the Northern public. Holding abolitionists in special contempt, the Wolverine lieutenant called them "cowards, disunionists; aye, murderers." The day before Lincoln's proclamation went into effect, Lt. Joseph Culver of the 129th Illinois "tremble[d] for the results." He worried that the thousands of Union troops from Kentucky and Tennessee might "refuse to fight," causing the Union army to possibly "be overwhelmed with superior numbers."[29]

Brig. Gen. Jefferson C. Davis spoke for many who doubted that emancipation would much help the Union cause. The proclamation "can do nothing but mischief," he stated. "I see no hope for the country if this abolition policy is to continue to rule at Washington. It is making the South more and more bitter every day and at the same time disgusting the army. The whole scheme is visionary and absurd." Davis's ferocious opposition to emancipation led him into conflict with Col. Hans Christian Heg of the Fifteenth Wisconsin. Heg described "quite a spat": "He [Davis] is a proslavery General, and he is down on the Abolitionists. I had some plain talk with him, and told him what I thought of proslavery Generals—I have no good feeling for him." As such, Heg would not serve under Davis in another battle. Such disputes over emancipation caused divisions between even the hardest-fighting commanders in the West.[30]

The fact that a good many western officers, like Davis, opposed emancipation in late 1862 and early 1863 is not surprising. Almost all these officers came from the Midwest, which had long been divided on the slavery question. The Democratic Party, fierce in its anti-emancipation stance, was especially strong in lower portions of the Midwest. Indeed, in the 1860 presidential election, 43 percent of the Midwest's popular vote went for the Democratic ticket. Politically, many officers were Democrats and generally unsympathetic to emancipation. The Midwest was also a region that manifested an especially virulent racism. Midwesterners feared massive numbers of black people entering their states, taking their jobs, and degrading their society. In the end, this officer opposition highlighted how the army was not quite ready to follow Lincoln in adding emancipation as a war aim. Attitudes lagged behind policy.[31]

Such discord would not last. The level of opposition to emancipation declined strikingly after the first few months of 1863 because officers came to realize its practical benefits and, in some cases, came to understand the harsh reality of slavery. Many officers actually went from opposing a war to free the slaves to supporting one. Emerson Opdycke, colonel of the 125th Ohio, noted in October 1863 how another colonel was "getting to be a 'red mouthed Abolitionist.'" For Opdycke, "this [was] a cheering sign, of a healthy change in sentiment." That same month, Illinois lieutenant Joseph Culver was no longer as fearful about the effects of emancipation as he had been. He was actually ready to correct the views of his brother, who had "no friendly feeling towards 'old Abe & his dear nigger.'" In fact, Culver had to straighten out the opinions of several family members, though conversions on the home front understandably did not always happen quite as fast.[32]

Just as practical considerations drove so many officers to support emancipation in the first place, they also helped explain these later conversions. At the end of November 1863, Maj. James Connolly of the 123rd Illinois noted how he used to argue with an abolitionist named Martha. While he was not "a *political* abolitionist" like her, he was now "a *practical* . . . abolitionist." For Connolly, political abolitionists were just "a canting hypocritical set of cowards, having courage only to support their peculiar opinions with their tongues." Unsympathetic toward emancipation for much of the war, Lt. Alfred Pirtle of the Tenth Ohio observed in September 1863 that "the 'inexorable logic of events' is rapidly making practical abolitionists of every soldier and should the war continue long enough the entire army will be more or less of that stripe." Reflecting on how much he had changed on the issue, Pirtle commented, "In fact I am so far gone myself that I don't feel any abhorrence when I see a negro armed and equipped in U.S. style." The Fourth Michigan Cavalry's William Van Antwerp had repeatedly expressed his opposition to emancipation in no uncertain terms. Then, at the end of August 1863 in a dramatic turnaround, he asserted: "I don't want to free the niggers, by any means, if the war can be brought to an honorable termination by any other means. But if it is absolutely necessary to free the niggers in order to save the Union I say let the niggers go." The continuation of the war was making the most unlikely soldiers turn emancipationist.[33]

This, however, was not the only reason that officers changed their opinions on emancipation. Some finally recognized the brutality of slavery. Marcus Spiegel, now at the head of the 120th Ohio, had been a powerful voice against emancipation around the time of the proclamation. Now he grew appalled by what he saw of slavery in Louisiana. Witnessing "more of what the horrors of Slavery" meant than he had hitherto known, Spiegel was happy that "the accursed institution" was soon ending. "Now understand me when I say I am a strong abolitionist," Spiegel informed his wife, "I mean that I am not so for party purposes but for humanity sake only." Soon, Spiegel would lose his life in the struggle to eliminate slavery. Near the end of the war, the lieutenant colonel of the Twenty-First Wisconsin, Michael Fitch, claimed that as far as he knew, the army was comprised of "all abolitionists." Many men who were made proslavery by "the arguments of [abolitionists] Phillips, Sumner, and Beecher" had been transformed "by the simple protestations and silent evidences of the cruelty of slavery [and] the poor demented negroes."[34]

Fitch was quite correct that many officers embraced emancipation during the latter stages of the war. In fact, it is notable how little opposition remained in 1864 and 1865. By then a clear majority supported emancipation. Writing from Lookout Mountain in Tennessee in July 1864, Capt. Jacob Ritner of the Twenty-Fifth Iowa felt all his sufferings were worth it because it was "only through this baptism of blood, [that] are nation, freed and purified from the blighting curse of slavery, shall lift her radiant forehead from the dust and crowned with the wisdom of freedom go on her glorious way rejoicing." The next month, an Illinois lieutenant, Clifford Stickney, also made it clear that he was pleased to fight for emancipation. When he received a commission in the U.S. Signal Corps from the president, Stickney was especially honored because he would now have "a memento . . . from the hero of the emancipation proclamation—Abraham Lincoln."[35]

While officers by and large came around to support emancipation—overwhelmingly so later in the war—the question of black troops proved to be much more difficult. When black men first entered the Federal service in late 1862, there was significant opposition among officers, and this often continued unabated until the end of the war. Some officers even denied that black troops had performed heroically in battles such as Port Hudson and Milliken's Bend. Much of this resistance to black troops stemmed from a strong aversion to the race. To be sure, more officers supported putting blue uniforms on black men, a stance driven by practical considerations, just like with emancipation. Many came to understand that black men would provide critical manpower for the army. But the numerous expressions of approval could not overshadow the substantial evidence of disapproval. Turning former slaves into soldiers became a far more divisive issue than emancipation.

Some officers who favored emancipation opposed black enlistment. Though Lt. William White of the Sixth Michigan was antislavery, he was "doubtful" about Maj. Gen. Benjamin Butler's black soldiers in Louisiana. While fully understanding the practical necessity for emancipation, the idea of organizing black regiments was "*worse* than ridiculous nonsense" to Assistant Surgeon Seneca Thrall of the Thirteenth Iowa. "Niggers will [only] *work if you make them do so*," Thrall claimed. "I do not believe you could pick out one thousand Negroes out of 50,000 who would *fight* with *loaded* guns, or who would not run at the first appearance of danger." Another pragmatic abolitionist, Capt. Channing Richards of the Twenty-Second Ohio, confessed in March 1863 that he had "no faith" in black troops, doubting that slaves governed for so long by the lash could "have the manhood left to make good soldiers." He believed they would "make trouble" in the army, could be better used in other ways, and would cause no end of difficulties with the enemy. And perhaps more telling, Richards "would certainly object to sitting at a court martial table with a dozen black captains" and thus understood why soldiers would not want to "mingle with them as equals."[36]

Michigan captain Harrison Soule echoed Richards's concerns and amplified the racial contempt. He told his wife in April 1863 that he could never tip his cap in respect for any black captain and, in fact, would not recognize any black soldiers. The ones already in the service in Louisiana were "a failure" because they were not "willing to run any risk in this Rebellion." The white soldiers did not want to serve with them, and very few would ever seek a commission in a black regiment. When Soule's wife disagreed, suggesting that black men were effective soldiers, the captain retorted, "I wish as fast as they organized them they might be sent to good old New England and about 40 thousand stationed awhile in Michigan where their worth can be appreciated properly." As the examples of Soule, Richards, and Thrall show, racial concerns largely drove opposition to black soldiers. Raised on the belief that black people were innately inferior, it was difficult for many Union officers to accept the fact that they would make capable soldiers. After all, soldiering took intelligence, commitment, and above all, courage, all qualities that former slaves supposedly lacked.[37]

Despite racial prejudices, some officers still supported black soldiers because they would help win the war. In the spring of 1863, this practical position began to pick up a significant following. An adjutant in the Seventy-Sixth Ohio felt enlisting black men "was a step in the right direction," as any slaves taken from the enemy were "a blow against their material strength and endurance." Capt. John Ferree of the Fifty-Fourth Indiana asked, "If they [black troops] can render assistance should they be denied the privilege?" His answer was emphatically no as he was ready to "congratulate" any black regiment that defeated the Confederates. When black troops were being organized in Helena, Arkansas, Wisconsin captain Thomas Stevens thought this "is as it should be" because the Union needed to "use every means we possess to conquer a peace by putting down this infernal rebellion." Lt. Henry Potter of the Fourth Michigan Cavalry informed his sister that black men made "good *fighting* soldiers" to the benefit of the Union. "Show me a man, who is down on negro soldiers," he wrote her, "and *I* will show you a *coward*, yes a *moral*, coward, and I believe God hates a coward."[38]

This growing support for black troops stemmed partly from the work of one man, Adj. Gen. Lorenzo Thomas. At the end of March 1863, Thomas had been given an extraordinary mission by Secretary of War Edwin Stanton: the organization of black regiments throughout the Mississippi Valley. The old career officer was entrusted to energize lagging recruitment efforts and commission suitable officers. But just as important, Thomas had to explain to the armies in the region the government's rationale for arming the former slaves.

It was a full-scale public relations campaign, and Thomas proved more than equal to the task. As he tirelessly traveled among the western armies giving speeches, officers reported largely favorable reactions.[39]

One of Thomas's first stops was Helena, Arkansas, where he made it clear that the army was going to arm every black man who was willing to serve. Maj. Gen. Benjamin Prentiss let his soldiers know that there would be no debate on this policy. Both generals drew cheers from the army. Witnessing the festivities, Assistant Surgeon Joshua Underhill of the Forty-Sixth Indiana described Thomas as "the very personification of a *venerable* hero," adding that "the enthusiasm of the army has never been as great since we left Indiana as it has been." Thomas himself reported that "the officers and men have new life infused into them" at Helena.[40]

After this rousing reception, the adjutant general continued his journey southward to meet the main part of Maj. Gen. Ulysses S. Grant's army, which had been trying every which way to capture Vicksburg. Thomas addressed various commands, emphasizing that using black soldiers was the policy of the land, and that anyone who refused to carry this out or openly disagreed with it would be dismissed. Slaves should be gladly received by the army and the able-bodied transformed into soldiers as soon as possible. Thomas explained that his goal was twenty regiments of black troops, and that he was ready to dole out commissions to worthy men to lead them.[41]

Along with Thomas, many of the most prominent generals in Grant's army gave speeches supporting the policy. Maj. Gen. John Logan, well respected by his soldiers and a fierce fighter, made an especially powerful impression. Any means, Logan argued, should be used to crush the rebellion, "whether Negroes, elephants, bears, lions or anything else." Serving as a Democratic congressman before the war, Logan would never have countenanced emancipation or black troops, but like so many other officers, military necessity made him embrace both. Another unlikely convert was Maj. Gen. Frederick Steele. Just the previous September, Steele had been willing to return slaves to their owners, but now told his soldiers that "the time had come to throw away gloves and use every means in our power to crush the infernal rebellion." An officer in the Twenty-Fifth Iowa, Jacob Ritner, had never heard "a better or more patriotic speech."[42]

These speeches generated much enthusiasm from the officers in Grant's army. An Illinois artillery lieutenant, George Throop, said of Thomas's message, "Good for him and the government." After hearing Thomas speak, Edward Stanfield, an adjutant in the Forty-Eighth Indiana, wrote his father: "I have great faith in this experiment although you may not have any. I dont think myself a lot lowered although negroes are made soldiers." Indeed, personal ambition no doubt contributed to this change in attitude. Capt. William Britton of the Eighth Wisconsin reported that forty applications from his regiment had been submitted for commissions in black regiments. On the same day, Maj. Luther Cowan of the Forty-Fifth Illinois noted Thomas's visit and how the most important topic in the army was now black troops. He observed, "We are now about to enter the time in history which will show the fallacy of the long entertained opinion that the negro could not be made to fight as a soldier." Cowan contended that officers who were not "ashamed or afraid" to lead black soldiers were "entitled to the highest respect."[43]

One soldier eager to command black troops was Jacob Bruner. Bruner had once believed that black people deserved to be slaves and that if freed, they should either be colonized outside the country or in South Carolina. But after Thomas visited the army, Bruner supported the new policy. The speeches by Thomas and others were "a great treat," Bruner told his wife. Arming black men was "considered the master stroke of policy," and the army received it "with shouts and acclamations of applause." The slavery issue "which has puzzled our fathers for 50 years is now being solved," Bruner concluded. Here was a great opportunity for a downtrodden race and, not coincidentally, for Bruner. The day after Thomas spoke, Bruner was discharged from his Ohio regiment to accept an officer's commission in the black Ninth Louisiana. This soldier who had earlier in the war decried the abolitionists as no better than the rebels died in June 1863 leading black soldiers at Milliken's Bend.[44]

Union officers increasingly took favorable notice of black men's battlefield exploits. After Milliken's Bend, Ulysses S. Grant himself stated, "I doubt not but with good officers they [black men] will make good troops." Commenting on the same engagement, Capt. William Britton of the Eighth Wisconsin asserted, "We don't want to hear any more about negroes not fighting." Britton talked with a black soldier who had been in the thick of the action at Milliken's Bend and became convinced that the black men would have fought to the last man. "I wish there were five hundred thousand of them in the field today," the captain declared. Lt. Col. George Currie of the Mississippi Marine Brigade was impressed with the fighting prowess of black men near Port Gibson, Mississippi. Despite several rebel assaults, the black soldiers "never wavered," he reported. "They had learned to endure under the lash, and they now displayed such desperate courage and determined endurance, that it amounted to heroism." When Confederate major general Nathan Bedford Forrest attacked Paducah, Kentucky, in March 1864, Capt. Irwin Eckels of the Thirty-Second Wisconsin noted that the black troops there "fought like tigers."[45]

A little over two weeks later, at Fort Pillow on the Mississippi River, Forrest's men massacred black troops trying to surrender. This episode enraged some Union officers and also helped change some minds. When he received news of the slaughter, Maj. James Connolly of the 123rd Illinois averred that "it will create a hundredfold more sympathy in the army for the negro than ever existed before, and will insure Forrest 'a strong rope and short shrift' if he ever falls into the hands of negro soldiers." The great cavalry raider, Gen. Benjamin Grierson, remembered that "the people of the North and civilized nations everywhere were appalled and viewed with repugnant horror the vile and inhuman atrocity." Particularly alarmed and angered were officers in black regiments. Lt. Rufus Kinsley of the Seventy-Fourth United States Colored Troops (USCT) tersely quoted scripture: "Vengeance is mine; I will repay saith the Lord." A surgeon in the Ninety-Sixth USCT, John Wilson, described the fort as "the scene of one of the most barbarous massacres on record, a fitting memorial of the evil passions fostered by slavery."[46]

Yet even as support and sympathy for black soldiers increased, there remained a considerable core of opposition—unlike what had occurred with the emancipation question. This extended even to top-level commanders. In April 1863, when it was reported that Brig. Gen. Willis Gorman was against using black troops, Ulysses S. Grant relieved him from command of the troops in Helena, Arkansas. That same month, Maj. Gen. William T. Sherman wrote to his wife, "I would prefer to have this a white mans war. . . . I cannot bring myself to trust negros with arms in positions of danger and trust." And Sherman never changed his mind on this question; former slaves would make good laborers, pioneers, cooks, teamsters, and servants but not combat soldiers. Right after the fall of Atlanta, Sherman put the matter this way to Henry Halleck: "I have gone steadily, firmly, and confidently along, and I could not have done it with black troops, but with my old troops I have never felt a waver of doubt." Although the value and ability of black soldiers was clearly evident by this point, Sherman's racial beliefs did not allow him to accept these facts.[47]

The opposition was even stronger further down the chain of command. An assistant surgeon in the Eighth New Hampshire, Hosea Smith, reassured his sister in July 1863 that he had applied for a position as surgeon not in a black regiment but in a Louisiana unit of mainly former Confederates. Earlier, Smith claimed that he would "rather be a small white man with little honor, than to be a big 'Black Man' with a good deal of glory." Some officers' racial fears were palpable. When black troops performed heroically at Milliken's Bend, John Henry Hammond was concerned that black people in the South would "become the masters + uproot the whites." Then, the North in turn would have to fight the former slaves and "destroy the force which the proclamation has let loose." Far from earning Hammond's respect, black troops instead inspired in him an apocalyptic vision of race war.[48]

If Hammond worried about the consequences of black men fighting effectively on the battlefield, other officers did not even believe they had fought well in the first place. When he read a report of black casualties at the battle of Port Hudson, Lt. Lucius Hinkley of the Tenth Wisconsin wrote that "the attempt to make the country believe in their courage, by such excessive laudation, is just humbug." Hinkley thought that the Union would find that black men were "never a match o[n] equal terms for those who have once ruled them, and never steady, and reliable as soldiers." Capt. Harrison Soule of the Sixth Michigan doubted that black men played such an active role at Port Hudson; the ones working near his camp were "consistent cowards." He especially took issue with an article claiming that black men had rescued the wounded Brig. Gen. Halbert Paine from the battlefield. "The writer of that article ought to have been choked in his infancy," Soule raged, "so his friends if he has any need not be disgraced by owning so miserable a relation." If any western soldiers captured this writer, Soule continued, they would most likely tie him to a tree and get "a good Buck Nigger detailed for about an hour to exercise his mouth upon him." In February 1864, another Michigan captain, William Ferry of the Fourteenth, denied that black troops had acted heroically at Milliken's Bend or Port Hudson. At the former, black men "would not stand firm" despite the best efforts of their officers. It was only because the gunboats arrived that the Confederates retreated. In the latter battle, Ferry contended that far from making a grand charge, black soldiers ran at the first cannonading and "flew like leaves before the blast . . . running, not to our camp, but thr[owing] down their guns + r[unning] for Dixie." Ferry informed his aunt that "facts take the romance . . . out of the reported bravery of plantation negroes."[49]

Not surprisingly, white officers who commanded black regiments often faced skepticism if not outright hostility. At the head of the Fourteenth USCT, Col. Thomas Morgan wrote how such men "were stigmatized as 'nigger officers.'" On New Year's Day 1864, an Ohio lieutenant colonel previously acquainted with Morgan received him frostily at a social event, commenting that he "did not recognize these nigger officers." Robert Winn of the Third Kentucky Cavalry noted that their surgeon, Nathan B. Chase, who was a nephew of Secretary of the Treasury Salmon P. Chase, told him that he would not administer medicine to "any man holding the ultra nigger view." When

Winn remarked that a Union colonel at the head of a black regiment had been burned alive, Surgeon Chase coldly responded, "Served him right—they ought to be all treated in that way."[50]

Chase spoke for many Kentucky officers who despised black troops. When black soldiers were ordered into East Tennessee, the Twenty-Seventh Kentucky's Lt. Col. John Hardin Ward objected in the strongest possible terms. "I consider this a wide departure from the legitimate cause for which we fight, an insult to every true soldier," he angrily wrote his department commander. Ward never even desired to see the American flag in the hands of black troops, promising to rescue it "from such disgraceful custody" if he did. It took the impassioned pleas of both Ward's father, Brig. Gen. William T. Ward, and Maj. Gen. Lovell Rousseau to get the Kentucky officer to withdraw his objection. General Ward emphasized to his son that the use of black men as soldiers was a question of policy to be determined by the government and not by army officers. For his part, Rousseau counseled Ward to not jump the gun, for he was "not yet called upon to serve by the side of negroes in the army and may never be." Col. Frank Wolford of the First Kentucky Calvary caused an even greater uproar. In March 1864, Wolford delivered a speech to a large audience in Lexington, Kentucky, in which he savagely attacked the Lincoln administration and called for resisting the enrollment of black troops. In response to this address, the president dishonorably discharged Wolford. Yet despite being arrested numerous times, Wolford continued his campaign against the president and black soldiers for the remainder of the war.[51]

There were good reasons why the question of black soldiers caused greater opposition than emancipation and lasted longer. Even though black men endured pay discrimination, served in racially segregated units under white officers, and often found themselves in support roles instead of frontline combat, the fact that they were soldiers still annoyed white troops. Black men in uniform seemed in some sense equal to their white comrades in arms, and this galled many white officers. It was one thing to free the slaves but quite another to see them serving alongside white men. Additionally, if black troops put their lives on the line in war, would they not be entitled to certain social and political rights in peace? The logic seemed clear enough, and most officers did not yet envision black people at the ballot box or in the halls of Congress. In short, the issue of black soldiers touched racial concerns and fears more closely than emancipation had.

At the same time, black soldiers and emancipation had both proved to be very divisive issues among western army officers. In fact, every time Congress and the administration moved in an emancipationist direction—from the Second Confiscation Act to the Emancipation Proclamation to black troops—they generated substantial discord in the army. To be sure, a few officers endorsed these measures before the government even adopted them, but others either lagged behind or never came around. From first to last, what mattered was the conviction that liberating the slaves and using them as soldiers would help the Union, hurt the Confederacy, and hasten the end of the war. Pragmatism counted for far more than morality or idealism. On one level, emancipation and the use of black troops were revolutionary changes, but the decidedly mixed reaction of the officers points to the limits of this political and social revolution. Many officers did in fact come to support black freedom, but mostly on grounds of expediency and to further their overarching goal of saving the Union. Perhaps this was all that could have been expected of them. After all, Lincoln himself argued for these policies largely on practical grounds, and his arguments had not fallen on deaf ears.

CHAPTER FOUR

Officers, Servants, and Race

While many western Union officers came to support emancipation and even the enlistment of black troops, their racial attitudes changed very little. Interactions with black people on the ground both reflected and reinforced these attitudes. Officers found black people exotic, curious, childlike, ignorant, animalistic, dirty, funny, pitiful, and ultimately, inferior. Some officers even abused former slaves. Yet, despite these hardened prejudices, officers could sometimes see individual black men and women as people with positive qualities. This was especially true for black servants with whom Federals sometimes formed long-lasting personal bonds. Servants played a vital role in an officer's day-to-day existence: cooking provisions, washing clothes, pitching tents, and tending horses. Some officers developed such affection for their servants that they brought them home. So servants significantly softened officers' racial attitudes on an individual level, but there was no profound transformation of how officers viewed race generally. In this regard, the war was not revolutionary at all.

This lack of revolution on race can be seen in the very word "servant." Officers consistently used the term "servant" to describe the black men and women helping them in camp. They understood well that this term had a significant cultural meaning in the mid-nineteenth century; white Southerners called their slaves servants, using these two words interchangeably. By using the same name for black people as slave owners did, Union officers were clearly implying that their servants should be subservient, docile, and most important, never treated as their equals.[1]

A key to understanding the racial views of many western officers was their midwestern background. Many white people considered any contact with black people to be degrading; they also believed black people would not work hard on their own to earn a living. This intense prejudice was especially prominent in the Midwest where there were many discriminatory laws. Several states barred black people from entering their territory. Across the whole region, black men were prohibited from voting or serving in the militia. In many places, black people could not marry white people, testify against white people in court, or serve as jurors. When it came to education, black children found themselves in segregated schools with poor facilities, inferior teachers, and a rudimentary curriculum. In the Midwest, black men and women were clearly second-class citizens, if they were citizens at all.

Custom and public opinion also reinforced this inferior status. Racial segregation was widely practiced in most public facilities or accommodations. Everywhere from churches to public transportation to graveyards, black people had their own sections. For white people, these practices seemed logical and natural, preventing the inevitable calamities that would result from race mixing. At the same time, black people faced what might be termed a culture of derision. They were ridiculed in newspapers and minstrel shows. Sometimes, hostility toward black men and women even turned violent. For example, white people rioted and attacked black people in Cincinnati in 1830 and 1841 when the black population in the city increased. This was the environment that had shaped the views of many officers in the western theater, and they brought their racial assumptions and prejudices into the army.[2]

At the same time, many of these officers had not seen many black people. After all, before the war the black population never even reached 1 percent of the total population in the Midwest. This meant that some officers were fascinated with these seemingly exotic people. Capt. Edward Miller of the Twentieth Wisconsin described in detail the different types of black people he came across: "Nigs of large stature and little nigs; nigs of the male gender and nigs feminine; ancient nigs with white hair and curly; nigs of more recent date with curly hair and black; nigs black as the ace of spades; nigs white as refined sorghum molasses." A soon-to-be lieutenant in the Seventy-Second Ohio, Jonathan Harrington, told his parents that "we have now got where we can See as many negroes as we wish. . . . It looks funny to see so many Darkeys [on plantations] at work together." Lt. Bennet Grigsby of the Forty-Ninth Indiana thought that if his family "could only see the number of negroes, men, women and children it would be the greatest sight" they ever witnessed. A captain in the Twenty-Eighth Wisconsin, Thomas Stevens, was captivated by the slaves on a plantation: "What a lot of negroes there were about! Little & big—dark and light colored—'boys' & 'girls'—it was an interesting crowd to look at."[3]

A few months later, Stevens noted how black women in Helena, Arkansas, were "*dress[ed] . . . to kill*" for church. "You can see them wearing their fine silk dresses, Lace shawls & mantillas," he wrote his wife. "Oh, it is gay! Black as the ace of spades, with lips on which you could hang a hat, they get on their fine attire on Sunday, and aint they grand?" Asa Slayton, a lieutenant in the Twenty-Fifth Michigan, also found black people laughable in their Sunday best. In Kentucky, he observed them "walking about as pompously as might the King of Dahomey" wearing their masters' old clothes, which were too big. But this was not their fault, Slayton claimed, for "uneducated in what is consistent, untaught in appropriateness, with the natural fondness of the African race for gaudy show, they are certainly but acting out their natures to the best of their abilities." In contrast, Illinois lieutenant Charles Wills thought plantation slaves looked dirty, ragged, and shabby, "clumsily ludicrous, with their close-curled wool, great white and black eyes, and heavyended motions."[4] Such diverse remarks reflected widespread racial assumptions: black people appeared slovenly in working clothes and foolish in fine clothes.

If officers sometimes found the appearance of black Southerners entertaining, they were even more amused by black people dancing. Col. Halbert Paine of the Fourth Wisconsin described how several officers "formed a ring and the Sambos and Dinahs danced for their amusement." Lt. William McCarty of the Seventy-Eighth Ohio wrote home, "I wish you could be down here one of these pleasant evenings and see some scientific dancing among the 'darkies.' It takes the rag off Corner Hall 'hoe downs' . . . [and] affords us great amusement I can assure you." Capt. Luther Cowan of the Forty-Fifth Illinois commented that "the boys have great times with the darkies, they dance and sing like a whole menagerie and circus." For often-bored officers, such scenes provided welcome diversion. Federal officers often encouraged and even instigated them. The chief engineer of New Orleans, Capt. Joseph Bailey, threw the 350 black men under his charge a beer party on Christmas Eve. There were "drunk toasts" as "a majority danced . . . played on the bones and sung songs." Bailey was delighted: "I would willingly give 50 barrels more if our friends at K.C. could have seen the fun." With contrabands no longer around their camp, Assistant Surgeon Thomas Winston and his fellow soldiers in the Ninety-Second Illinois lamented, "We all miss this [dancing and singing], but must suffer until father Abraham makes all the blacks free."[5]

Maj. James Connolly of the 123rd Illinois became so fascinated by the "regular 'Plantation Dance'" near his headquarters that he described it in detail. The characteristics "of the genuine plantation negro," he observed, were "far more grotesque and mirth-provoking than the broadest caricatures of

'Christy's Minstrels.'" When dancing, "they kick, and caper and shuffle in the most complicated and grotesque manner their respective fancies can invent." Their singing was "a sort of barbaric chant" that Connolly had never "heard from the lips of white mortals." When he passed a plantation, Connolly had the chance to watch young slaves dancing to the music of Union bands; "they capered around like little imps" as the other slaves stood in wonder of the Union column. Laughing "at their comicalities" to the point of tears, Connolly commented, "There is as much difference between the negroes we see in the North and the plantation negroes of the South, as there is between a cultivated gentleman and a clown in the circus ring."[6] When some officers witnessed black people dancing, they saw it as a spectacle, something to laugh at during the trials of war. Black Southerners to them appeared ludicrous, and in some cases, interactions with recently freed slaves simply reinforced racial stereotypes.

Many officers mocked black speech. John Greene of the Twenty-Sixth Indiana escaped from a Confederate prison with the help of slaves. He recounted how they prayed for him and the Union: "Oh, Lawd, bress dat good man Marsa Linkum; an' help de army ob Uncle Sam. Bress all dem po' sojers whut's kilt by ball o' cannon, or elsewhat. Bress dem whut's in de prezon pen, O Lawd; dey done suffer 'nuff. Help dese yer po' prez'ners whut lay out in de cole night and de win'; gib 'em stren'th ter tromp on de junny, an'ter reach dem Union line." Soldiers almost always used exaggerated dialect in rendering such quotations. Upon seeing Col. Halbert Paine's Fourth Wisconsin, one slave became joyous. According to Paine, he gleefully shouted, "Oh bress de good God. Dis I been prayin' for a long time. I tink I nebber see de Yankees. Massa say you hab only one eye and eat us all up. Lor' amassy. Tank God. Whoop." Even high-ranking officers made fun of the way black people talked. Although Adm. David Porter admired a black man's courage so much that he eventually took him home and used him as a coachman, he still ridiculed his speech. Defending his courage, the black man reportedly said to Porter, "I ain't no coward. Dis nigger stan's by his colors to de las'. If you was half as frightened as dis chile you'd swim fo' de sho'. I've got what you call de moral courage, sar." Black people who treated officers kindly and even earned their respect could still be described with a kind of comic condescension.[7]

Though officers laughed at black men and women, they also pitied them. A surgeon in the Ninth Illinois Cavalry, Charles Brackett, treated former slaves free of charge even though "they make me nearly as much trouble as our whole Regt." This was because he could not take "from the poor wretched beings anything they have though many of them have money,

& many fine things stolen mostly from those once their masters." As another Illinois doctor, Elijah Burton of the Seventh, watched black people arrive at a contraband camp, he remarked, "It is difficult to conceive what is to become of all these people—In slavery these are to be pitied—freed all at once & unprepared for the thing they are just as bad." Burton saw "[a] mournful sight. . . . Mothers with babes at the breast—little ones just able to walk hanging on. . . . All seem terribly tired & hungry." During the Red River campaign, Capt. George Burmeister of the Thirty-Fifth Iowa witnessed several pathetic scenes along the march. In particular, he focused on an elderly man and woman who struggled to move forward with the Union troops. Hardly able to walk, the woman frequently sat down and only continued on because the man coaxed and eventually pulled her. "It was a sorry sight indeed to see these negroes suffering so much," Burmeister wrote.[8]

Some officers sought to alleviate such suffering. Captain Burmeister gave some meager crackers to a slave who was poorly clothed and had been badly treated by his master. The slave was elated to have a delicacy he had not enjoyed for over a year. Surgeon John Bennitt of the Nineteenth Michigan told how his unit provided food for a famished black family that had fled into their lines. Even though they were short on provisions, "it was too pitiful to see those women & little children travel all day on foot without food."[9] Many officers viewed black people as dependent creatures who, for the most part, had nothing and could do little for themselves. Seeing them in such a destitute state could reinforce notions of their inherent helplessness.

Added to such notions was a widespread belief that the former slaves were not only ignorant but stupid. "I have not yet seen among the contrabands the *first* inteligent Nigger," wrote Capt. John McDermott of the Ninety-First New York. "Employ + treat them ever so well + kind + invariably they will turn out thieves and liars." McDermott believed it was a "self evident fact" that black people were "a lower order of beings, And advance in intelligence only in proportion to the amount of white blood *amalgamated*." An officer in the Forty-Fifth Illinois, Luther Cowan, observed that black people in Louisiana "seem but a grade above a beast, manifest no signs of human intelligence scarcely. They stand or sit in the gates or by the roadside in groups, staring with wonder on the Yankees, hardly knowing whether to run or not." Lt. Charles Wills of the Seventh Illinois Cavalry characterized plantation slaves as "a miserable, horrible-looking, degraded set of brutes," which the most "copper savage" could not be below "in any brute quality."[10]

Higher-ranking officers echoed such beliefs. Maj. Gen. William T. Sherman remarked that the people emerging from slavery were "a poor, ignorant class of human Beings, that appeal to all for a full measure of forbearance." Describing black men and women following the army during the Vicksburg campaign, James Wilson, who was inspector general of the army at that time, asserted, "It was pitiful to see their ignorant upturned faces as they struggled through the mud." Adm. David Porter was even more explicit about his views. On the Steele Bayou expedition, slaves chopped down trees "with as much glee as children would feel at setting fire to a hay-stack" to impede Porter's advance. This led the admiral to claim that a slave "was too accustomed to implicit obedience to his master to refuse to do anything imposed upon him. He was too ignorant to have formed any opinions on the subject of doing something to deserve liberty. Oppression was second nature to him, obedience one of Heaven's first laws."[11]

Many of these descriptions made the former slaves appear subhuman. When the assistant surgeon of the Eighth New Hampshire, Hosea Smith, lost his horse and black servant in a battle, he wrote his sister, "Dont I have the luck with my *dogs, colts,* and niggers that I pet." Officers often grouped black people together with animals. Maj. Samuel Wells of the Fiftieth Indiana estimated that the town of Russellville, Kentucky, had a population of "about 1,000 souls—leaving out the negroes and dogs. The negroes being very numerous and the dogs about as plenty as the fleas in Vallonia, [Indiana,] in midsummer." Commanding Company G of the 114th Ohio in Mississippi, Capt. Ephraim Brown remarked that "the Chief produce of this parts are Niggers dogs + mules the Country is full of that kind of stock."[12]

Some officers made such comparisons even more explicit. While Maj. Thomas Taylor of the Forty-Seventh Ohio wrote about Tennessee slaves "grinning at us like apes," Capt. Harrison Soule of the Sixth Michigan observed that black residents in Baton Rouge were "thicker around than rats and many not much larger." A soon-to-be lieutenant in the Chicago Mercantile Independent Battery, George Throop, offered this unflattering description: "The only thing that seemed to render them [black people] unlike monkies was their power of speech, and with some, that was almost anything but human." Lt. George Shaffer of the Nineteenth Michigan believed that former slaves would be good soldiers because, unlike white men, they were used to being "driven around." Thus, the black man was "just the animal we want" to go into the army and save white lives, argued Shaffer. Despite his abolitionist views, cavalry commander Benjamin Grierson characterized black people as animals. The general recalled that the crowd of black refugees blocking his retreat in February 1864 in Mississippi was "an enormous undisciplined herd.... And, like beasts, they huddled together and would not budge." Spurring his horse to the front of the crowd, Grierson told them to follow him, and they "flocked like sheep" out of his way.[13]

In point of fact, these officers did not even want to be around black men and women. "All the negroes in the Army are almost worthless and I but express what is almost a universal wish, when I say that I wish they were all in some other world," remarked Ohio lieutenant Alfred Pirtle. The contrabands were becoming so "trifling" that Pirtle would "not be surprised to hear of a 'black burying' any day in our army." Capt. Eli Griffin of the Sixth Michigan was disgusted with the way black laborers ruined his clothes trying to wash them, and he angrily declared, "I am sick of Niggers and wish them in Halifax or some other port." A fellow Michigan officer, Maj. Elisha Mix of the Eighth Michigan Cavalry, wanted to go home for a few days to "get away from 'orders' and 'Niggers.'" Frank Jones, a lieutenant in the Thirteenth Ohio, believed that black people were "the cause of their own depravity and indolence as well as the source of all their troubles" and was more than pleased that he had so far avoided associating with them. "Thank god that I have never had anything to do with their darkies! and I only pray that in the end . . . this War . . . may result in the entire freedom of our country from further troubles about the *cursed* niggers," asserted Jones.[14]

Unsurprisingly, given such attitudes, black people in the army suffered a good amount of abuse in many different forms. A Union chaplain teased Illinois assistant surgeon Humphrey Hood's servant "about his *wool*." When the servant made it clear that he did not appreciate it, Hood harshly scolded him. "I threatened to recall his recollections of Massas old cow hide," Hood wrote, "if he didnt learn to be more respectful towards our visitors." Previously, Hood had tried to convince his servant "that he did very wrong in running away from his master." An officer in the Seventy-Sixth Ohio, Charles Miller, explained how one servant was teased so badly that he feared for his life. The soldiers persuaded him that bears were lurking in the woods near the camp and "were partial to colored folks; the meat was sweeter." Then, one night, Maj. Willard Warner "enveloped himself in a huge buffalo robe and growled and scratched" at the servant's tent until he eventually was so scared that he fled the camp for a nearby river. Officers also swindled black Southerners. Lt. John Hartzell and a fellow soldier of the 105th Ohio bought three ducks from a slave with an advertisement that resembled a five-dollar greenback, getting back two legitimate dollars in the process. "We both thought that was good business and very smart to cheat a poor old darkey so," maintained Hartzell.[15]

At times, the abuse grew violent. The skillful engineer Col. Joseph Bailey of the Fourth Wisconsin physically abused black men as he constructed his miracle dam that saved Adm. David Porter's fleet during the Red River expedition. It was "Fun, yes fun ... hewing Negroes down with a shovel, tying up some Banks politician Niger officers by the thumbs," stated Bailey. "No pen can picture the many funny scenes that happened during the construction of this emence work." Pvt. Robert Winn in the Third Kentucky Cavalry remarked how his regiment stationed in Edgefield, Tennessee, was given orders each evening to "Rock (i.e. Pelt) every Nigger out of Town you find in the Streets." They ended up harming some black waiters in a Wisconsin regiment. Lt. Henry Potter of the Fourth Michigan Cavalry forced black people who allegedly lied to him to "get on their Knees and own up Everything," and then he "double-quicked them 3//4 of a mile up and down [a] hill." Another Wolverine officer, Capt. William Ferry of the Fourteenth, reported that Union officers and enlisted men terribly abused black women in contraband camps. "The negro women were debauched by our soldiers," Ferry lamented. "They were herded together like cattle, + the soldiers went among them picking out as they might fancy here + there one to satiate lust brutal lust." As a result of this brutality, Ferry claimed that a Christian black man named "old Jack" went willingly with his family back to slavery: "Of the two evils he chose the least."[16]

Like Ferry, some officers—especially those who most pitied the poor slaves—sympathized with black Southerners who were mistreated by Union soldiers. On Christmas Eve 1862, Union troops tossed a pound of powder down the chimney of a black family's house, blowing it up and killing a sick woman. Surgeon Charles Brackett of the Ninth Illinois Cavalry railed against his comrades: "Miserable cowardly dogs only could commit such an outrage on poor defenceless people as these are. . . . How Brave for an armed man to kill a helpless sick woman." Less than a week later, just as the final Emancipation Proclamation was about to go into effect, Brackett reported that "the besotted, ignorant soldiery" attempted to murder the regiment's black butcher. During the Red River campaign, Capt. George Burmeister of the Thirty-Fifth Iowa was furious at the conduct of soldiers who plundered black shanties, stealing money and valuables. Later on, one Iowa soldier reportedly raped an old black woman in front of her family. "Oh, God, what a fiendish act this was," exclaimed a mortified Burmeister. Illinois captain Charles Wills also talked about soldiers being "d——d thieves" and stealing from black people. This was a "lower business than I ever thought it possible for a white man to be guilty of," contended Wills, "and many of them [black people] are learning to hate the Yankees as much as our 'Southern Brethren' do. The army is becoming awfully depraved."[17] Yet, while these officers denounced such abuse, they generally still harbored deep racial prejudices.

But significantly, when it came to individual black men and women, officers' racial attitudes sometimes softened. On a personal level, officers sometimes saw a particular black person in a favorable light, especially when that person had helped them or the army in some way. This was particularly true of officers' servants. A black servant might remain with an officer for several years, helping him with daily tasks and sharing the trials of surviving in the army. Naturally, officers developed personal bonds with their servants that in some cases lasted beyond the war. Many came to see their servants as human beings with admirable qualities and occasionally would bring them into their own households. Rarely did officers attribute such positive traits to the black population as a whole, and often they characterized former slaves in a very negative way. So good experiences with servants and other black people helped officers rise above the dominant racial prejudices of their time and place in a limited way.[18]

Officers found some black preachers especially impressive. The chaplain of the Seventy-Ninth Ohio, James Stillwell, attended a black Methodist church service in Savannah, Georgia. Even though the black preacher was untutored, Stillwell had "not heard such Stories of eloquence for a long time from any one, either black or white." During an impressive sermon, Stillwell "laughed outright with gladness" several times and went up to talk to the preacher after the service. He found out that the man had taught himself to read and write as a slave, enduring many whippings in the process. Deeply impressed, Stillwell declared, "The old gentleman is a man of much natural talent, if he had the advantage of a liberal education would undoubtedly be a *Star preacher*." Iowa captain George Burmeister attended a black religious meeting and remarked, "One of the best prayers I ever heard was uttered by a colored man." The assistant surgeon of the Ninety-Second Illinois watched an illiterate man "as black as a stack of black cats" deliver a prayer very well. The whole affair seemed "remarkable" to him.[19]

Capt. William Vermilion of the Thirty-Sixth Iowa gave a particularly positive description of a black preacher who delivered a sermon to his regiment. The former slave "used better language and was undoubtedly a more intelligent man and a better preacher" than a white one he knew from back home. Speaking for the first time to white people and in the open air, the preacher prayed for the U.S. government and the Union soldiers. "I wish I could get to tell some of our one horse rebel [Copperhead] preachers in Iowa," Vermilion wrote, "that there is a slave or a man here in Little Rock who has always *been a slave* who is now a better preacher and a smarter man than they are. *Poor insignificant whelps that they [the Copperheads] are.* How I do love to hate them." Having spent their lives in bondage, such black preachers appeared all the more extraordinary.[20]

Yet individual black men and women did not necessarily have to display remarkable talent to draw favorable attention from officers. Simply assisting the army helped win positive comments. While leading a foraging expedition through guerrilla-invested territory in Arkansas, Capt. James Madison Bowler of the Third Minnesota was aided by a runaway slave who "knew the country to perfection." The slave successfully guided Bowler and his men to every residence in the area, and the captain thought that when it came to black people, he was "one of the most intelligent I ever saw." George Bradley, the chaplain of the Twenty-Second Wisconsin, received information about the Confederates from an old black man he believed "to be a warm Union man, and also quite intelligent." Bradley had earlier encountered an even more famous black man, the legendary Robert Smalls, who had gained his freedom in 1862 by seizing a Confederate steamer in Charleston, South Carolina, and piloting it out to the Union blockading squadron. Smalls had transported Bradley and his regiment across a river near Savannah, Georgia, in the same steamer. This was an "honor" for Bradley, who described Smalls as "a mulatto, short, thick set, full face, bright, keen eyes, and withal a smart looking man." Despite his clear racial prejudices, Adm. David Porter missed the "truthful and intelligent contrabands, in whom I was wont to repose confidence" when they were no longer around. "They were so faithful in adherence to their protectors," he noted.[21]

Often, black Southerners also provided Union officers with food and water. An adjutant in the Seventy-Sixth Ohio, Charles Miller, told how a "kindly" black woman gave water to the men on the march. "The negroes seemed to take a secret delight in administering to the wants of the Union soldiers," he observed. Miller procured "a hasty corn dodger" from another black woman, remarking that "it was one of the sweetest morsels I ever partook of." Another Ohio officer, Lt. George Landrum of the Second, informed his sister that they were living on a variety of foods, including raspberries and cherry tarts, thanks to an old black "friend" who was "always sending . . . something nice." Lt. Henry Dwight of the Twentieth Ohio dined in luxury because of the kindness of a black couple. After enjoying juicy chicken, crisp bacon, hot corn dodgers, eggs, and sweet potatoes, Dwight happily noted that the supper "was to cheer the hearts of the travellers." He praised the black man who served him: "Our sable host waited on the table with grave dignity, and answered our questions with a reserve. . . . He was a Union man to his heart's core, and he refused to take pay [?] for the supper."[22]

Black people sometimes furnished food for officers in the most dangerous of circumstances. When officers fled Confederate prisons, they often had to rely on the aid of slaves as they tried to reach Union lines. Black men and women risked their lives to help these Yankee officers and, in the process, earned their esteem. An officer in the Fifth Iowa, Samuel Byers, asserted, "The slaves universally were the prisoners' friends, and they knew a hundred times more about the war and its object than their plantation masters ever supposed." When Byers escaped from a prison in South Carolina, a black man hid him in his cabin in Columbia within earshot of a Confederate general's headquarters until the city fell to Union forces. In appreciation, Byers gave his black protector money and provisions and even dedicated his later prison memoirs to him. When Lt. Col. William McCreery of the Twenty-First Michigan and his fellow officers made a daring escape from Libby Prison in Richmond, Virginia, they relied on a black man who was "intelligent, [and] thoroughly acquainted with every foot of the country" to guide them past a Confederate picket line. "If good deeds are recorded in Heaven," a grateful McCreery wrote, "this slave's name appeared in the record that night." Another escapee from Libby Prison, Capt. Isaac Johnston of the Sixth Kentucky, commented on how black people were the officers' friends during their escape, and white people were their foes. "We contrasted the duplicity—nay, almost perjury, of the civilized white man who had betrayed us into the power of our enemies," Johnston noted, "with the fidelity of the African slave who had proved so kind and true, and felt that under the dark skin beat the nobler heart."[23]

Lt. Edward Dickerson of the Forty-Fourth Wisconsin found slaves instrumental in his successful prison escape. As he journeyed from a South Carolina prison to Maj. Gen. William T. Sherman's army, slaves gave him directions, fed him, allowed him to sleep in their quarters, and told him which plantations not to visit. Dickerson was especially taken with a remarkably knowledgeable elderly slave. "He could give a better history of the lives of Generals Scott and Jackson and Taylor, and all of those old fellows than I ever saw in print," Dickerson thought. "He had the finest memory of any man I ever met, he could quote the Bible from end to end and in good language, more correctly by far than we could." Officers saw these individual black men and women as intelligent, good hearted, and heroic when they helped the officers in very perilous situations. Literally fighting for their lives, officers had no other options but to turn to black people for aid. And when black people came to their rescue, officers saw them as people rather than members of an inferior race that was regarded with so much disdain.[24]

But for most officers, it was their servants who tempered racial prejudices. This is not surprising since servants helped officers in so many ways around camp. Capt. Samson North of the Seventy-Fourth Indiana informed his wife that he had a servant "to do my cooking, wash my clothes, black my boots and I am learning him to shave me." Maj. Henry Eggleston of the First Wisconsin Cavalry was assisted by "a contraband who takes care of my Horse, blacks my Boots; brushes my clothes and makes himself generally useful." Leading the Fifteenth Wisconsin, Col. Hans Christian Heg had a sixteen-year-old servant to do all his hard work. "My Negro works good—Blacks my Boots, makes my bed . . . he is a good boy," Heg stated. "He says he will go with me where ever I go."[25]

Given such valuable services, officers soon came to see servants as a necessity. Capt. Thomas Stevens of the Twenty-Eighth Wisconsin described a servant as "first rate" but evidently lost him when the army left Helena, Arkansas. Less than two months later, Stevens hired another servant and hoped he would work out: "I need some help, especially when on a hard march or after it." An adjutant in the Forty-Eighth Indiana, Edward Stanfield, did not know if he could make it without a personal servant: "Such a one is almost necessary—to make pies—get food + water and a great many other things." Stanfield eventually had at least two different servants.[26]

Servants were paid for all of their hard work. While pay was not standardized for servants, they made about ten dollars a month, depending on the regiment and the officer they served. Capt. Thomas Stevens told his wife that his regiment paid its black cooks ten dollars a month, and three dollars of that could be in clothing. The servants of Lt. Col. William Ward of the Thirty-Seventh Indiana made a bit more. In February 1864, his servants earned eleven dollars a month in wages. This was very similar to a Union private's pay of thirteen dollars a month. Indeed, both Ohio chaplain Lyman Ames and regular army officer Edgar Wilcox noted that servants were to be paid the same as privates. Sometimes, servants received pay from the government and other times they were paid directly by an officer or group of officers. It appears that when servants were on the regular payroll, their pay was drawn by an officer and then given to them. This practice could lead to dishonesty. In the Ninety-Sixth Illinois, officers drew the extra pay for a servant even when they did not have one. Lt. Evangelist Gillmore did this and felt a little guilty about it, but he concluded, "I am in reality just as entitled to a servants pay if I do my own work as if I employed them." After all, Gillmore reasoned, "when you are with Romans you must do as Romans do." Regardless of this unscrupulous behavior, many officers greatly valued their servants, and the servants received a decent wage for their labor. Undoubtedly, this filled many of the former slaves turned servants with pride and enthusiasm for the Union.[27]

While assisting officers around camp was the most common function for servants, some assumed more extraordinary roles, such as tending to officers when they were sick or wounded. Capt. Nathan Paine of the First Wisconsin Cavalry reported to his sister that when he and two fellow officers had to go to the hospital, they took their attendants and cooks with them. "Every dainty the market afforded we have had in good shape," wrote Paine. "[We] have had good medical attendance and good care in every way." In far direr circumstances, Capt. Oscar Jackson of the Sixty-Third Ohio had a black servant who tended to him in the hospital after he was grievously wounded. When Jackson went home to recover, he took the woman back to Ohio. Capt. Eli Griffin of the Sixth Michigan was shot during the siege of Port Hudson, and his servant was "faithful as could be," washing his wounded arm twice daily. Henry Kircher, an officer in the Twelfth Missouri, was seriously wounded in the battle of Ringgold Gap, and his longtime servant, Louis, traveled all the way home with him to nurse him back to health.[28]

At times, officers and servants even went into battle together. Lt. Charles Nelson of the Fifteenth Wisconsin fought with his black servant, Peter Thomas, in many battles. "We were in the battles of Chickamauga, Mission[ary] Ridge, Dalton, Resaca, and Dallas," Thomas remembered. According to Surgeon Charles Brackett of the Ninth Illinois Cavalry, the servants in his regiment fought near Helena, Arkansas, "bravely using knives, bludgeons, & fire arms with telling effect. A few of them were killed." This made Brackett believe in using black men as soldiers: "I am satisfied they will do well for soldiers, & expect to hear of most effective fighting from Jim Lanes Regts when they get in the field."[29]

With black servants doing so much to aid Union officers and their cause, it was natural for officers to come to appreciate and even admire them in spite of racial prejudices. Capt. Luther Cowan of the Forty-Fifth Illinois believed his new servant was "very intelligent," though he thought little of the race in general. Another Illinois officer, Charles Wills, would rather have had black people "dumped into the Gulf" than have them in his state, but he still regarded his regiment's black cook as "a splendid nigger, [who] seems to think the world of us boys." Assistant Surgeon Thomas Winston of the Ninety-Second Illinois described the black servants that helped him in very complimentary terms. Bob Riddle was in charge of washing at the hospital, and despite knee problems, Winston asserted, "he can out run any man in the house ... or [do] anything else that requires strength or agility." Winston trusted Riddle so much that he told his wife that if she ever visited him, he could have Riddle watch their son. Much later, Winston stated that his servant in charge of the kitchen was "proving himself to be a very fine little fellow. He is superior to the great mass of white boys."[30]

Higher-ranking officers had similarly good experiences with servants. Maj. Gen. Ulysses S. Grant employed an escaped slave named Bill, who proved very faithful to his famous chief. Bill eventually served Grant in many ways, including acting as his valet and waiter. According to one of Grant's staff officers, Horace Porter, Bill "was devoted, never known to be beyond call, had studied the general's habits so carefully that he could always anticipate his few wants, and became really very useful." After serving Grant in both the eastern and western theaters of the war, Bill accompanied him to the White House. Porter summed up Bill's loyalty: "In his humble way he was as faithful and devoted to his chief as the famous Roustan." Roustan had been the bodyguard of Napoleon Bonaparte. Brig. Gen. William Hazen acquired a very valuable black servant during the Atlanta campaign who remained with him long after the war. "His accomplishments proved to be more varied and perfect than I ever knew possessed by any other individual," Hazen maintained. "He was a thorough groom, valet, cook, laundry-man, and butler. He could darn my stockings, mend my clothing, sew on my buttons, forage from the country, keep my mess-accounts, and take full charge of arranging my headquarters; and he actually did or caused all this to be done excellently, and with the least amount of care on my part."[31]

Like Grant and Hazen, officers often formed personal bonds with their servants. Brig. Gen. James Garfield characterized his servant as "very intelligent and thoroughly honest and faithful," adding that he "has much more than ordinary Negro talent." Garfield noted that his servant was "greatly attached to me and I believe he would die for me cheerfully if it were necessary." Michigan captain Henry Clubb performed a marriage service for a black servant. "He is a smart fellow," Clubb thought, "and declares he will also stay by me all his life if I will keep him." Maj. Gen. Oliver Howard found a servant named Sam in Chattanooga and became very fond of him. "'Sam' continues [to be] the best man in the world," Howard gushed. "He reads to me every night and morning, and keeps up his interest in the Bible."[32]

Some officers believed it was important for their servants to become educated. "I want a primmer for my young contraband," Assistant Surgeon Humphrey Hood of the 117th Illinois wrote his wife. "He is 14 years old and appears to be quite a sharp little rascal. I think he will learn quickly and I want to try the experiment. I want a primmer with large colored letters."

Lt. Summer Nash of the 115th Ohio reportedly instructed a black man, who was most likely a servant, how to read and spell. Illinois assistant surgeon Thomas Winston promised his servant a spelling book and told him "that he must occupy his spare time in learning to read and write." Winston also inquired into his servant's moral and religious background and wanted him to join the Methodist Episcopal Church in the North after the war. In seeing to the intellectual and even moral development of their servants, officers were recognizing the basic humanity of individual black people. This seemed a far cry from seeing black people as animalistic or clown-like.[33]

Lt. Thomas Smith of the Seventy-Ninth Ohio described his servant, Butt, as "a quiet, innocent, industrious, and . . . *honest* fellow." Butt was a runaway Kentucky slave who cooked for Smith, and they became very close. Indeed, Butt would not go to sleep for the night if Smith was still awake. When Butt suddenly died, Smith grieved deeply. "In his death," Smith lamented, "I have not only lost a faithful servant, but a poor honest man, for whom I felt a strong regard almost if not quite worthy of the name of friendship." Smith added, "I am too much disturbed to write all about it to night." The Ohio officer attended to every last detail of the burial, including laying the body out, having soldiers build a coffin, and selecting the gravesite. Butt was buried in "a beautiful place" next to Kentucky Union soldiers. During the war, officers saw many of their men die or be badly wounded, but the fact that Smith was so touched by Butt's death was a testament to the special relationship between officer and servant.[34]

But it is important to point out the limitations of this relationship. Indeed, some of the language Union officers employed to describe their servants mirrored the way slaveholders characterized their favorite slaves. Masters would use words like "faithful," "industrious," and even "intelligent" when talking about prized slaves such as drivers or personal body servants. Undoubtedly, some owners also felt genuine affection for particular slaves. But the master-slave relationship was far different from the officer-servant one. While servants were free or soon would be, slaves were the property of their masters. As free men and women, servants were compensated for their labor and did not have to worry about being constantly mistreated or sold on a whim. Officers and servants were far from equal partners in the relationship, and given the racism of Union soldiers, the army was not always a very pleasant environment for black people—but being a servant was an improvement over being a slave.[35]

Some servants were quite pleased with their positions. Capt. William Britton of the Eighth Wisconsin wrote that his servant was "the happiest negro in the army." Another Wisconsin officer, Maj. John McMynn, had a servant who was happy to serve him even beyond the war. "He was almost wild with joy, when I told him he could go home with me," McMynn reported to his wife. Other black men and women showed their desire to be servants through their actions. Col. Hans Christian Heg explained to his wife how a female slave named Mary Ann disguised herself as a man and traveled a great distance with the army in hopes of aiding the Union. Heg obliged the former slave and, to her great satisfaction, made her a servant to a regimental doctor. Grant's servant Bill also would not be denied in his quest to serve; he started laboring for officers at Grant's headquarters whether or not they wanted him to. In short, Bill insisted that he would serve and then made himself useful. Servants consistently demonstrated their loyalty and affection for Union officers and formed close relationships with them.[36]

This connection became so powerful that some officers brought their servants home with them. Surgeon John Wilson of the Ninety-Sixth USCT told his wife that he was bringing his "intelligent and faithful" servant home. "He is a very good house servant," Wilson claimed, "and has been with the Regiment from the formation of it." Lt. William McCarty of the Seventy-Eighth Ohio planned to take his servant, who he believed had "a high moral character," north if he ever got back there himself. McCarty described this servant very positively: "He is quiet & reserved and honest to a fraction. I can trust him to do any errand and he always brings the exact change back." Officers often saw the black servants they were willing to take home as upstanding individuals who could contribute to their families' welfare. Capt. Joseph Culver's longtime servant, Albert Green, did not leave Culver's family until after he married.[37]

Officers considered the servants they brought home to be exceptional black people. Capt. John Corden of the Sixth Michigan asserted that his female black cook and laundress "is not like the common run of 'niggers[.]' [S]he is as smart as a whip and naturally intelligent only has no education." Corden was certain that his family would be "delighted" with his servant, telling his wife that "she is so faithful neat and clean.... You will find her to be worth a dozen of white girls to have in the house." Lt. George Shaffer of the Nineteenth Michigan discussed taking home his black cook, who was "the best negro I ever saw," along with a good female worker. They were different from the "saucy thieving negroes in that country," Shaffer explained to his wife.[38]

Corden and Shaffer both sought their wives' permission to make black servants part of their households. Other officers also wanted approval from home and explained to their families the value and positive qualities of their servants. "Don't you want a Nigger waiter," Lt. Albert Rockwell of the Twentieth Wisconsin teasingly wrote his sister. "I have got the smartest darkey that travels." Rockwells servant, Jeff, had formerly served as a cook for a Confederate general. Rockwell reported that Jeff "makes a chicken pie that would hurt no one to eat, and give him some flour and water . . . and he will turn out as good bread as any woman." Jeff even wore a Union uniform, making him "as proud as any *other officer.*" At the end of the war, Capt. Orville Chamberlain of the Seventy-Fourth Indiana asked his father if he should bring his black servant home. "He is a trusty fellow, and is devoted to me," Chamberlain told him. "He can + will do a good deal of work, and I think that we can use him to a good advantage."[39] Undoubtedly, one of the reasons officers were so concerned with getting their families' endorsements was because not only were they bringing someone new into the house, but that person was black. Understanding dominant racial prejudices, they probably felt especially compelled to explain the good traits and abilities of their servants.

Officers naturally weighed their children's reactions. Col. Ralph Buckland of the Seventy-Second Ohio wondered what his young son "would say to a black man." Capt. George Lennard, an aide-de-camp to Brig. Gen. Thomas Wood, acquired "rather a smart good negro" named Dick shortly after the battle of Shiloh and expressed his intention to take him home and "set him free." Lennard remarked to his wife, "Just imagin how Gertie & Sailie would look if Pa was to bring a negro home with him from the war." In fact, Lennard's children were apparently pleased about the prospect, and for his part, Dick was ready to do anything to amuse them. Sometime after the battle of Stones River, Lennard sent Dick to his home in Indiana. Lennard himself was killed during the Atlanta campaign, and this news fell particularly hard on Dick, who mournfully noted, "I shall ever regret the loss of my best friend who brought me to the land of liberty."[40]

Other officers sent their highly valued servants home during the war to help their families. In January 1863, Col. Hans Christian Heg of the Fifteenth Wisconsin offered his servant, "one of the best negro boys that I have yet found," to his wife. "He has been so faithfull to me that I can not doubt but that he will be just as faithfull to you," Heg reassured her. The brave Heg, however, never got home; he was killed that same year at Chickamauga. In February 1864, Assistant Surgeon Nelson Sisson of the Ninety-Second Ohio dispatched his servant to Ohio. The servant agreed to stay with Sisson's family until the war was over. "I think he will be a good hand," Sisson noted. Not every servant worked out so well. By early 1863, Brig. Gen. James Garfield's servant, Jim, was at his home assisting his wife but not doing a very good job. Garfield angrily commented: "I am disgusted with Jim. I don't want anything to do with that stubborn kind of laziness and wrong-headedness which he has manifested. As soon as you can get along without him, send him off."[41] Notwithstanding Garfield's experience, officers realized how much benefit servants could be to their families in their absence.

Deeply caring for their own families, officers came to profoundly sympathize with the plight of servants who had been separated from their families. Leading a brigade at Chattanooga in December 1863, Col. Benjamin Scribner heard a servant's story that "touched the tenderest spot in me." The man's wife and children had been sold away despite his loyal devotion to the master. Wanting to rescue his family, the servant asked Scribner's permission to go beyond Union lines, which the colonel granted. A few days later, the servant came back with his wife and one of his children. Assistant Surgeon Humphrey Hood of the 117th Illinois learned that his teenage servant had been separated from his parents and then reflected on his own children: "I wonder how Georgie and Fannie would feel if their Pa was sold away from them so that they would never see him again and their Ma taken away and made to work for somebody else and they left with people who did not care for them?" Another surgeon, Charles Brackett of the Ninth Illinois Cavalry, had sympathy and respect for his elderly servant who had lost all his children to the auction block. Brackett poignantly described the circumstances to his wife: "Only think this man as smart by nature as his master, & as smart anyhow as any of our whites who cannot read & write has worked for seventy years under the lash; his children all sold away from him, & alone in his old age he has now nothing but the rags with which the chivalry have clothed him."[42] This expression of genuine empathy demonstrates how much officers had come to see their servants as human beings.

There were some important reasons that so many officers viewed their servants positively at a time when there was so much racial prejudice. For one thing, servants helped officers enormously in camp, where officers spent most of their time; they often described these actions in detailed letters home. But servants' roles went beyond camp drudgery. Going off to war, officers no longer had families to look after their possessions, health, and general needs. Servants carried out these vital functions and in so doing became a nurturing force amid wartime suffering and a partial substitute for family. Perhaps this at least partly explains why officers were eager to have servants become part of their households when the war ended. They distinguished these special people from the nameless black men and women they often regarded with scorn and contempt.

This is not to say that all officers developed close relationships with their servants. Some had servants who did not work out very well at all. Col. Halbert Paine of the Fourth Wisconsin thought he had found a good servant but then overheard the servant express sympathy for the Confederates after the battle of Stones River. Paine quickly got rid of him. During a skirmish around the same time, Lt. John Hartzell of the 105th Ohio had a servant run away with an immense store of supplies. This was particularly galling to Hartzell, for he was arguing with other officers over who had the best servant. An officer in the Third Illinois Cavalry, Robert Carnahan, became extremely frustrated with his own servant. "My *nigger* is sick and cant cook," he reported to his wife. "I dont think niggers have any right to get sick. I will not put up with it much longer." Lt. Lucius Hinkley of the Tenth Wisconsin harshly derided his servant's work ethic. "I have got the laziest specimen of *animated* beings, in existence, in my employ," he informed his mother. "When he chops wood we have to look across a post to see whether the axe moves, and I don't think it an exaggeration to say that I can do more work, at anything in half an hour, than he will do in all day."[43]

Lt. Alfred Pirtle of the Tenth Ohio described his servant, Bill, at length. Bill was most likely a slave Pirtle brought with him from Kentucky, and at first, they got along well. As Pirtle wrote home at the end of June 1862, "Bill was attentive and did every thing he could and took care of my things." Soon, however, Pirtle grew frustrated with Bill and even threatened to force him to work on fortifications. Pirtle complained that Bill did a poor job of attending to his horse and got drunk. By early 1863, Pirtle was ready to get rid of Bill, and in February, he threatened to cane him, contending, "He is not worth the Ordnance that would blow him to the middle of next week." The following month Pirtle gladly hired out Bill to someone else, declaring "happy riddance." Pirtle wrote his mother, "A greater scoundrel in a small way I never saw." Clearly, not all servants caused officers to see individual black people more favorably, but these bad experiences were more the exception than the rule.[44]

Yet no matter how much officers might respect individual black Southerners, there was no profound transformation in their racial attitudes. During the last stages of the war, officers continued to express their prejudices. As he marched through Georgia, Chap. George Bradley of the Twenty-Second Wisconsin sneeringly observed, "Some plantations seem to swarm with little woolly heads." While being held in a Confederate prison in Charleston, South Carolina, Capt. Alvah Skilton of the Fifty-Seventh Ohio commented that the black fire companies were not very good because "they work as only a negroe does." In December 1864, Maj. James Connolly of the 123rd Illinois called the slaves laboring on rice plantations near Savannah, Georgia, "filthy, ignorant wretches," remarking that they "were scarcely a single remove[d] from brutes, and they speak a broken sort of English that I can scarcely understand." Around the same time, Capt. Thomas Smith of the Seventy-Ninth Ohio described slaves close to Savannah as "the queerest specimens of humanity I ever saw . . . and . . . *smaller* than common people. They have a kind of gibberish language, that is no language at all." Two days after Smith wrote this unflattering description, Maj. Seymour Howell of the Sixth Michigan mentioned that his unit had celebrated Christmas Eve with a minstrel show, "which, if black faces, and high collars are a criterion, was a success, most decidedly so."[45]

As the war came to a close, customary racial attitudes still prevailed. In March 1865, Maj. Oscar Jackson of the Sixty-Third Ohio lamented how poorly many Union soldiers treated former slaves. "The silly prejudice of color is as deeply rooted among northern as among southern men," Jackson contended. "Very many of our soldiers have as yet no idea of treating the oppressed race with justice." Four days before Appomattox, Capt. Charles Felker of the Forty-Eighth Wisconsin confirmed Jackson's observation when he described black residents of Missouri. "Niggers are quite plenty," he told his wife: "Little black niggers with a great row of ivory in front and yellow niggers and big niggers and all very dirty niggers." Less than a month later, Felker wrote from Kansas that "the niggers are as usual lazy and shiftless and dirty." Daniel Sheiler, an officer in the inspector general's office of the Fourteenth Corps, made it clear that he still regarded black people as an inferior race despite emancipation: "The niggers all seem to be as black as they were before President Lincolns Amanicipation Act, although they deny their niggership, and now call them selves white colored."[46]

Such officers would hardly support any efforts toward racial equality. Many in fact never even mentioned race as an issue directly involved in the war. Even if these officers ardently supported emancipation, they showed little sympathy for expanding black rights. Capt. William Moore of the Tenth Wisconsin was committed to eliminating slavery, particularly the horror of black women laboring on plantations. Yet he would not have these women "placed on a level with our own wives & mothers." Assistant Surgeon Albert Hart of the Forty-First Ohio was an abolitionist but still thought it was evident "that a long time must elapse ere they [black people] will be fit for all the privilege[s] of freedom." While he explained to his sister the absolute necessity for emancipation, Capt. Channing Richards of the 22nd Ohio still made it plain that "I am no advocate of negro equality. I believe in the superiority of my own race and color, and I am fully satisfied that the less the two races are brought in contact, the better for both."[47]

Naturally, officers who were less supportive of emancipation condemned any move toward racial equality even more strongly. An officer in the Twelfth Missouri, Henry Kircher, feared serving near a black soldier, for a bullet might wound the black man and then him, causing his blood to mix with black blood. This improbability was unacceptable to Kircher because, as he wrote his father, "I am not far enough advanced in civilization that I don't know the difference between white and black anymore." Kircher was very concerned that white people would be degraded to the level of black people if they fought with them. "What is a white who forgets that he stands above the African? Then he is no better," Kircher argued. Capt. William Ferry of the Fourteenth Michigan unequivocally rejected the idea of racial equality. "The two [races] can never prosper with equal privileges," he contended. "The inferior race must be controlled by the superior for the greatest good to the greatest number. It is the growing + strengthening sentiment of the Army here, who see + know what the negro race is + what is their capacity." Wisconsin colonel Joseph Bailey succinctly expressed his opinion on the question: "The Negro is not the equal of the white man and no scratch of a pen can make him so." If emancipation had been a divisive issue for western Union officers, there was a much broader consensus on racial issues.[48]

One of the foremost Union commanders, William T. Sherman, strongly opposed any hint of racial equality. At the end of October 1864, he wrote to Secretary of War Edwin Stanton, "I much prefer to keep negros, yet for some time to come, in a subordinate State, for our prejudices, yours as well as mine are not yet schooled for absolute Equality." Sherman greatly feared that granting black people any kind of equal rights would lead to additional bloodshed. As the war ended, he explained to Salmon P. Chase, the chief justice of the Supreme Court, that he was not ready to support black equality because it "might rekindle the war whose fires are now dying out, and by skillful management might be kept down." Sherman did not want to risk the violent upheaval that he believed was a likely consequence of pushing equality for the freed slaves.[49]

Sherman especially opposed black voting rights. "My belief is that to force the enfranchised negroes, as 'loyal' voters at the South, will produce [a] new riot and war," Sherman remarked to his prominent brother, Senator John Sherman. "My army won't fight in that war. . . . The time has not yet come [for black voters]." Other Union generals joined Sherman in opposing black suffrage. In command in North Carolina at the end of the war, Maj.

Gen. John M. Schofield strenuously objected to giving black men the ballot because of legal and, more important, competency issues. He explained to Grant "the absolute unfitness" of black men to vote: "They can neither read nor write. They have no knowledge whatever of law or government. They do not even know the meaning of the freedom that has been given them, and are much astonished when informed that it does not mean that they are to live in idleness and be fed by the government." Maj. Gen. James Wilson believed that black people had been impeded in their moral and intellectual growth in slavery and were certainly not equals of white people. "As a class they may be deceitful, idle, inclined to theft, and pitiably ignorant," Wilson claimed. Viewing black people in such a degraded state, Wilson was not ready to grant them voting rights. Like Sherman, he also worried that black enfranchisement would precipitate more violence in the country.[50]

After the war, many junior officers also continued to oppose black suffrage. Differing with his wife on the subject, Capt. George Squier of the Forty-Fourth Indiana contended that the Radical Republicans were only pushing for black voting rights out of a desire to gain political advantage. They were trying *"to organize a hybrid party on the platform of Negro suffrage."* Squier was not pleased that black men were getting so much attention; he thought that people had "Nigger on the braine." Lt. Samuel Evans of the Fifty-Ninth USCT said he would vote against extending the franchise to black men because "the unsettled [state] of our country would be augmented for the minds of the people are not prepared for it [and] [n]either is the darkie prepared for it." Evans, however, would consider giving black men the vote sometime in the unspecified future. At the end of the war, most Union officers were not yet ready to accept black people as full citizens.[51]

The war never radically altered the racial attitudes of most Union officers. It represented no moment of enlightenment or transformative experience. On the whole, officers continued to view black people as inferior, incapable, and even subhuman. Freeing the slaves, which many officers only supported as a practical necessity to win the war, was very different from seeing black people as anything close to equal with white people. But experiences with black men and women, particularly servants, often tempered racial prejudices on an individual level. Officers made very positive comments about their servants, whom they had come to know and respect. They did not see their servants as equals but nonetheless as human beings with very good traits—so good, in fact, that they were ready to take them north and make them part of their households. This softening of racial attitudes, however, almost never extended to the black population as a whole. In that regard, there was much less change. This persistent racial prejudice of Union officers helps explain why the North eventually retreated from Reconstruction and acquiesced in segregation and disfranchisement. The Civil War had eliminated slavery but had hardly solved the problem of racial prejudice. Nowhere was this more evident than in the minds of the officers who led the Union to victory.

CHAPTER FIVE

A Practical Army of Liberation

How the Union Army Carried Out Emancipation in the West

After the final Emancipation Proclamation went into effect in January 1863, western armies generally liberated slaves quite vigorously. In fact, they became the key instrument for bringing freedom to Southern slaves. As Union forces penetrated deeper into Confederate territory on expeditions and raids, officers routinely brought in slaves who took refuge in Union lines. But always driving this emancipation policy first and foremost were practical military considerations. Many officers supported emancipation because it would help win the war, and this was exactly how they carried out the policy. As much as possible, officers focused on freeing slaves for the army's benefit, often targeting able-bodied men who could be of most use as teamsters, pioneers, laborers, and most important, soldiers. Given these military priorities, officers frequently grew frustrated when they had to deal with slave women and children flocking to their camps. They saw these people as a military burden and usually sent them to hellish contraband camps or to labor for wages on plantations. In the politically sensitive border states of Kentucky and Missouri, emancipation was especially slow and conflict ridden. Yet even there, military necessity forced commanders to eventually adopt increasingly emancipationist policies. A few officers did support emancipation for moral reasons, but moral imperatives had very little influence on emancipation policies in the field. Union commanders and their subordinates consistently implemented very practical policies when it came to freeing slaves. In short, wherever the Union army operated, slaves were liberated and put to military use.

This became apparent during the 1863 campaign of Maj. Gen. William S. Rosecrans and his Army of the Cumberland in Tennessee. Rosecrans was a West Point–trained soldier who had little taste for politics. In 1860, he had cast his ballot for Stephen Douglas. Distinguishing himself on several battlefields during the first year and a half of the war, Rosecrans rose to command the Army of the Cumberland after Buell's missteps in the 1862 Kentucky campaign. At the end of December 1862 and the beginning of January 1863, Rosecrans won an important victory at the battle of Stones River near Murfreesboro, Tennessee. Clearly, Rosecrans had proved himself an effective battlefield commander. Like Grant, he would also carry out the orders of his superiors on thorny political questions such as emancipation. Regarding that issue, Rosecrans reportedly declared: "I am bound to obey the orders of the government, not to inquire why they are issued. I shall obey." Rosecrans not only saw emancipation as a military obligation but also believed it was a practical necessity for the Union to prevail. With these attitudes, Rosecrans was willing to destroy slavery wherever his army went in Tennessee.[1]

Even though Tennessee was exempt from the Emancipation Proclamation, Rosecrans's army would, for all practical purposes, liberate many of the state's slaves under the Second Confiscation Act, which allowed the army to seize slaves belonging to rebels. In this instance, when the army confiscated them, they essentially emancipated them as well. In late January 1863, Rosecrans spelled out his policies for confiscating slaves, and it was clear that military priorities guided him. He directed that slaves be taken in and employed as teamsters, laborers, medical attendants, cooks, and servants. Rosecrans's goal was to return the soldiers who would otherwise be doing these jobs to their regiments, thereby adding to his effective force. All such employed slaves would receive wages and clothing (taken out of their pay), and no unemployed slaves were permitted to remain in camp. Officers were to exercise "great caution in the employment of women in any case where it might lead to immorality." Rosecrans further ordered that slaves be taken first from men in the Confederate service, then from those who had disloyal sympathies, and finally, as an absolute last resort, from Unionists. In the last case, loyal slave owners were supposed to receive the money their slaves earned from the army, but this rarely happened. It was too difficult to determine which slaves belonged to loyal masters, much less properly compensate the masters. In any case, Rosecrans had signaled his desire to target slave property—primarily that of rebels—and use it for the benefit of his army.[2]

These orders brought every slave who could be used for military purposes into encampments in central Tennessee. In February, Lt. George Landrum of the Second Ohio observed about the area around Murfreesboro: "There are not men enough left to cultivate the ground; the whites are all in the Rebel army; the blacks are coming in to us, and are being used as teamsters and put to work on the fortifications. In either case they never can be made slaves again.... They are willing and ready to do anything to help us in the 'good cause.'" Six weeks later Lt. Thomas Smith of the Seventy-Ninth Ohio noted similar developments in Gallatin, Tennessee: "Slaves are entirely worthless property in this country now. All who want to come to town [can] work in the hospitals[,] drive gov teams[,] clean streets, work on the fort or are sent off to Murfreesboro to dig. None are refused. Nor is it the calculation that they are ever to be returned to their masters Union or Reb." By the beginning of August, the quartermaster at Nashville estimated the number of black people employed in Rosecrans's department to be between 10,000 and 11,000. As Rosecrans intended, black Southerners were providing vital labor for the army, which freed up countless men for service in the ranks. This point was stressed by Maj. Gen. Joseph Reynolds, who noted how in about three months' time he had procured enough slaves from hard-core rebels to drive all his teams, increasing the strength of his companies "by the same number of able-bodied soldiers."[3]

Regardless of Rosecrans's wishes, many black families did in fact enter Union lines. Under pressure from Washington, Rosecrans relaxed his restrictions on women and children, and some officers were already allowing them into the camps anyway. Col. William Lyon, for example, admitted all escaped slaves into his lines at Fort Donelson. But slaves of no practical use to the army were, for the most part, viewed as a military burden, and officers had a difficult time figuring out what to do with them. "The Negro question is becoming one of very great practical difficulty," Rosecrans's chief of staff, Brig. Gen. James Garfield, informed Salmon P. Chase. "The trouble arises with the swarms of Negro women and children that flock to our lines for protection and support.... We should be obliged to duplicate our issue of rations in less than two months if we took them up to feed and protect.... The General and I have spent many earnest hours in studying the question, but we fail to solve it in any way hopeful for them." Many former slaves ended up living in squalid conditions in contraband camps or in Union-controlled Tennessee cities. The fact that the army often employed the able-bodied men in black families meant that black women and children were in a very vulnerable position with no means of support. The army would not always provide for or protect them even if their family members worked for Union forces. Pursuing an emancipation policy dictated by military priorities, the army simply shoved aside these unemployable black people so they would not impede its operations.[4]

Rosecrans's active operations in the summer and fall of 1863 focused on capturing the strategically vital city of Chattanooga. His army's drive into Middle and East Tennessee brought his soldiers into contact with a white population of varying political loyalties. In Middle Tennessee, the Union army ran into a mostly rebel population. This area had been politically divided in 1860, with some counties showing strong Southern Democratic support and others roughly splitting between the Southern Democratic and the Constitutional Union Parties. As a whole, though, this region voted strongly for secession in 1861. In fact, in nearly all the counties the army passed through, more than 90 percent of the people had voted in favor of separation from the Union. But the army met a very different population when it moved into East Tennessee, a mountainous region that consisted of many Unionists who had demonstrated weak support for secession. Indeed, many East Tennesseans welcomed Rosecrans's soldiers with enthusiastic displays of kindness and assistance. Understanding this sentiment, Lincoln had long urged the liberation of East Tennessee and the seizure of Chattanooga. It is worth noting that in forcing the Confederates to evacuate Chattanooga, the Union army also maneuvered through northeastern Alabama and northwestern Georgia, where the population was generally more rebellious.[5]

Just as the political landscape changed during the course of Rosecrans's movement, so did the concentration of slaves. In Middle Tennessee, the counties had large numbers of slaves. For example, in Rutherford County, where Rosecrans started his campaign, there was a population of nearly 13,000 slaves in 1860, which accounted for almost 47 percent of that county's population. The army also ran into significant slave populations in Bedford and Franklin Counties, which had over 10,000 slaves combined. The slave population, however, dropped off as the army advanced into East Tennessee. There, poorer, self-sufficient farmers worked on less fertile land with often very few or no slaves. Hamilton County, where Chattanooga was located, had only 1,400 slaves in 1860, and that was a high number relative to other East Tennessee counties. While these numbers give a general sense of the slave populations the army encountered, a note of caution is particularly necessary here. Unlike in earlier discussions involving military operations and numbers of slaves, this campaign took place in 1863, not 1861 or even 1862. Moreover, the Union army under Maj. Gen. Don Carlos Buell had already come through part of this region in 1862 during his failed campaign to take Chattanooga. Buell was forced to retreat, but his army's presence caused movement in the slave population, as some slaves courageously sought refuge in Union lines.

So these numbers of slaves should not be taken as close to or completely accurate but only as very rough estimates.[6]

Wherever the Army of the Cumberland went across this region, its officers took in slaves. When Rosecrans was preparing for his drive on Chattanooga during the summer, his army continued to liberate slaves for military use. Indeed, the general ordered raids into the enemy's country for this purpose. On the same day, July 10, Rosecrans instructed both Col. John T. Wilder and Maj. Gen. David Stanley to seize all "able-bodied male negroes" from rebels during their expeditions. Wilder succeeded in taking at least 800 slaves as he swept the country clean around the Duck River. These former slaves would eventually fill a black regiment.[7]

During his campaign into north Alabama, Maj. Gen. David Stanley took in between 600 and 1,000 slaves to drive teams or work on fortifications. Stanley recounted how they captured the slaves in Huntsville as they left their Sunday church services, sorting out the able-bodied ones. "I think we had nearly one hundred of them in tall silk hats, white coats and pants, a most woe-begone and weeping collection of darkies," Stanley recalled. "But their distress was as nothing compared to that of their white masters when they found we had impressed their men servants." The army gave the slaves the option of returning to their masters the next day if they desired, but none did. Freedom was always better than slavery even if it meant performing hard labor for the Union army.[8]

Assessments of Stanley's policy varied greatly. Brig. Gen. John Beatty declared: "This is a blow at the enemy in the right place. Deprived of slave labor, the whites will be compelled to send home, or leave at home, white men enough to cultivate the land and keep their families from starving." On the other hand, Capt. William Van Antwerp of the Fourth Michigan Cavalry was disturbed by Stanley's lack of concern for slave families. "Many of them [able-bodied male slaves] have to leave their families, and ten chances to one if they ever see them again," Van Antwerp lamented. "I think it is about as bad as separating families by selling them. I can see no difference for my part, and you will know what a tremendous howl was always raised by the abolitionists about the sin of selling parents from their children ... and I think the way we are separating them is equally as great a sin."[9]

Regardless of individual objections, however, Rosecrans's officers continued to bring in slaves. Besides those capable of labor, they wanted any slave who could provide information about the enemy. At Chickamauga Creek in Georgia, Col. Charles Harker took in a slave who eventually gave him invaluable intelligence regarding Confederate general Braxton Bragg's army.

Harker was so moved by this slave that he wrote, "I desire respectfully to call the attention of the general commanding . . . to the fact that information of such vital importance to our safety was derived from a negro. . . . It has taught me that . . . we should endeavor to elicit information from every conceivable source, and that the most humble may be profitably used in the promotion of our great cause." The next day Col. Emerson Opdycke of the 125th Ohio took in Bragg's personal servant and gathered intelligence about Confederate movements in Georgia. The Army of the Cumberland increasingly found that liberated slaves could be of great value during a military campaign.[10]

At the same time as Union forces were welcoming slaves into their lines in Tennessee, Maj. Gen. Ulysses S. Grant was emancipating huge numbers of slaves along the Mississippi River. During the first half of 1863, Grant relentlessly campaigned against the key Confederate stronghold at Vicksburg. These operations took him into the heart of cotton country and wrecked slavery in the process. As Inspector General James Wilson observed, "Wherever our columns went there freedom went also, and every colored man and woman that could walk eagerly embraced it." In plantation areas, "our army was the precursor of agricultural disorganization and distress as well as of emancipation. Farm work was practically at an end and idleness, the negro's nearest conception of freedom, everywhere prevailed." Slaves rightly came to view the Union army as liberators, the force that was making emancipation happen on the ground.[11]

There were huge numbers of slaves to free in the heart of Mississippi. According to the 1860 census, there were 436,631 slaves in the state. This very large slave population made up over 55 percent of the state's overall population. Only in South Carolina did slaves comprise a greater percentage of the state population with a little over 57 percent. In slave-rich Mississippi, Grant's army campaigned in the regions where slaves were the most concentrated: the Mississippi Delta and along the Mississippi River below Vicksburg. Here, fertile soil made for rich cotton yields and some of the wealthiest planters in the South. In Issaquena County, just north of Vicksburg, 92.5 percent of the population was in bondage. The counties Grant went through on his final and successful drive on Vicksburg consisted of enormous slave populations. In 1860, there had been over 100,000 slaves in these Mississippi counties and Louisiana parishes. Even considering the dislocation caused by war and the fact that the Union navy had previously been in the region, there still would have been a multitude of slaves within the Union army's grasp. But even as Grant brought emancipation to so many slaves in the Mississippi River valley, he sought to take advantage of this revolutionary upheaval to advance his military objectives.[12]

Indeed, during this campaign Grant was beginning to understand that to achieve these objectives he had to destroy the Confederacy's economy and means to make war, which of course included slavery. In particular, Grant wanted to target civilians with pro-Confederate sentiments. This was not a problem, as a rebel white population generally surrounded him in Mississippi. Mississippi had been a fairly reliable stronghold for the Democratic Party before the war, and the state gave a heavy majority of its support to Southern Democrat John C. Breckinridge in 1860. Breckinridge, an ardent defender of slavery and the rights of Southerners to expand the institution, captured nearly 60 percent of the overall state vote and won a majority of the vote in over three-fourths of Mississippi's counties. Constitutional Unionist candidate John Bell drew significant strength from the counties along the Mississippi River, where conservative Whig ideology remained potent, especially among the large plantation holders. But secessionist sentiment only increased in the state after the election, and although cooperationists of different stripes had a significant presence among the delegates at Mississippi's secession convention, the immediate secessionists were able to easily defeat them. The final vote on secession was eighty-four to fifteen in favor of leaving the Union. Almost all the counties Grant campaigned in voted for a majority of secessionist delegates and those delegates voted for secession. Pockets of Unionism remained in Mississippi, particularly in the northeastern section of the state and in Natchez. And certainly Grant's men would encounter Unionists or disaffected Confederates during the Vicksburg campaign, but pro-Confederate sentiment was much more the norm. Perhaps this helps explain Grant's eventual willingness to liberate huge numbers of slaves and use them for the benefit of his army.[13]

Like Rosecrans, Grant wanted to use the labor of former slaves. In early 1863, he began constructing a canal to bypass Vicksburg, and his troops were suffering under the strain of such arduous work. One of Grant's corps commanders, Maj. Gen. John McClernand, reported that all of the fatigue duty was "bearing heavily upon the strength and spirits of the men. Prevalent sickness, and exposure to rain and mud are telling with fearful effect." Grant quickly sought help from slaves. "Collect as many able bodied negro men as you can conveniently carry on your transports, and send them here to be employed on the canal," he instructed Col. George Deitzler. Deitzler sent 100 slaves the next day. Capt. William Vermilion of the Thirty-Sixth Iowa commented that there were sixteen regiments laboring on the canal along with "all the negroes they can get."[14]

While the army's high command was working out these policies, junior officers were welcoming useful slaves into their lines. Commanding a company of the Twenty-Eighth Wisconsin, Capt. Thomas Stevens noted, "Negroes are coming in every day, bringing horses, mules, wagons & other property. They are kept within the lines, and will be fed, & kept busy if we have work for them to do." Another captain, Ephraim Brown of the 114th Ohio, remarked, "There were dozens of niggers [who] would come to us and say Capt. I will give you this mule or these two mules which ever they chanced to have and wait on you till de end of de war if you will take me with you[.] I can cook or wash your clothes sir[.] [E]very Capt in the reg has got one but me." Assistant Surgeon Seneca Thrall of the Thirteenth Iowa described how in Greenville, Mississippi, black people pleaded to be taken with the departing Federals: "Massa, don you want a boy to take care of your hoss, black your boots, do anything [you] want, oh, Massa, take me with you, do take me with you." At the last minute, the Union soldiers relented and drove the black people onto their boats, all the while standing between them and Confederate guerrillas, many of whom had been their masters. It was easy to see how freeing this particular group of slaves offered direct military benefits. Indeed, many black men and women realized why the army might want to emancipate them and so eagerly tried to explain their own value.[15]

But Grant also found that more slaves came in than his army could effectively use, and in February 1863, he prohibited any more unemployable slaves from entering Union lines. He explained that "the nature of the service the army is now called on to perform" makes "it impracticable to transport or provide for persons unemployed by [the] Government." Officers could still send out details to collect able-bodied black men "whenever the services of negroes are required," but no other slaves could find refuge in Grant's camp. There would be no more large groups of women, children, and the aged to impede the campaign against Vicksburg. In fact, as Grant noted, many masters moved their able-bodied slaves away from the grasp of the Union army. In the end, this was a purely pragmatic policy—take in useful slaves when needed and keep out the rest. Yet by adopting it, Grant had closed off his lines to many slaves, and Washington eventually would not tolerate such a limited emancipation policy. At the end of March, General-in-Chief Henry Halleck reminded Grant that "it is the policy of the Government to withdraw from the enemy as much productive labor as possible. So long as the rebels retain and employ their slaves in producing grains, &c., they can employ all the whites in the field. Every slave withdrawn from the enemy is equivalent to a white man put *hors de combat.*" So reprimanded, Grant ended his prohibition against slaves coming into his camps.[16]

Washington, however, soon initiated a program that provided work for former slaves the army could not employ. In April 1863, Adj. Gen. Lorenzo Thomas outlined a plan for settling black Southerners on abandoned plantations along the Mississippi River. There, the freed slaves could work the land, earn wages, and become self-sufficient. But most important, they would not be a burden on the government anymore. The plantations would be leased to Northerners and Southern Unionists who were expected to make them profitable enterprises and "to feed, clothe and treat humanely all the negroes." Guarding the plantations would be the responsibility of black soldiers, whom Thomas was just then beginning to recruit in earnest. Posted at various garrisons along the river, black troops would not only hold crucial territory for the Union, but also be in an ideal position to operate against Confederate guerrillas. Thomas and Grant saw all this as a sound military policy that would place a loyal population along the crucial supply artery of the Mississippi River, provide troops to guard it, and relieve the army from dealing with thousands of slaves they could not use. Despite these military advantages, however, the program proved less advantageous for the former slaves themselves. Many indeed found themselves in a situation akin to slavery, receiving brutal treatment from harsh lessees who often defrauded them of their wages.[17]

With Thomas's labor system offering a viable way to deal with the many slaves who came into his lines, Grant could focus on the military benefits of emancipation. During his final, decisive campaign against Vicksburg, military considerations guided how Grant carried out emancipation. When Brig. Gen. Frederick Steele led an expedition into the Deer Creek country of Mississippi, Grant ordered him to "encourage all negroes, particularly middle-aged males, to come within our lines." Grant was clearly thinking about getting black men he could use in the army and, at the same time, denying their labor to the South. As he wrote to Steele, "It is our duty ... to use every means to weaken the enemy, by destroying their means of subsistence, withdrawing their means of cultivating their fields, and in every other way possible." Steele's division stripped the country clean, seizing and destroying anything of military value and taking in huge numbers of slaves. An officer in the Twenty-Fifth Iowa noted how slaves "come in by scores, as fast as we can provide for them." They were "organizing all the able-bodied men into military companies; several hundred are enrolled already." An adjutant with the Seventy-Sixth Ohio, Charles Miller, observed around 300 slaves trailing the army and commented about enlisting the men and employing the women as cooks and washerwomen. Both of these officers believed that the army was doing the right thing in freeing slaves for military advantage.[18]

Steele's campaign served in part to divert Confederate attention as the main body of Grant's army marched south of Vicksburg, crossed the river below the city, and attacked it from the rear. During these operations Grant's army continued to free militarily valuable slaves. Indeed, not able to take his animals across the river, Grant reported, "We picked up all the teams in the Country and free Africans to drive them" on the other side. In Raymond, Mississippi, a Southern woman remarked that black women who came into Federal lines "were put to washing for the hospital. They wash from daylight until dark," only receiving food rations. At Grand Gulf, Lt. Bennet Grigsby of the Forty-Ninth Indiana informed his family, "We have recruited a regiment of Negro soldiers here this week.... There is an order to recruit twenty negro Regiments here; one Regt. drew their guns yesterday." Capt. John Foster of the Fourth Independent Company, Ohio Cavalry, led a reconnaissance to the plantation of Confederate president Jefferson Davis, liberated his slaves, and put them in the pioneer corps.[19]

Using former slaves as pioneers was a common practice in Grant's army as it tried to capture Vicksburg. In March 1863, Grant had ordered 300 freed slaves added to the pioneer corps of each division in the army. "These contrabands," Grant remarked, "will be used for fatigue duty as far as practicable, for the purpose of saving every soldier possible to the ranks." During the siege of Vicksburg, the labor of black pioneers was extremely valuable. The chief engineers reported that the black men "proved to be very efficient laborers when under good supervision." Col. John Whiting of the Eighty-Seventh Illinois thought black pioneers were so important that when they were ordered away from his command, he complained to Maj. Gen. John McClernand: "Now, General, it is a hard case to require the soldiers (white) to do heavy military duty and also heavy fatigue duty, I have several times suspended work, for a short time, on the fortifications.... I hardly know how I am to get along unless I can have some more Contrabands." Samuel Jones of the Twenty-Second Iowa mentioned that while his regiment dug trenches at night, black men dug them during the day. Officers often freed black people to perform hard labor and camp drudgery, but acting in these capacities, former slaves were great assets to the army.[20]

Grant also liberated slaves to deny their labor to the Confederate army. He ordered Brig. Gen. Peter Osterhaus to have the cavalry bring in all black people, along with teams and cattle, so that Confederate general Joseph Johnston's army could not use them in efforts to raise the Vicksburg siege. Osterhaus himself used former slaves to destroy the roads and bridges that

Johnston's men would have to travel. A much larger cavalry expedition under Maj. Gen. Frank Blair also destroyed supplies and freed slaves that could aid Johnston's army. "I brought with me an army of negroes, nearly equal to the number of men in my command," boasted Blair.[21]

Even after Vicksburg's capitulation, Grant sought to prevent Confederates from using black labor. In paroling Confederates after the surrender of the city, he denied rebel officers permission to take their servants with them, asserting that the black men were now free. Servants could only go with officers voluntarily. But Confederate officers still tried to force their servants into accompanying them, which angered Grant's commanders. "I solemnly protest, as an officer of the United States Army, against the manner in which Confederate officers are permitted to intimidate their servants," fumed Maj. Gen. John Logan. Because of this intimidation, no servants were permitted to leave with officers except under extreme circumstances. Confederate commander Lt. Gen. John Pemberton protested, but to no avail, for Union officers had no desire to let Confederates retain the services of their slaves.[22]

While Grant was emancipating slaves in Mississippi as a largely military measure, one of his corps commanders, Maj. Gen. Stephen Hurlbut, was doing the same thing around Memphis. Hurlbut brought in able-bodied slaves to fill black regiments. An officer in what would eventually become the Fifty-Ninth USCT, Samuel Evans, described the process: "The way we recruit [is to] mount a squad of about 50 men, ride out into the country where the darkies are, take all the negros (able bodied), all their mules (able bodied) and any gun that can be found in the hands of Citizens." Freeing slaves to put them in the military pleased Evans. "My doctrine is that a Negro is no better than a white man and will do as well to receive Rebel bullets and would be likely to save the life of some white men," he pragmatically asserted. Around the same time, Pvt. Rankin McPheeters of the 126th Illinois told his wife that he and about fifty other privates "have been detailed to go to the country to morrow to press negroes from secesh farmers into the service." McPheeters was "calculating on having a rich time" and thought there were enough black men in the area to form three regiments.[23]

If slaves could be brought in by Grant's army to serve as soldiers or laborers, they could also provide intelligence about the enemy and the enemy's country. The commander of the Thirtieth Iowa, Col. Charles Abbott, took in seven slaves from Vicksburg and sent them straight to Grant because of their knowledge about the rebel position. "One of them has been in the Artilery service," maintained Abbott, "and can tell you the possition & numbers of almost every gun from Vicksburg down to Warrenton." Abbott hoped Grant would permit the black men to travel north once he obtained intelligence from them. Maj. Gen. John McClernand seemed to constantly rely on black Southerners for information about enemy forces and local geography during the most critical stages of the Vicksburg campaign. One "intelligent negro," who had been driving teams in the country for fourteen years, helped acquaint McClernand with the roads the army would have to travel. Grant himself reported that a black man helped him decide the best point to cross the Mississippi River with his army. As Grant tightened the noose around Vicksburg, black people kept his army informed about the sagging spirits of the Confederate army in the city and of the other rebel army that was supposed to relieve the city. Indeed, just a little over a week before the Confederates capitulated, Maj. Gen. Edward Ord told Grant that a black man had come in from Vicksburg who was a servant to a Confederate general and stated that he thought "the men wont stand it a week longer." Grant could certainly put great faith in the information that black Southerners almost continuously provided his army.[24]

Even though military considerations might have determined how and why the army embraced emancipation, the key point for the slaves was freedom. The slaves understood this fact well and consistently greeted Grant's soldiers as saviors and liberators during the Vicksburg campaign. On his daring raid, Col. Benjamin Grierson observed that the slaves were overjoyed to see his troops despite being told that the Yankees were beasts and would sell them off to Cuba. "Among themselves they [the slaves] imagined God was sending the Yankees, like angels, on purpose to make them free," Grierson remarked. Grierson's cavalrymen did take plenty of slaves with them, including one poor man who had been cruelly chained up by his master for trying to run away. Capt. George Burmeister of the Thirty-Fifth Iowa also noted the slaves' positive reaction to the army. "The colored people manifested great joy at our approach," Burmeister wrote, "and told us they prayed constantly for our success and had been praying for this time for many years. Many a 'God Bless You' was sent after us as we passed them." Capt. David Sparks of the Third Illinois Cavalry commented how slaves regarded them as "their friends and deliverers." One slave woman was so overjoyed to see him and his men that she gushed: "Bless God, I knowed you'd come; I knowed you was Northern soldiers; bless de Lord; I knowed you'd come. I told our folks you'd come and dat you was de prettiest people in the world. I am a Northern lady."[25] Slaves fully comprehended that the Union army was the means for carrying Lincoln's Emancipation Proclamation into effect. The army's mere presence undermined slavery and gave slaves a sanctuary from which they never could be returned to bondage. It mattered little to the slaves that many army officers saw emancipation more as a military measure than a moral one.

After the Vicksburg campaign, the high command confirmed that the army had wrecked the peculiar institution and freed the slaves. "The people of the North need not quarrel over the institution of Slavery," Grant wrote in August 1863. "What [Confederate] Vice President [Alexander] Stevens acknowledges [as] the corner stone of the Confederacy is already knocked out. Slavery is already dead and cannot be resurrected." A little over two weeks later, Maj. Gen. William T. Sherman remarked to Henry Halleck: "Slavery is already gone, and to cultivate the land negro or other labor must be hired. This of itself is a vast revolution."[26]

As slavery died in the area that summer, Grant wanted to make sure that all freed slaves who could be were employed in some way by the army and not wandering about independently. "It will be the duty of the provost-marshal at every military post," he ordered, "to see that every negro within the jurisdiction of the military authority is employed by some white person." Grant provided an extensive list of possible roles they could fill, including soldiers, pioneers, teamsters, servants, cooks, and nurses. Employed black people had to have certificates that showed "how, where, and by whom they are employed." If able-bodied black men were found idle, they could be "pressed into service." Unemployable black people would be sent to contraband camps where army officers would try to find them suitable work such as harvesting crops from abandoned plantations. Grant's chief goal was to ensure that former slaves who could help the army were doing so, and those who could not did not become a military burden.[27]

In the late summer and fall of 1863, many black Southerners found themselves employed in the army. Many labored on the fortifications at Vicksburg to spare white soldiers from such arduous duty. One of Grant's corps commanders, Maj. Gen. James McPherson, received the following instructions: "No more details of white troops will be made for work on the fortifications in the vicinity of Vicksburg, at present. Negro troops will be brought here for that purpose. During the present hot weather it is necessary to save our men as much as possible from fatigue duty in the sun." Like the slaveholders, officers apparently assumed that black men were quite suited to drudgery and arduous labor. McPherson made sure that this labor policy was carried out. "All negroes with arms in their possession and all able-bodied negroes who are found doing nothing will be arrested and sent in here, to work on the fortifications," he ordered in mid-August. Later, Sherman instructed one of his brigade commanders to send any black refugees to Vicksburg for employment.[28]

Junior-level officers noted how the army was working former slaves hard in Vicksburg. Capt. Robert Braden of the Twenty-Sixth Indiana commented on how 2,000 black men had come in "and are now busily at work here saving the soldiers a great deal of hard labor." Lt. Albert Rockwell of the Twentieth Wisconsin emphasized how poorly black people were being treated. "Niggers are at a discount down here. They are lying along the river bank dying by the dozens every day," Rockwell informed his mother. "They are used to load and unload boats, and other work, and then turned loose until they are wanted again. Not half as well cared for as *Government Mules*." This difficult fatigue duty was the type of freedom that the army offered to many slaves.[29]

If black men were working hard in Vicksburg, their families were suffering greatly outside the city and at various other points along the Mississippi River. Dr. James Bryan, a medical inspector who had been dispatched to the area, informed the secretary of war that there were around 10,000 black women and children right beyond Union lines here. The children, who made up a majority of the group, "suffer[ed] very much from exposure and want of proper protection." Bryan suggested to Stanton that all these people be employed in some way so that they could support themselves. Many people during this time believed that working was the key to overcoming illness. So, like Grant, Bryan wanted the freed slaves to be engaged in some kind of labor.[30]

While Grant ensured that freed slaves were being employed in the most militarily beneficial way, he also urged Mississippi planters in the areas controlled by Union forces to free their own slaves. "It is earnestly recommended that the freedom of negroes be acknowledged," Grant stated, "and that, instead of compulsory labor, contracts upon fair terms be entered into between the former masters and servants.... Such a system as this, honestly followed, will result in substantial advantages to all parties." Sherman echoed these sentiments, giving the following advice to citizens of Warren County, Mississippi: "You must do as we do, hire your servants and pay them. If they don't earn their hire, discharge them and employ others." Grant and Sherman wanted planters to start a free labor system themselves and recognize the inevitable end of slavery. After all, the army itself could use only so many freed slaves.[31]

If planters did hire their former slaves, Grant did not want his army seizing them for military service. At the end of August 1863, he instructed Brig. Gen. Marcellus Crocker to enlist slaves belonging to planters who showed no willingness to give up on the Confederacy or adopt free labor. A little over six weeks later, Grant directed General McPherson to have his cavalry recruit black men still held by rebels. "Where planters have hired their negroes in accordance with established regulations," Grant advised, "recruiting officers should refuse to receive or harbor them about their camps." Grant was trying to protect both Southern Unionists and those who were now willing to return to the Union and end slavery. This protection was part of the general's larger efforts to encourage Unionism among the people of Mississippi. Grant had some fertile ground to advance this objective. After the fall of Vicksburg, some white Mississippians became demoralized and disenchanted with the Confederacy.[32]

As Grant was managing the collapse of slavery in much of Mississippi, Maj. Gen. Nathaniel Banks was dealing with slavery's demise in Louisiana. In late 1862, Banks had replaced Maj. Gen. Benjamin Butler as commander of the Department of the Gulf. Like Butler, Banks had been a Massachusetts politician before the war. He began his career as a Democrat, but switched to the Republican Party amid the sectional debates of the 1850s. A nationally prominent political figure, Banks served as both Speaker of the House of Representatives and governor of Massachusetts. On the divisive issue of slavery, Banks proved himself a moderate, opposing the expansion of the peculiar institution but not willing to agitate for its abolition. When the war began, Banks was quickly made a major general despite his almost complete lack of military experience. Banks received this important commission because of political considerations. Unfortunately for the Union, this political general was a disastrous battlefield commander. In the spring and summer of 1862, Banks suffered terrible defeats against Confederate general Thomas "Stonewall" Jackson in Virginia. But Banks had shown himself loyal to the Lincoln administration and remained popular among many people in the North. Banks also possessed considerable political skill. For all these reasons, Banks was dispatched to Louisiana to command Union forces in the Gulf.[33]

The general, however, faced a complex situation in the state when it came to the issue of slavery. The Emancipation Proclamation exempted thirteen parishes in southern Louisiana under Union control, but it still applied to the rest of the state. It was impossible, however, to maintain slavery in those exempted parishes. There the Union army had already confiscated numerous slaves under the Second Confiscation Act, and many others had wandered into Federal lines seeking refuge. None of them could be returned to their masters by law. In January 1863, it was estimated that between 70,000 and 100,000 black people had entered Union lines.[34]

Banks tried to make use of the ones he could. Able-bodied men were put to work on fortifications at Camp Parapet near New Orleans. Charles Bosson of the Forty-Second Massachusetts recalled how they would send out the black men in gangs. Detachments of soldiers swarmed into the countryside to bring in more black men for fortification labor. In just two such expeditions, Bosson reported that 1,000 slaves were seized. But there were too many black people in army lines to use effectively. Capt. John McDermott of the Ninety-First New York commented on how black people in Baton Rouge had congregated in a college. "It is a curiosity to take a peep (provided you hold your nose) into what was once a large and beautiful institution of learning/college, but now filled to the roof with tangible ignorance and depravity in the shape of Niggers All sizes + colours. They have in + about it over 3000," McDermott wrote. "They are not a notch above the beasts of the field such an idea as modesty never occurred to the mass. What a burden upon Government to feed them."[35]

Banks came up with a way to make the people less of a burden for his army. Building on what Butler had done previously, Banks turned to a system of contract labor in February 1863. Unemployed black people had to enter into labor contracts with planters for a year at a time. While former slaves were permitted to pick their employers, they were required to stay with them during the term of their contract. Banks outlined the duties of both laborers and planters: "Laborers shall render to their employer, between daylight and dark, ten hours in summer and nine hours in winter, of respectful, honest, faithful labor, and receive . . . just treatment, healthy rations, comfortable clothing, quarters, fuel, medical attendance, and instruction for children." Additionally, black laborers would receive wages based on a specific scale or be given a portion of the crop. Banks was very optimistic about this labor policy, calling it "the best act of my life." But if the system was successful in keeping black people employed, preserving order in the region, and maintaining the plantation system, it did not always operate to the benefit of the workers. As was the case with Thomas's labor system in the Mississippi River valley, black laborers were subjected to a brutal plantation regimen that resembled slavery and, in some cases, did not even provide wages. Famed abolitionist Frederick Douglass angrily claimed that Banks's system "makes the [Emancipation] Proclamation of 1863 a mockery and delusion." Yet this system did allow former slaves more freedom than they had before and permitted at least some to earn wages for the first time in their lives.[36]

Banks soon had more black men and women on his hands. In the spring of 1863, his army moved into the Teche country of Louisiana to drive out Confederates and secure provisions and horses. En route, his army liberated thousands of slaves. George Smith, a soon-to-be lieutenant in the Union First Louisiana, told an elderly slave woman, "We have come to free you all." With tears rolling down her cheeks, the woman ecstatically proclaimed: "May de Lor' bress you all. Ise been prayin' and prayin' for you dis many years. Now my eyes see dat de good Lor' has heard my prayer. Bress his holy name! Now Ise gwine ter die in peace." Most slaves did not have to be told and understood very well that the arrival of the Union army meant freedom. "Indeed every plantation we passed from Opalousas to Alexandra," Smith observed, "had its complement of these simple hearted beings [slaves] crowding to see us as we passed; all frantic with joy, some weeping, some blessing, and some dancing in the exuberance of their emotions." An aide-de-camp on Banks's staff, George Hepworth, similarly noted how slaves "crowded to the highway to see us pass, and clapped their hands, and sang and prayed, as banner after banner, beneath whose folds to-day there are no slaves, went by." Hepworth permitted male slaves who had been separated from their wives to go reunite with them. He also took one overjoyed young slave as a servant. As the slave was leaving the plantation with Hepworth, he declared himself "all right now for de fust time in my life." This former slave eventually enlisted in the army as an engineer.[37]

In fact, Banks was looking to enlist many of the slaves that he had freed. In May 1863, the general announced that he would organize a "Corps d'Afrique" composed of eighteen regiments from all branches of the service. Banks viewed this measure as an entirely pragmatic one. The corps was not "established upon any dogma of equality or other theory, but as a practical and sensible matter of business," he wrote. "The Government makes use of mules, horses, uneducated and educated white men, in the defense of its institutions. Why should not the negro contribute whatever is in his power for the cause in which he is as deeply interested as other men? We may properly demand from him whatever service he can render." Banks clearly saw freeing the slaves as a way to gain additional soldiers for his army.[38]

Union officers and recruiters tried to enlist every able-bodied black man they could but specifically targeted unemployed men in the cities. An African Corps recruiter remarked, "Every male negro who was found about the streets was taken up and put in the [work house]. If they were able-bodied, they were scared into enlistment." Black men were forcibly taken off plantations and pressed into the service, even when they had been hired according to Banks's labor regulations. The situation grew so bad that the department superintendent of black labor was "constantly besieged by persons both white and Black . . . some enquiring for their servants, others for their sons and Brothers some of whom have been forcibly seized while performing important duties."[39]

Some officers warned that heavy-handed methods to enlist black men would anger the loyal population. Brig. Gen. W. H. Emory reported anxiously to Banks that "the forced emigration and the enlistment of negroes" in the parishes around New Orleans "have made the population here very unsettled." When the Union cavalry was ordered to scout along the Fausse River and "collect all the able-bodied black men" for the army, Brig. Gen. Charles Stone was furious. "I regard this as a false military move," Stone argued. "The district opposite is one containing a large number of small farmers, the best disposed to the Government I have seen in this State. Their negroes are few, and are reported to be contented and quiet. If they are forcibly taken from their homes and put into the ranks, we shall gain a few worthless soldiers . . . and shall at the same time make hostile a region now friendly." Despite these protests, recruitment continued in earnest. By August 1863, Banks reported having almost twenty-one regiments of black troops organized, totaling 10,000–12,000 men. Banks thought these regiments had been crucial to his recent military success. "The regiments raised thus far," Banks informed Lincoln, "have been of great service in this department. I think it may be said with truth that our victory at Port Hudson could not have been accomplished at the time it was but for their assistance."[40]

While Banks's black troops did render great military assistance, more often than not they found themselves performing fatigue duty. "Many high officials outside of Washington have no other intention than that these [black] men shall be used as diggers and drudges," Brig. Gen. Daniel Ullmann complained. At the end of September 1863, Capt. Harrison Soule of the Sixth Michigan summed up these black men's wretched existence: "They are made soldiers or at least they carry a Gun and are draged around by some miserable White officers—who never held half so prominent a position before and who curses and swears and drives around the nigger worse than they were ever drove before."[41] As in so many other places, many Union officers could not care less about the welfare of freed black people.

In addition to recruiting emancipated slaves as soldiers, Banks's army also used them for other military tasks. At the direction of Banks, Maj. Gen. William Franklin ordered the cavalry to bring in all able-bodied black men from the country between the Teche Bayou and Mississippi River to work as teamsters. No women and children were supposed to be taken by the cavalry. Franklin also directed that liberated black men be employed in the artillery "as drivers of battery wagons, forges, and caissons." Plenty of officers brought in black people as servants to perform various menial duties around camp. Capt. John Dinsmore of the Ninety-Ninth Illinois informed his wife, "I have two or three Negroes in the Company to Cook to Wash for the men. I have one all the time to . . . Pitch . . . my tent." Michigan captain Harrison Soule commented how black servants in their camps "follow along doing all the Drugery and working as they never have done before and getting nothing but their grub + a few old clothes." Banks and his officers were finding all kinds of ways to take advantage of freed slaves.[42]

In point of fact, Banks's emancipation policies—even though they aroused far more controversy—were similar in many respects to those of Grant and Rosecrans. All three generals freed slaves for the practical use of the army. They all saw slave liberation as a way to supplement their military strength and put more white men back into the ranks. Black people were often put to work doing jobs that white men did not want to do, such as building fortifications or cooking and cleaning around camp. Freed slaves of little military value usually ended up in contraband camps, or in Mississippi and Louisiana, laboring on plantations. But even though military priorities dominated, all three armies freed thousands of slaves from bondage. Indeed, emancipation advanced with the armies. Understanding this, slaves constantly greeted the troops with cheers and powerful emotions. They were happy to help the Union in any way they could, even if it meant performing lowly tasks. In the end, this was a small price to pay for freedom.

Carrying out emancipation in the border states of Kentucky and Missouri proved far more difficult and politically dicey. Both states were exempt from the Emancipation Proclamation but were still subject to the provisions of the Second Confiscation Act. This meant that slaves belonging to rebels could be seized and used by the Union army. Unionists' slaves were still protected under the law and the army could not touch them. But officers had a difficult time determining whether a slave was the property of a Unionist or rebel. Sometimes, officers had to depend on the testimony of the slaves themselves, who naturally claimed their masters were disloyal. In addition to this confusing situation, the border states were absolutely critical to the Union cause, and nothing led to more political turmoil there than the emancipation question. Therefore, army commanders and Lincoln often exercised caution in attacking slavery in the border states. The last thing they wanted to do was alienate crucial Unionist support. When officers did try to move against slavery there, they often clashed with Washington officials, state authorities, or their own commanders. Lincoln had tried to induce the border states to enact some plan for gradual, compensated emancipation and did not want the army hindering that effort. Military considerations, however, would eventually push the army to adopt increasingly emancipationist policies in Kentucky and Missouri.[43]

At the beginning of 1863, pro-emancipationist general Samuel Curtis commanded Federal forces in Missouri. Curtis had vigorously carried out the Second Confiscation Act during the second half of 1862, even going as far as to issue "free papers" to the slaves seized under the act. He continued to confiscate slaves in Missouri during 1863, claiming to take in only rebels' slaves. "Negroes that belong to loyal citizens we have to regard as owing service to their masters, and we must respect the legal rights of loyal masters," Curtis wrote. When a confiscated slave belonging to a Confederate soldier was locked up in jail, a Union provost marshal ordered his immediate release. Hundreds of slaves were protected by the army at Cape Girardeau, and some reportedly made armed nighttime raids on nearby plantations to liberate family members. Curtis ordered an end to the raids, but the protection of slaves continued.[44]

Whatever care he might have taken, Curtis's policies on various matters, especially slavery, alienated conservative Unionists in Missouri, including the state's governor, Hamilton Gamble. They pressured Lincoln to remove Curtis, which the president did in May 1863, replacing him with the much more conservative Maj. Gen. John M. Schofield. Lincoln told Schofield that he had made the change "because of a conviction in my mind that the Union men of Missouri, constituting, when united, a vast majority of the whole people, have entered into a pestilent factional quarrel among themselves, Gen. Curtis, perhaps not of choice, being the head of one faction, and Gov. Gamble that of the other." Lincoln hoped Schofield could better navigate Missouri's treacherous political terrain and chart a middle course between the different Unionist factions.[45]

Schofield did have extensive experience dealing with Missourians. As the Civil War loomed in 1860, Schofield was teaching physics at Washington University in St. Louis, a position that allowed him to meet some of the prominent people in the state. With these connections along with his military background, which included training at West Point, Schofield was the ideal candidate to muster in Missouri troops early in the war. Politically, Schofield was a moderate Democrat who was primarily concerned with saving the Union. He quickly proved himself a fine combat officer with his heroics at the battle of Wilson's Creek. In November 1861, Schofield was given direction of the Missouri State Militia. In this capacity, he gained an acute appreciation for the complicated political and military situation in Missouri, particularly the potent guerrilla activity throughout the state. So all of his experience in Missouri made Schofield seem like a good replacement for Curtis, but mediating between the various political factions in the state would prove problematic, to say the least.[46]

Indeed, this was nearly an impossible task. As Curtis had favored the radicals in Missouri, Schofield very quickly came to identify more with the conservatives. Nothing better illustrated this than Schofield's policies on slavery. The general later recalled how he had put a stop to Curtis's "radical theory of military confiscation." He no longer allowed provost marshals to issue "free papers" to escaped slaves. Instead, they were instructed to list the property, including slaves, of any rebel within their jurisdiction, provide witnesses that could testify to the person's rebel sympathies, and report all this to the provost marshal general. Then, the matter was "turned over to the civil authorities." Schofield wanted the courts to carry out confiscation. While Curtis, and for that matter Rosecrans, interpreted the Second Confiscation Act broadly, Schofield held to a narrower interpretation. He aligned himself with Missouri's conservative state administration on the issues of slavery and confiscation. "A simple sense of duty," Schofield asserted, "compelled the military commander to act in these matters [concerning confiscation] more in harmony with the State government than with the radical party." Schofield did embrace "universal emancipation . . . as one of the means absolutely necessary to a complete restoration of the Union," but in the case of Missouri, he wanted the state to emancipate its own slaves.[47]

The state had moved in that direction during the summer of 1863 when a convention had approved a plan for gradual emancipation, though this process would not be completed until 1870. Even then, black people over forty would remain slaves for life, and those under twelve would be required to serve their owners as apprentices until they were twenty-three. Both Lincoln and Schofield supported this plan. Lincoln liked the idea of abolishing slavery gradually in the state, "believing as I do that gradual can be made better than immediate for both black and white, except when military necessity changes the case."[48]

Military necessity, however, did soon change the case, and the army in Missouri adopted much more emancipationist policies. The need for black troops led the army to assume the role of liberator. In September 1863, Schofield advised Washington: "I believe the able bodied negroes in Missouri will be worth more to the Government as soldiers than they are to their masters as laborers. . . . Moreover I believe it would be a great benefit to the state as well as to the negro to have him transformed from a slave into a soldier." Schofield soon received orders from the president to recruit black men in the state. The general then laid out regulations for recruitment in his department. All of the black men enlisted would be immediately free. If the slave of a loyal master volunteered, the master would be compensated up to $300 for the loss of his property. Provost marshals were to carry out the recruitment. "The exigencies of the war require that colored troops should be recruited in the State of Missouri," Schofield explained to his officers.[49]

This recruitment of black troops in late 1863 and early 1864 fatally undermined slavery in the state. The army received thousands of runaway slaves into the ranks, emancipating every one of them in the process. Union officers were instrumental in enlisting black men. Commanding the District of Central Missouri, Brig. Gen. Egbert Brown encouraged black enlistment and insisted that no obstructions be tolerated. "Any persons who shall interfere with or attempt to discourage the enlistment of negroes will be reported . . . to these headquarters, in order that they may be brought before a military commission or general court-martial," ordered Brown. The department's assistant provost marshal general, Lt. Col. A. Jacobson, discussed with all the provost marshals in the state "how the recruiting of colored men could be pushed more actively and vigorously." Jacobson stated that the army intended to use recruiting parties to bring in black men, and that it was their duty to protect "discharged soldiers in their undoubted right to their freedom." Ultimately, the Union army took in more than 8,300 Missouri slaves and made them soldiers. This constituted almost 40 percent of military-age black men in the state. By the spring of 1864, slavery in Missouri had been thoroughly wrecked by the needs of the Union army. As in so many other places, the army freed slaves for military purposes but, in doing so, destroyed the institution of slavery.[50]

The army eventually attacked slavery in the neighboring border state of Kentucky as well, but here the process was even slower and more delicate. During the first half of 1863, top commanders in the state remained reluctant to tamper with slavery. A Kentucky slave owner, Brig. Gen. Jeremiah Boyle, prohibited any slaves from entering army camps and ordered any slaves found there to be expelled. Boyle believed that meddling with Kentucky slavery harmed the Union cause, and he feared the possible effects on fervent Unionists like himself. Regarding emancipation policy, Boyle wrote, "I trust the Government will not do anything 'to alienate a loyalty that has proved true amid fire and blood.' Kentucky has vindicated her loyalty in the fiery ordeal of battle." Similarly, Boyle's department commander, Maj. Gen. Ambrose Burnside, instructed his officers neither to help Kentucky slaves escape nor employ them without their owners' consent. Moreover, he forbade interference with civil authorities trying to recover escaped slaves. In other words, Burnside did not want his troops freeing slaves in the state.[51]

Before coming to Kentucky, Burnside had, at best, a mixed military record. Early in 1862 he enjoyed success in operations against the Confederates on the North Carolina sounds. But in September 1862, Burnside's leadership was uninspired at the battle of Antietam. His greatest military failure came less than three months later at the battle of Fredericksburg, where he led the Union army into a disastrous debacle. While strong for the Union, Burnside was certainly no rabid abolitionist. Indeed, he had been a Democrat before the war. As a professionally trained military officer, Burnside did eventually come to accept emancipation as a practical necessity for the Union war effort. Yet he was not about to alienate the loyal citizens of Kentucky by interfering with slavery in the state.[52]

But despite Burnside's orders to the contrary, lower-level officers in Kentucky seized slaves. Just as in the fall of 1862, this led to conflict with their superiors. The Eighteenth and Twenty-Second Michigan got into a particularly bitter feud with one of Boyle's commanders, Brig. Gen. Mahlon Manson, over fugitive slaves coming into their lines. As the Michiganders were about to leave Kentucky and join Maj. Gen. William S. Rosecrans's army in Tennessee, Manson ordered them to expel the slaves from their camp. Col. Charles Doolittle, in temporary command of both regiments, refused. Manson then tried to intimidate the Michigan men by ordering other Union regiments to surround them. Pvt. Morris Hall of the Eighteenth recalled that Manson "even plant[ed] a battery of artillery at each end of our command and bearing upon us." The determined Wolverines still would not give up their slaves. "Our guns were loaded and bayonets fixed and we stood ready for any action which the emergency might require," stated Hall. Fortunately, there was no bloodshed as Burnside allowed the regiments to proceed to Nashville with the slaves.[53]

The Twenty-Third Michigan also found itself embroiled in controversy over taking fugitive slaves in Kentucky. At least twice, they were ordered to expel slaves from their lines, and General Boyle allowed sheriffs to scour the regiment's camp for slaves. These measures, however, proved futile. Capt. Oliver Spaulding described how his regiment foiled General Boyle, whom he called "an ardent and persistent slave hunter." When the slave catchers approached "regimental headquarters exhibiting their written authority," recounted Spaulding, "a kind of telepathic word ran through the camp and was caught both by the sought 'nigger' and the camp guard; he got outside the lines, and the camp search proved fruitless." Later, the black people returned to the regiment. Sometimes, slaves were able to escape Boyle's grasp permanently by accompanying officers, who were detailed to guard trains, to

Nashville. In the end, these Michigan regiments successfully resisted returning slaves even if the owners were from Kentucky.[54] But the slaves liberated through the individual actions of regiments were relatively few, so slavery would remain largely intact as long as the high command stuck to its policy of noninterference.

In fact, slavery was so well protected that Kentuckians were able to re-enslave black people hailing from Deep South states. There were numerous complaints about freed slaves moving with the army through Kentucky being seized and sold back into slavery. When Congressman Frank Kellogg of Michigan visited Louisville in the spring of 1863, he fumed over the abuse of freed slaves: "Colored men from Arkansas Tennessee Miss and other Rebel States who have Certificates of their freedom signed by Generals in the field are seized—imprisoned, and sold for costs &c—The temptation to kidnap them is very great as the man who takes them up gets $75 each & the Jailor is well paid also and these poor fellows have no friends to help them. . . . This infernal treatment of such men ought to call down the vengeance of Heaven on all who permit it." Around the same time, the provost marshal in Louisville, Orlando Moore, stopped a slave auction at the courthouse. Moore contended that the slaves "were legally entitled, under the President's proclamation, to their freedom, but . . . were imprisoned and dragged from jail to the auction block, by proslavery tyrants, to be sold to the highest bidder." President Lincoln read about the auction in the newspaper and was appalled. Secretary of War Stanton ordered Burnside "to take immediate measures," so slaves "entitled to protection from the Government" would never be reenslaved. The general complied, ordering that slaves freed by war measures were "entitled to their freedom, and no one in this department has a right to interfere with that freedom. Any sale of such persons in this department is void."[55]

Carrying out this order, General Boyle, at the beginning of May 1863, directed that all slaves freed further south be released from jail and put to work for the Union army. In Louisville, they were to labor "on the redoubts and fortifications in process of construction." Boyle urged caution and thought it best for Kentucky officers to execute this policy. This was presumably because Boyle only wanted "freed" slaves from deeper south, not Kentucky slaves, liberated from the civil authorities. Boyle actually set up a three-man commission in Louisville (not surprisingly, two members were Kentucky officers) to determine the status of captured black people. If they were free under the proclamation, the commission was to "give them certified declarations of the fact of their freedom under the War measures of the Government." Emancipated slaves that now came to Kentucky could not be reenslaved but were free to work for the army.[56]

Yet the army in Kentucky soon required more labor than liberated slaves from other states could provide. So policy shifted toward extensively using Kentucky slaves for military purposes. Acting at Burnside's direction, in August 1863, Boyle ordered 6,000 slaves impressed in central Kentucky to labor on military roads. Building these roads was a "necessity," according to Boyle. Slaves between the ages of sixteen and forty-five were eligible for impressment, but only a certain number could be seized from each owner. The idea was to sustain agricultural production at the same time. Even given this limitation, however, Burnside still ordered 8,000 more slaves to be impressed to build a railroad. Impressment was different than confiscation in that the black people were returned to their owners after the work was complete, and the owners were compensated. The owners were in essence hiring out their slaves for the army's use. But this was not how it always worked. Impressed black Kentuckians often mingled with freed slaves, making it difficult to keep track of them. Some most likely attached themselves to the many Union regiments moving through the state. Whatever the intention of the policy, impressment, too, undermined slavery in Kentucky.[57]

Military considerations pushed the army to impress Kentucky slaves, but they would eventually drive the army in a much more emancipationist direction. In particular, the use of slaves as soldiers would lead the army to liberate thousands of Bluegrass bondsmen. Kentucky had the largest black population of any border state and could thus furnish crucial manpower to the Union cause. For a long time, however, fear of alienating Kentucky Unionists and even sparking violent resistance had caused the administration and the army to hesitate, even when recruitment was proceeding almost everywhere else. Indeed, many Kentuckians, including the state's governor, Thomas Bramlette, opposed enlisting black soldiers. But by the end of February 1864, Congress authorized the enrollment of all able-bodied slaves between the ages of twenty and forty-five, with compensation for Unionist masters.[58]

This recruitment job fell to Brig. Gen. Stephen Burbridge, a Kentucky slaveholder who had taken Boyle's place as commander in the state. This was no easy task, for Burbridge faced determined opposition. In mid-March 1864, Governor Bramlette sternly warned: "I am determined to execute our laws—and if any man violates them he must abide the penalty. The forcable abduction of slaves—the enlistment without consent of owners enticing them to run away etc are all crimes against the known laws of the land, and instead of commanding the commission of crime it is the duty of officers to arrest the violators & hand them over to the Civil Magistrate for trial." Around the same time, Bramlette considered issuing a proclamation urging resistance to enlisting slaves but was talked out of it by a group of prominent Unionists who worried about a potentially disastrous clash with Washington. Bramlette took his grievances all the way to the president, meeting with him in Washington. The two reached an agreement on several issues concerning black recruitment. First, and most important, if a county filled its quota of soldiers with white recruits, no black men would be recruited. Any black volunteers were to be organized in camps outside Kentucky, and recruiting was to be conducted only by officers authorized to do so.[59]

The agreement did not last, as Kentucky counties fell short of their quotas. This opened the way for Burbridge to begin recruiting and enlisting black men aggressively throughout the state. In April 1864, Burbridge directed his provost marshals "to receive and regularly enlist . . . all able-bodied negro slaves . . . who may apply to them." Any loyal "owners" of such recruits were to be given certificates so they could later be compensated. Lt. Col. Thomas Fairleigh, who drafted this order, hoped that recruiting these black troops would "be favorable to the success of our aims and the restoration of our country."[60]

Fairleigh would not be disappointed. At last, given the chance for freedom, Kentucky slaves joined the army in huge numbers. Burbridge's adjutant, Capt. J. Bates Dickson, observed that slaves were "flocking in by hundreds—far beyond the ability of the provost-marshal to attend to them—to enlist. This matter is one that has created considerable excitement in many districts." After a visit to Kentucky, the judge advocate general of the army, Joseph Holt, reported to the secretary of war at the end of July 1864: "The recruiting of colored troops in Kentucky is proceeding most satisfactorily. About 10,000 have already been enlisted, and this number, it is believed, will be doubled in sixty days. They have for some time been coming in at the rate of about 100 per day." Ultimately, 23,703 black Kentuckians became Union soldiers, which represented 57 percent of military-age black men in the state. As in Missouri, the raising of black troops provided a pathway to freedom for so many slaves that it dealt a deathblow to Kentucky slavery.[61]

Indeed, wherever Union armies operated in the western theater in 1863 and 1864, emancipation was carried out for the army's benefit. Western officers consistently freed slaves so that the army could use them. Southern slaves were seen as valuable manpower that needed to be taken away from the rebels and used by the Union. From the army's perspective, this policy carried an ironclad logic. As a military institution, the Union army's goal first and foremost was winning the war, and emancipation should serve that end. Moreover, on a personal level, many Union officers primarily supported emancipation because of its practical benefits to the Union cause. The fact that so many carried out the policy in this militarily pragmatic way was a direct reflection of these attitudes. Officers' prevailing racial beliefs help explain why many of them were more concerned with former slaves' ability to help the army than with their welfare. But even though the army liberated slaves for their military value, they still liberated them. Freedom literally advanced with the army. So ultimately, the army did help bring about a social revolution, albeit an unintended one.

CHAPTER SIX

William T. Sherman and His Officers

The Reluctant Emancipators

In April 1864, Maj. Gen. William T. Sherman wrote his brother, Senator John Sherman, a revealing letter on emancipation. "Too much stress has been laid on the Negro," the general complained. "It is used as a touch Stone, a test. It should not be, but treated as any other minor question. The Negro question will solve itself. The Government of the United States is the Issue. Shall it stand or fall? If it stands it can in Some way control Negros as well as whites, but if it fall another combination will grow up that will govern all discordant Elements with an iron hand for the world will go on.... Let us manage the Whites & Niggers and all the Physical resources of the country & apply them when most needed. Let us accomplish great results."[1] Less than a month later, Sherman began his decisive drive on Atlanta. During this critical campaign and those that followed, Sherman focused on military success and restoring the Union, not liberating slaves. He wanted to free only able-bodied slaves who could be employed by his army. All others were a military burden and should remain on the farms and plantations. But as hard as he tried, Sherman found it impossible to deal only with slaves who had military value. Thousands of slaves determinedly followed his army's columns through Georgia and the Carolinas. In fact, numerous slaves enjoyed their first taste of freedom at the heels of Sherman's army. So ironically, the general who was probably least interested in assuming the mantle of a liberator led an army that freed thousands.

Sherman had never been very enthusiastic about emancipation or black people. He had opposed the Emancipation Proclamation at the time it was issued and had long believed slavery to be a valuable system that reflected the natural order of society. But at least by late 1863, Sherman had come to accept the end of slavery as a necessary and inevitable consequence of the war. He often argued that secessionists killed slavery by rebelling. The death of the institution became "the natural, logical, and legal consequence of the acts" of white Southerners: "The South has made the interests of slavery the issue of the war. If they lose the war, they lose slavery." Indifferent to the morality of the matter, Sherman viewed emancipation as simply a practical measure. He displayed little if any sympathy for the oppressed slave. "I care not a straw for niggers," Sherman bluntly admitted just a few weeks before he captured Atlanta. Despite his repeated contact with black people and slavery, Sherman's racial prejudices only seemed to harden.[2]

In the spring of 1864, Sherman assumed overall command in the West. In March, Gen. Ulysses S. Grant had been promoted to commander of all Union armies and headed east, entrusting his western armies to Sherman. Sherman had proved to be Grant's most reliable lieutenant, serving with him from Shiloh to Vicksburg to Chattanooga. Now Sherman was to move against Confederate general Joseph Johnston's forces in Georgia as Grant squared off against Confederate general Robert E. Lee's army in Virginia. This was part of a grand Union offensive to put simultaneous pressure on the Confederacy's two most important armies. In this campaign, Union forces intended not only to defeat Confederate armies but also to destroy the South's military resources and will to fight.[3]

As Sherman prepared for the campaign that ultimately would bring the Confederacy to its knees, slavery was dying all across the Union-occupied South. During 1863, Federal forces had shattered the institution in the Mississippi Valley and in Tennessee. From Nashville, Maj. Gen. Lovell Rousseau observed, "Slavery is virtually dead in Tennessee, although the State is excepted from the emancipation proclamation. Negroes leave their homes and stroll over the country uncontrolled. . . . It is now and has been for some time the practice of soldiers to go to the country and bring in wagon-loads of negro women and children to this city." "All parties agree," Surgeon John Bennitt of the Nineteenth Michigan informed his wife, "slavery is virtually abolished in Tennessee already." While in McMinnville, he remarked, "There are a great many negroes here, but they are no longer held in slavery by their masters. They only stay with their masters if they please."[4] The Federal army had wrecked slavery everywhere it went, and Sherman was about to do the same in Georgia.

Yet, in May 1864, when Sherman's army advanced from Chattanooga into northern Georgia, it ran into relatively few slaves because planters had often fled the area with their bondsmen. Capt. Charles Wills of the 103rd Illinois noted that "all the negroes and stock have been run off" near Dalton, Georgia. About two weeks later Wills still did not see any slaves: "The planters in this country own thousands of negroes, and they've run them all off down this road. They are about two days ahead of us." Sherman himself remarked, "Negroes are as scarce in North Georgia as in Ohio."[5] As far as these slaveholders were concerned, Sherman's army might as well have been filled with abolitionists.

Besides slaveholders moving their slaves away from the advancing Union army, another reason Sherman's men did not encounter huge numbers of slaves was the nature of the region in which they were campaigning. The mountainous region of North Georgia was not replete with slaves. Only about 6 percent of Georgia's total slaves, according to the 1860 census, resided in the counties Sherman's army marched through on its way to Atlanta. In almost all of these counties, slaves comprised less than 30 percent of the population, and in many of them, they made up far less. For example, in Whitfield, Milton, and Paulding Counties, slaves accounted for 17.2 percent, 13.4 percent, and 8.1 percent of the population, respectively. With fewer slaves, North Georgia's culture and economy were quite different from those of the cotton belt, which ran through the central and southwestern parts of the state. Rather than cotton, North Georgia farmers grew grain products and often engaged in subsistence agriculture. They had a strong sense of community and family and valued their independence and freedom from outside interference.[6]

With these characteristics, North Georgians developed a different political outlook from those in the plantation belt. Long a stronghold of the Democratic Party, North Georgia powerfully endorsed Southern Democrat John C. Breckinridge in 1860. Much of this support grew out of party loyalty that had been entrenched in the region for decades. Even though they voted for Breckinridge, many North Georgians opposed immediate secession, electing cooperationist delegates to the secession convention. Secessionists in the plantation belt had worried about the feelings of North Georgians on disunion, and with good reason. In the end, the state voted to secede 208 to 89, with a significant amount of the opposition coming from North Georgia. But once Georgia left the Union and joined the ranks of the Confederacy, most North Georgians became generally supportive of the rebel cause. As the war progressed, some of these people became disaffected with the idea of a Confederate nation, especially when Sherman's army brought the war to their doorsteps. Sherman destroyed war resources across the region and freed some of the slaves.[7]

Sherman quickly put to military use those black Southerners he emancipated. The general especially employed former slaves as pioneers to relieve his soldiers from digging trenches. "I endeavored to spare the soldiers this hard labor," Sherman recalled, "by authorizing each division commander to organize out of the freedmen who escaped to us a pioneer corps of two hundred men, who were fed out of the regular army supplies, and I promised them ten dollars a month.... These pioneer detachments became very useful to us during the rest of the war, for they could work at night while our men slept." Like other Union commanders in the West, Sherman saw black people as a source of army labor. Black Southerners were being worked so hard by Sherman that Adj. Gen. Lorenzo Thomas complained that they were forced to labor "in many instances" more than they did as slaves.[8]

Sherman believed black people were best suited to perform such menial tasks and ferociously resisted any attempt to recruit black soldiers in his army. In June 1864, Sherman issued the following directive: "Recruiting officers will not enlist as soldiers any negroes who are profitably employed by any of the army departments." This order drew the ire of Lorenzo Thomas, who wanted as many black men as possible recruited. Sherman bluntly told Thomas: "I believe that negroes better serve the Army as teamsters, pioneers, and servants.... I confess I would prefer 300 negroes armed with spades and axes than 1,000 as soldiers." The general explained that he did not want to recruit too many able-bodied black men as soldiers because then there would be no one left to look after black women and children. But the real problem was that Sherman did not believe black men were capable of serving in the Union ranks. As he succinctly put it to a Massachusetts recruiter, "The negro is in a transition state, and is not the equal of the white man." Sherman's racial prejudice thus limited former slaves to certain roles in his army.[9]

Sherman's army especially welcomed black Southerners bringing military intelligence. Sherman instructed Maj. Gen. James Steedman to reward slaves who brought news about enemy positions and movements. An officer in the Seventh Pennsylvania Cavalry, Heber Thompson, reported a slave coming into the picket line who explained that the Confederates were moving all their soldiers from Atlanta to the front and fortifying the Chattahoochee River. Another cavalry regiment, the Eighth Michigan, received information from black women under far more dire circumstances. During Maj. Gen. George Stoneman's aborted raid to liberate the Union prisoners at Andersonville, the Michigan cavalrymen were forced to depend on female slaves to get back to Union lines. The black women guided the Federal troopers through the Georgia countryside, at one point even lighting their way across a stream at night with torches. Capt. James Wells commented, "There was just enough light to reveal the desperate earnestness depicted on the faces of these slave girls ... who had entered upon this task that might prove death or torture to them." Slaves were willing to risk all to aid Sherman's army even if it was not the most idealistic liberating force.[10]

The army continued to liberate slaves for military purposes as it closed in on Atlanta. Striking the Macon and Western Railroad in late July, Union cavalry under Brig. Gen. Kenner Garrard freed 100 or more slaves. Col. George Gallup of the Fourteenth Kentucky noted how these former slaves were soon formed into "working parties." With the loss of only two soldiers, Maj. Gen. George Thomas reported that the raid had brought in "a fair lot of fresh horses and negroes." Other cavalry expeditions achieved similar results. In early August, Grant told Sherman to employ "as many negroes as you can get for teamsters, company cooks, pioneers, &c., and keep the enlisted men in the ranks." Emancipation remained primarily a military measure.[11]

After Atlanta fell in September, the army made sure that all freed slaves were doing something productive. Every free black male found in the city "without proper authority" was seized and put to work on fortifications. Commanding a brigade in Atlanta, Col. James Selfridge of the Forty-Sixth Pennsylvania stated that his men took in sixty-six black people and either turned them over to the quartermaster or made them officers' servants. All servants had to carry very detailed papers to prove that they were properly employed, which Chap. Lyman Ames of the Twenty-Ninth Ohio filled out for his servant, Henry Owen.[12]

While in Atlanta, Brig. Gen. Alpheus Williams took in a family who had walked over thirty miles "with what worldly goods they could carry to get away from slavery." They labored hard for Williams and earned his affection. He especially admired Phoebe Simms, "a most excellent cook, washer, and sewer. Indeed, the best colored servant girl I ever saw, pious, steady, industrious, and wonderfully intelligent." When the army left Atlanta, Williams sent the family north with a letter of commendation hoping they could find employment. He wanted them to go to his hometown of Detroit, Michigan. Even as emancipation policy was driven mostly by military considerations, there were still a few instances where officers looked out for the welfare of freed slaves. In this case, Williams's personal relationship with a black family clearly drove his attitude and actions.[13]

For his part, Sherman remained committed to freeing slaves to help his army, but he remained skeptical about enlisting black soldiers. In September 1864, he told Henry Halleck, "Let us capture negroes, of course, and use them to the best advantage," but "we want the best young white men of the land . . . to fight for their country." Using black troops was like "fighting with 'paper' men" to Sherman. When he heard people say, "Is not a negro as good as a white man to stop a bullet," he thought, "Yes, and a sand-bag is better." Some of Sherman's officers agreed. Capt. William Van Antwerp of the Fourth Michigan Cavalry was outraged at abolitionists who wanted to enlist black soldiers. "They can send their agents down here to recruit negroes," he fumed, "but they have not manhood enough to go in to the army themselves. Gen. Sherman is fixing that class of sneaks that come to him, and if they show themselves among the soldiers, they will get a double dose." Van Antwerp thought Sherman was the best Union general and "he is all right on the nigger question."[14] Although many Union officers endorsed black troops by this point in the war, many still did not. The issue remained a divisive one until the end of the war.

However adamant Sherman and others might have remained in their aversion to black soldiers, the army was still a powerful force of liberation. Writing from Georgia, Michigan captain Henry Potter emphasized the vital role the army had played in emancipating slaves: "Every slave that has been freed has gained his liberty by and thro' the army—and no negro not freed by the army, has been freed at all—as far as the army goes into the *'Confederacy,'* the slaves are used for Army purposes, and have their freedom."[15] As with other Union forces, the advance of Sherman's army meant freedom for countless slaves. Whatever Sherman's sentiments, he was a powerful liberator.

This fact became even more apparent when Sherman began his famous March to the Sea. In November 1864, Sherman abandoned Atlanta and his supply line as the two wings of his army marched toward Savannah, Georgia. The goals of this march were to destroy Confederate military resources and sap the spirit of the Southern people. Sherman explained to Grant, "If we can march a well-appointed army right through his territory, it is a demonstration to the world, foreign and domestic, that we have a power which [Jefferson] Davis cannot resist." The general was sure that many in the South would reason that such a march "is proof positive that the North can prevail." It was a daring strategy to defeat the Confederacy swiftly.[16]

This was the perfect region to strike at the will of the Confederate people. The central-Georgia plantation belt had been largely untouched by the war up until this point, and the white civilians there were generally pro-Confederate in sentiment. This most populous region of the state demonstrated strong support for secession in 1861 and provided more than its share of soldiers for the war effort. Politically, the area had been divided before the war, with a very strong Whig presence in the region. In the counties that Sherman's army marched through, the citizens, in fact, split their vote in 1860 between Southern Democrat John C. Breckinridge and Constitutional Unionist John Bell. But many of these Bell voters ended up endorsing secession. Located in high-slaveholding counties, these former Whigs, like Democrats, keenly perceived a threat to slavery and their society and joined the Confederacy. When Sherman and his men got into this region, white citizens still showed their support for the Confederacy and hatred of the Union, but some citizens had also started to become disenchanted with the war effort.[17]

One group that was happy to see Sherman was the enslaved black population, and there were huge numbers of slaves in the area. Slavery was concentrated in the central plantation belt and the rice belt along the Atlantic coast. Marching through the heart of Georgia, Sherman's men came into contact with large numbers of people in bondage. According to the 1860 census, Sherman went through counties with over 116,000 slaves in them. In over half those counties, the slave population made up a majority of the total population, and sometimes it was much greater than that. For example, in Morgan, Putnam, and Burke Counties, the enslaved comprised over 70 percent of the population. Most of the area of Sherman's march was where cotton was king. Cotton dominated the economy of this region, and the planters' plantation culture shaped its values and beliefs. Once Sherman reached the coast, he entered an older region of the state, the rice belt. Here, large numbers of slaves toiled in especially dangerous conditions on rice plantations. These plantations were some of the most lucrative in the South. In this area, there was already significant dislocation of the slave population because of Union naval and army operations earlier in the war, but undoubtedly, some slaves remained. Yet even though there were massive numbers of slaves in Sherman's path as he marched to the sea, the general simply was not that concerned about them.[18]

Sherman's focus was on ending the war, not freeing slaves. On the march, he at best embraced emancipation as a strictly pragmatic measure to help his army. Able-bodied black men of military use could accompany his columns. Indeed, Sherman directed his officers to use black men as much as possible to fill pioneer battalions. But officers were urged to keep slaves of no immediate military value away from their commands. No refugees "should be encouraged to encumber us on the march," the general cautioned. "At some future time we will be enabled to provide for the . . . blacks who seek to escape the bondage under which they are now suffering." Needing to move quickly and cut loose from his supply lines, Sherman did not want his army slowed down by numerous black women and children.[19] It is important to note that these orders did not explicitly exclude black families from Union lines; they were more advisory in nature. At this point in the war, it would have been politically difficult, if not impossible, for a Union army commander to bar black people from his lines.

The general, however, did his best to discourage black Southerners from following his army. Near Covington, Georgia, Sherman informed an elderly black man named "Uncle Stephen" that the army "wanted the slaves to remain where they were, and not to load us down with useless mouths, which would eat up the food needed for our fighting-men." The general went on to tell the slave that he "could receive a few of their young, hearty men as pioneers." Later, he reiterated this message to a reportedly "intelligent" and "dignified" black man who spoke with him for half an hour about various subjects, including the battle of New Orleans. Despite his deep racial prejudice, Sherman was usually polite to individual black men and women, often assuring them that their freedom would result from the war. One of Sherman's aides, Maj. Henry Hitchcock, commented, "The General has a capital way of talking to these [black] people,—frank, pleasant and unaffected, without being familiar, and they respond with a mingled respect and confidence which shows how well he understands them." But however he treated them personally, Sherman was clear that he only wanted to free those that could be of assistance to the military.[20]

Hitchcock and other staff officers communicated Sherman's policies to the slaves. While at the plantation of a particularly cruel slave owner, Hitchcock talked with two female house servants, strongly discouraging them from following the army. He told one, "Better stay where you are, we don't want women to come with us,—we have long marches to make." Only able-bodied men should accompany the army. Hitchcock admitted, "Two words of encouragement from me would have brought her along." Sherman's chief commissary officer, Col. Amos Beckwith, took in a few "stout negro men" and employed them as teamsters but would not allow their families to come with them. Yet not everyone on Sherman's staff was happy about turning black women and children away from the army. Capt. George Nichols thought it was "heartrending . . . to refuse them liberty." He noted how one woman wanted to see her family in Savannah after many years of separation and another wanted to reunite with her son in Macon.[21] Whatever their personal attitudes though, Sherman's staff certainly understood their chief's military priorities when it came to emancipation.

This understanding extended to most officers in the army. Sherman's generals focused on liberating slaves of military value. Commanding the

Fourteenth Corps, Brig. Gen. Jefferson C. Davis reported that his command took in about 1,340 black Georgians, "mostly able-bodied males," during the march. These former slaves were employed as officers' servants and pioneers. Additionally, almost half of them were detailed for heavy fatigue duty rebuilding King's Bridge near Savannah. Brig. Gen. Giles Smith instructed his division to bring in only able-bodied black men and turn them over to the pioneer corps. Brig. Gen. William Hazen tried to limit the black people accompanying his division to pioneers, cooks, and servants. The former slaves serving in these capacities had to have tickets from the provost marshal.[22]

Lower-level officers followed suit during the march to Savannah. Maj. John Widmer of the 104th Illinois noted that his regiment alone brought in and employed twenty black people. Another Illinois officer, Maj. Charles Wills, remarked, "An immense number of 'contrabands' now follow us, most of them able-bodied men, who intend [on] going into the army." An officer in the Seventy-Ninth Pennsylvania, Michael Locher, reported freeing "25 able-bodied male negroes" as one of the fruits of the campaign. Maj. F. H. Rolshausen of the Eighty-Second Illinois stated that his unit took in eleven slaves as servants and cooks. "My command has never lived any better since in [the] service as while this tramp was made," the major contended.[23]

Echoing Rolshausen, Maj. James Connolly of the 123rd Illinois discussed how the liberated slaves served their new bosses. "The negro walks along beside the soldier, with his knapsack and cooking utensils strapped upon his back, thus relieving the soldier of his load, and helping him along," Connolly observed. "What soldier *wouldn't* be an abolitionist under such circumstances." Benefiting from former slaves personally could thus reinforce pro-emancipation feelings.[24]

Yet as much as Sherman and many of his officers wanted to free only able-bodied male slaves of military use, they could not keep women, children, and the elderly away from the army. Understanding that advancing Federals meant freedom, slaves of all types followed Sherman's bluecoats whether they were wanted or not. Lt. Col. Michael Fitch of the Twenty-First Wisconsin reported: "On the march to the sea . . . negroes flocked to our columns by the thousand. They knew by instinct that the old flag led to freedom." He saw "Darkies of all sizes and ages." Lt. Alfred Trego of the 102nd Illinois described the great variety of black Southerners following the army: "One woman had her child fastened on her back like the Indian custom. Another wore Pantaloons with a short dress to her knees. Another had black silk and very large hoops. Some were in carriages, others on horseback. Some little children walking and almost worn out." Lt. Col. Andrew Hickenlooper recalled:

"Among the poor ignorant untutored negroes there was everywhere evidenced faith that the coming of the Yankee army was to bring them freedom from bondage. They turned out in full force to hail their deliverers, and in the most extravagant terms thank God for the 'Day of Jubilee.' Although given no encouragement thousands of these poor blacks left their humble homes, laden down with home plunder and caring for their little ones as best they could, fell in behind the various columns of marching soldiers and trudged along with no idea where they were going except that they were on the highway from slavery to freedom." As with other Union armies in the West, slaves saw Sherman's men as their liberators.[25]

No single figure loomed larger for some slaves than Sherman himself. The adjutant of the Thirty-Second Illinois, Fenwick Hedley, asserted that black people greeted all the troops as "their deliverers," falling to their knees and blessing them. But "they manifested an ardent anxiety to see General Sherman, and in some instances addressed him or spoke of him with a reverence and extravagance of expression which they could not have exceeded had he been the Savior of mankind." Sherman confirmed this when he wrote his wife, "It would amuse you to See the negros, they flock to me old & young they pray & shout—and mix up my name with that of Moses, & Simon, and other scriptural ones as well as Abram Linkum the Great Messiah of 'Dis Jubilee.'" A particularly poignant instance occurred on the plantation of Confederate major general Howell Cobb near Milledgeville, Georgia. An elderly black man there could hardly believe that his deliverer had finally come and just kept staring at Sherman until the general convinced him that the Yankees "he had been dreaming [about] all his life" were really there. The newly freed slave had an additional reason to be overjoyed, for he found among Sherman's escort his former master, Lt. David Snelling. Snelling was a Confederate deserter who had joined the Union army. Overcome with emotion at seeing Snelling alive and well and in a Yankee uniform to boot, "the slave fell on the floor [and] hugged the lieutenant around the knees."[26] As a practical military man, Sherman never wanted to free any more slaves than could be used by the army; he was always thinking foremost about military success, not emancipation. But marching his army through the heart of Georgia attracted thousands of slaves and made him a liberator in spite of himself.

The slaves did not care that Sherman was unenthusiastic about freeing them. For them, the important thing was that they were getting their freedom, and many of them would do anything to help the army that was making this a reality. They proved to be invaluable sources of information. Lt. Col. Andrew Hickenlooper thought the knowledge the slaves had of army movements was "wonderful." They "could communicate to us absolutely reliable detailed information in regard to the movements of the enemy, not only in our immediate vicinity; but the most intelligent had in some mysterious way been made acquainted with the achievements, disasters, or victories of the forces operating in Tennessee, Virginia or on the coast." Maj. Gen. Oliver Howard would have agreed, as he received important intelligence from black people about the Confederate defenses at Savannah, including the key stronghold of Fort McAllister.[27]

Slaves reinforced Sherman's objectives by helping the army seize valuable property from their masters. In one night, according to Chap. George Bradley of the Twenty-Second Wisconsin, twenty slaves brought forty of their masters' mules and horses into Union lines. Slaves happily showed Federal soldiers where important items were hidden on plantations. "They very readily tell us where anything is concealed, and seem well pleased when we find various articles," remarked Bradley. Sometimes doing this endangered the life of the slave. Maj. Charles Wills of the 103rd Illinois discussed how a female slave was abused horribly for revealing where her mistress hid mules and horses: "Milly [the mistress] took half a rail and like to wore the wench out. Broke her arm and bruised her shamefully." But black Southerners seldom wavered in their willingness to help the Union army. As Capt. Oscar Jackson of the Sixty-Third Ohio asserted, "They hail us as deliverers and are true and loyal under all circumstances."[28]

Despite black people's brave assistance, Sherman and most of his officers viewed many former slaves as little more than a military burden. The long train of black refugees following Sherman's columns was seen as a drain on the army's time and resources. An officer in the Twenty-First Wisconsin, John Henry Otto, called them a "great hindrance" and a "nuisance." He remarked: "The crowd [of black people], like a rolling snowball, would increase from day to day.... They would not leave us if told to do so.... There were thousands of them and I wondered many times what would be done with them." Lt. William Pittenger of the Thirty-Ninth Ohio complained: "We are becoming encumbered with contraband. Hundreds of women and children are following our trains—suffering much. Better that they remain at their homes."[29]

The army brass agreed that the black refugees were an impediment to the military. Brig. Gen. William Carlin grumbled that "several thousand of these useless [black] creatures were allowed to follow the different corps of the army, encumbering the trains and devouring the subsistence along the line of march so much needed for the soldiers." Brig. Gen. Jefferson C. Davis fumed, "Useless negroes are being accumulated to an extent which would be suicide to a column which must be constantly stripped for battle and prepared for the utmost celerity of movement." Officers were not pleased about liberating slaves of no military value whose bothersome presence slowed down the advance toward Savannah.[30]

General Davis found a heartless solution to the problem of black women and children trailing his corps. In early December 1864, Davis's column reached the formidable obstacle of Ebenezer Creek near Savannah, Georgia. Harassed by Confederate cavalry and falling behind other Union commands, Davis felt great urgency to get across the creek as quickly as possible. This made the "useless" black refugees who were following his column seem like a dangerous impediment. So after his soldiers crossed the creek on pontoon bridges, Davis promptly ordered that the bridges be taken up before the black people could cross. The black refugees were now stranded and easy prey for the Southern cavalry, who they feared would reenslave or kill them. Some had also just been separated from their families, as Davis permitted the able-bodied black men to cross the bridge with his troops. Thus out of sheer desperation, some of the former slaves jumped into the creek and tried to swim across, many drowning in the process. This incident was one of the saddest examples of Union callousness toward black Southerners during the war. While Davis was certainly acting out of hard-nosed military considerations, he in fact displayed little sympathy for emancipation.[31]

Davis's fateful decision at Ebenezer Creek produced a mixed reaction among Sherman's officers. Maj. Henry Hitchcock fervently defended Davis, claiming that the black people were a "great hazard to the very existence of his corps, perhaps to the whole army." If Davis had to deploy to fight the enemy, Hitchcock maintained, "the presence of the negroes ... would have added *three hours* to the operation." This was an unacceptable risk, as Davis's "first duty" was the safety of his troops. By contrast, Illinois major James Connolly was outraged by Davis's "inhuman" and "barbarous" act. Witnessing the sad scene at the creek, Connolly let Davis's staff know what he thought: "The idea of five or six hundred black women, children and old men being thus returned to slavery by such an infernal copperhead as Jeff. C. Davis was entirely too much for my Democracy." Connolly thought he might receive a reprimand for his vociferous protest at the creek but did not care. "If he [Davis] undertakes to vent his spleen on me for it, I have the *same rights that he himself exercised in his affair with Nelson*," Connolly declared, referencing the famous incident when Davis shot and killed his former commanding officer, Maj. Gen. William "Bull" Nelson.[32]

Avoiding such controversy, most of Sherman's commanders did not resort to such harsh measures to rid themselves of black refugees. They might have tried to discourage slaves from following the army but did not force them to leave. Commanding the Twentieth Corps, Brig. Gen. Alpheus Williams advised the weak and elderly to stay at home, but they came anyway. "Negroes of all ages and of every variety of physical condition from the infant in its mother's arms to the decrepid old man, joined the column from plantations and from cross-roads, singly and in large groups, on foot, on horseback, and in every description of vehicles," Williams wrote. By the time his corps reached Savannah, Williams had over 2,500 former slaves with him. Military burden or not, the army still provided a refuge for thousands of emancipated slaves.[33]

At least one commander did not view the former slaves as an encumbrance. Division commander Brig. Gen. Absalom Baird was a strong abolitionist (and nephew of the famed social reformer Gerrit Smith) who viewed emancipation as a moral imperative. Maj. James Connolly, who served on Baird's staff, noted how large numbers of black men and women came into the division's lines and received sympathetic treatment. "I believe they have taken a fancy to our Head Quarters," Connolly wrote, "for they come to us with all their little complaints; get all the waste victuals from our mess, and make their little camps as close to us as they dare." The freed slaves stayed away from Brig. Gen. Jefferson Davis's headquarters, for "they find no sympathy there." Baird cared about the slaves, but he also understood that they might have important information for the army. "He [Baird] delights in talking with these contrabands when we halt by the roadside and in extracting information concerning their 'masters and mistresses' from them," Connolly remarked. Even those officers who saw emancipation in moral terms recognized the practical advantage that could be gained from using former slaves.[34]

Yet Baird's views regarding emancipation proved to be the exception to the rule. Sherman felt little sympathy for the black refugees who trailed his army to Savannah. He continued to see them as a military burden and wanted to rid his army of them as soon as possible. The general told the secretary of war, Edwin Stanton, that once Savannah fell, "my first duty will be to clear the army of surplus negroes, mules, and horses." This language itself revealed Sherman's low regard if not outright contempt for the race. Nowhere did he express any positive idealism about freeing so many. At the end of his march, Sherman noted that there were "at least 20,000 negros, clogging my roads, and eating up our subsistence."[35]

The general's seemingly callous policies drew fire from Washington. Some high-ranking officials thought Sherman's army should have been kinder to slaves and freed more of them. The secretary of the treasury, Salmon P. Chase, sharply criticized Sherman for treating black people as little more than dumb animals. An advocate for racial equality, Chase lectured Sherman on his unenlightened attitudes. "You are understood to be opposed to their employment as Soldiers, and to regard them as a set of pariahs, almost without rights," Chase told Sherman. Frustrated by this criticism, Sherman explained the military problems posed by large numbers of slaves following his army: "If you can understand the nature of a military column in an enemys country, with its long train of wagons you will see at once that a crowd of negros, men women and children, old & young, are a dangerous impediment." Sherman added, "Now you know that military success is what the nation wants, and it is risked by the crowds of helpless negros that flock after our armies." Around the same time, Henry Halleck wrote Sherman privately that there were some people close to the president saying that he had "manifested an almost criminal dislike to the negro," and that he was "not willing to carry out the wishes of the Government in regard to him [the black man]." These unnamed critics often cited the incident at Ebenezer Creek. The general bristled at all this attention to black people, asking Halleck: "But the nigger? Why, in God's name, can't sensible men let him alone?" Sherman said that the idea that black refugees were forced out of his army so they would be murdered by Confederate cavalry was a "cock-and-bull story" and "humbug." At Ebenezer Creek, Gen. Jefferson C. Davis left slaves behind "not because he wanted to leave them, but because he wanted his bridge." Sherman again referred to the military difficulties of taking along huge numbers of slaves, claiming that "if it be insisted that I shall so conduct my operations that the negro alone is consulted, of course I will be defeated." Sherman stoutly defended his policies against the salvos of criticism coming from Washington, but this did not silence them.[36]

In January 1865, Edwin Stanton visited Savannah to discuss Sherman's policies toward freed slaves. The secretary of war particularly wanted to know what happened at Ebenezer Creek and shared with Sherman a critical newspaper account of the event. Sherman defended Davis's actions, asserting that Davis had no "hostility to the negro." But then to make sure Stanton was convinced, Sherman sent for Davis and let him explain everything himself. Whatever Davis said to Stanton evidently satisfied the secretary. Stanton asked Sherman to set up a meeting with some black Georgians so he could ask about their thoughts on the war and the commanding general. Stanton conducted an extensive and extraordinary interview with a group of twenty black people, mainly ministers. The group showed a keen understanding of the war's issues and the meaning of emancipation. Moreover, they made it clear that their people were devoted to the Union cause. "If the prayers that have gone up for the Union army could be read out," they told Stanton, "you would not get through them these two weeks." As for the general: "We looked upon General Sherman, prior to his arrival, as a man, in the providence of God, specially set apart to accomplish this work, and we unanimously felt inexpressible gratitude to him.... We have confidence in General Sherman, and think that what concerns us could not be under better hands."[37]

After gathering all this information, Stanton became convinced that black Southerners could care for themselves if put on abandoned plantations, and he urged Sherman to draft an order to do just that with the freed slaves that had followed his army. Under the secretary's careful guidance, Sherman produced his famous Sea Island order, which allowed freed slaves to settle on the islands off the coasts of South Carolina and Georgia. Finally, black people were given the opportunity to own their own land. "No white person whatever, unless military officers and soldiers detailed for duty, will be permitted to reside; and the sole and exclusive management of affairs will be left to the freed people themselves," Sherman ordered. The military would protect the black settlements with a general officer supervising the whole operation. Sherman regarded this plan as a temporary war measure. What probably pleased him the most was that it allowed him to get rid of the black refugees encumbering his army. An officer in the Twenty-First Wisconsin, John Henry Otto, believed that the Sea Island order was promulgated "to dispose of the army of negroes who had followed us." Maj. Gen. Oliver Howard recalled that the order immediately had good effect: "Idle masses were sent from cities and villages and from the various army columns to find relief and to set out upon a course of thrifty industry which was hopeful and helpful to their future."[38] With this policy in place, Sherman had satisfied Washington on the emancipation question.

But Sherman still had plenty to worry about, for he was making final preparations for his campaign through the Carolinas. He wanted to destroy Confederate morale and military resources there just as he had done in Georgia. Ultimately, he hoped to come up in the rear of Gen. Robert E. Lee's army, which was at that time bottled up in Petersburg, Virginia. During this march, officers in Sherman's army carried out emancipation like they had in Georgia. They focused on freeing slaves for military benefit and made some efforts, mostly in vain, to discourage black women and children from following the army. Long trains of refugees still trailed behind the army's columns. Interestingly, Sherman never directly ordered his commanders to discourage this as he had right before the March to the Sea. He probably realized it was futile and wanted to avoid any further problems with Washington over emancipation issues. But as soon as he could, Sherman disposed of the black refugees, which he still saw as an annoying burden. For their part, many slaves continued to help the army in any way possible and to view the Union troops as liberators. Once again, Sherman's army had freed thousands and, in the process, helped destroy slavery across the Carolinas.[39]

From the beginning of the campaign, Sherman's generals wanted to make sure freed slaves were assisting the army. From Pocotaligo, South Carolina, Maj. Gen. Frank Blair requested that black men be sent from Beaufort to serve as pioneers for his corps. "I have fatigue duty enough to occupy them here in making roads [and] wharves, in which I am now compelled to employ my troops," Blair wrote. As he began the march, Brig. Gen. William Hazen directed his brigade commanders to use "all unarmed men and superfluous servants" in the pioneer corps and take in all the able-bodied black men they could for that purpose. These black men received ten dollars a month plus rations.[40]

As the army wrought a path of destruction through the Carolinas, officers liberated plenty of slaves to serve as pioneers. Leading a company of the Seventy-Eighth Ohio, Capt. Cyrus Roberts noted how black men rode "our captured animals to camp" and then became pioneers. Lt. John McQueen of the Fifteenth Illinois Cavalry found 200 slaves hiding in a swamp and put them in the pioneer corps. Maj. Gen. Oliver Howard's chief of artillery, Maj. Thomas Osborn, commented: "Our superior pioneer organization is of great value to us now. It is composed mostly of negroes and is probably superior to that of any other Army."[41]

In addition, officers acquired valuable servants. About a month before he took in the pioneers, Capt. Cyrus Roberts brought in a slave with two mules and two horses and hired him as his servant. The slave had been serving the Confederate army but now was freed to help the Union cause. Sometimes, black people themselves volunteered their services. Near Cheraw, South Carolina, Lt. Henry Hurter of the First Minnesota Light Artillery mentioned that a black woman presented his battery "with a young recruit," who most likely became a servant in the unit.[42] Any slave that could be of assistance to the army was welcomed into the lines. This included slaves possessing information about the enemy or local geography.

As in almost every other major western theater operation, slaves were an indispensable Union resource during the Carolina campaign. Col. James Wilson took in two slaves who had escaped from Charleston and obtained very specific information about Confederate defenses and manpower. In addition to learning the precise disposition of rebel forces in and around the city, Wilson received a detailed description of Confederate works: "Toward

Charleston... is the Five-Mile Fort, being two works, one on each side of the road, each mounting about four guns. The guns are black and... are not field pieces. There are no rifle-pits near these forts.... Two miles and a half from Charleston there are rifle-pits crossing the dirt, road, extending on the right, going from here about half a mile to a marsh, and on the left about half a mile." Brig. Gen. Absalom Baird relied on black people to calculate distances along the march. During a raid to destroy the railroad bridges near Simonsville, South Carolina, Illinois captain William Duncan received intelligence from slaves about the strength of rebel forces in the area. Right outside Goldsboro, North Carolina, slaves warned Assistant Surgeon Samuel C. Rogers of the Thirtieth Iowa about nearby Confederate bushwhackers and then helped him and another soldier escape from them. The black Southerners were even able to identify a couple of the bushwhackers.[43]

Despite black people's invaluable assistance, soldiers sometimes treated them cruelly. In Robertsville, South Carolina, Brig. Gen. Alpheus Williams was outraged by the "disgraceful and demoralizing" pillaging of homes, which included those of free black people. Just a week later, Maj. Gen. John Logan had problems with his plundering soldiers, leading him to forbid his men "from wantonly taking the few rags belonging to the poor negroes, who have in so many instances befriended our soldiers on their escape from rebel prisons." Some soldiers had no problem stealing from slave cabins. As if such actions were not bad enough, soldiers also committed sexual assaults. "No colored woman or girl was safe from the brutal lusts of the soldiers—and by soldiers I mean both officers and men," explained a female missionary from the North. In Columbia, South Carolina, there were several cases of soldiers raping black women. A white Southern woman recalled that the slaves "became thoroughly disgusted" with the Union soldiers and "vowed vengeance for the base treatment their women had been subjected too."[44]

Sometimes even black soldiers were treated poorly by their white compatriots. Capt. Cyrus Roberts of the Seventy-Eighth Ohio told how his men, dressed in clothing that made them resemble Confederates, "charged up" to some unsuspecting black troops "and demanded them to surrender." The black men quickly laid down their arms, which were new, bright muskets. The Ohio men took the new guns and gave the black soldiers their rusty weapons in exchange. They then let the black men go, informing them that they were really Union soldiers. A disgruntled black soldier "said he wanted to get back to live with his Massa in Kentucky—that he was draf'd in the Army and was tired of Yankees." Despite the cruelty of the army at times, most black people did not share such sentiments. As Chap. George Bradley of the Twenty-Second Wisconsin observed, "Many of our soldiers treat them roughly, still they look upon Sherman's army as their great deliverers, and they wish the Yankees success in whipping the rebels."[45]

Bradley's point was well taken, because thousands of slaves—men, women, and children—joined Sherman's army during its campaign in the Carolinas. Just like during the March to the Sea, the army became a magnet for all those seeking freedom. There were some attempts by officers to prevent refugees from following the army, but these efforts proved ineffective. When Union forces moved out of Columbia, South Carolina, they were followed by huge numbers of black people, which was not surprising since the city had just been burned. Maj. Gen. Oliver Howard recalled a vast "refugee train" behind his columns. "It consisted of thousands of people . . . mostly negroes," he observed. Surgeon Elijah Burton of the Twelfth Illinois was moved by this exodus: "The most interesting sight today was the crowds of refugees . . . & It looks melancholy indeed to see so many wom[e]n & little children start out without friends & on foot to find a home. Little black children not over six years trudging along—& then mothers carrying babies—How I pitied them."[46]

By the time the army reached North Carolina, it had accumulated even more former slaves. Maj. Charles Wills of the 103rd Illinois wished his sister "could see the crowd of negroes following us. Some say 2,000 with our division." Like in South Carolina, some of Sherman's men continued to be cruel to black Southerners. One slave recounted how the Union soldiers "stold ever'thing they could lay hand's on an' tored up ever'thing scand'lous." This slave thought that the soldiers had no concern for black people and just wanted to punish the South by freeing the slaves. She was correct about the practical views of many of Sherman's officers—and certainly of many of his enlisted men as well—regarding the emancipation issue.[47]

Sherman himself had developed no humanitarian impulse when it came to freeing slaves. As before, he viewed the slaves following his army as a tremendous military burden. "They are a dead weight to me," the general bluntly told Maj. Gen. Alfred Terry. He complained that they "have clung to our skirts, impeded our movements, and consumed our food." By the time the general reached Fayetteville, North Carolina, in March 1865, he was more than ready to get rid of the thousands of refugees (including some white people) who were following his army. He decided to send them from Fayetteville to Wilmington on the coast, where they could no longer impede his military operations. The refugees were provided with wagons, rations, and a 200-man guard for their journey.[48]

As the long line of refugees left the army, Sherman's officers expressed different emotions. An adjutant in the Thirty-Second Illinois, Fenwick Hedley, was amused by the whole procession: "Here was a cumbersome, old-fashioned family carriage, very dilapidated, yet bearing traces of gilt and filagree.... On the driver's seat was perched an aged patriarch in coarse plantation breeches, with ... his gray grizzled wool topped off with an old-fashioned silk hat.... Elsewhere in the column a pair of 'coons' rode in a light spring wagon, one urging the decrepit horse to keep up with the procession, while the other picked a banjo, and made serious attempts to sing a plantation song." By contrast, Brig. Gen. William Hazen felt pity for those refugees receiving rations: "A drizzling rain was falling, and it was a singular and pathetic sight, as the refugees, without shelter from the weather, of all ages and both sexes, with skins from the fairest Saxon to the blackest Ethiopian, some with delicate patrician features, and some of the most grotesque negro type, came forward in turn, and held out their hats, bonnets, handkerchiefs, aprons, and their skirts . . . to receive the army bounty." Just a short time before, Maj. Oscar Jackson of the Sixty-Third Ohio had been deeply moved by the "painful privation[s]" suffered by the refugees: "I have seen them dying on the road in wagons, carts, etc. In one wagon today, while they were halted at a swamp, a child was born and at the same time close by was another wagon with an aged negress in a dying condition." More officers expressed sorrow or pity for the refugees. They might be a military burden, but seeing so many people in such a desperate state evoked some sympathy.[49]

With the departure of these refugees, Sherman's dealings with slaves and emancipation questions largely ended. The war would be over in just six more weeks, and Sherman had just about completed his devastating campaigns through the South. Even at this late date, though, Sherman still sounded irritated about having to deal with slaves and slavery. At the end of March 1865, he claimed to have proved himself more loyal to the cause than any political abolitionist and argued, "I believe the honest, working People of the United States agree with me, to fight to maintain the Government according to the form bequeathed to us, and not to carry out any pet speciality." Sherman continued: "I have always thought we mixed up too many little side issues in this war. We should make a single plain issue & fight it out." The experience of liberating thousands of slaves had not made Sherman any more enthusiastic about emancipation.[50]

From beginning to end, Sherman remained a reluctant liberator who never saw emancipation as a moral imperative. At best, it was a practical measure that logically resulted from the war and had to be implemented. But even if emancipation made some pragmatic sense, Sherman was not particularly pleased with the results. He harbored deep racial prejudices and despised abolitionists. He worried that emancipation issues were looming too large in the Union war effort. During his famed marches in Georgia and the Carolinas, Sherman tried to carry out emancipation on a strictly military basis to benefit the army. He and his officers willingly took in slaves that they could use and discouraged all others. Yet thousands of black refugees had still joined Sherman's columns. Regardless of what army officers thought, many slaves viewed them as liberators and would not pass up an opportunity to gain freedom. Some slaves even saw Sherman as a man sent from God to liberate them, and this image proved enduring at least for one man. At the general's funeral in 1891, an old black man fell to his knees in prayer as Sherman's casket passed him.[51] For this man, results mattered more than intentions.

CONCLUSION

How Transformative Was the Civil War?

By the time Maj. Gen William T. Sherman finished his devastating campaign in the Carolinas in the spring of 1865, slavery was in its death throes everywhere in the western theater and, for that matter, in the Confederacy. A few months before, Sherman had bluntly told his wife, "Slavery is dead and the Negro free."[1] Union armies had marched through almost every area of the West and destroyed slavery in the process. The institution that had been the mainstay of the South for generations was now gone forever. The western armies had seemingly helped bring about a social revolution that would redefine the American nation.

Understanding what happened in the western theater is essential to telling the emancipation story. It was in this large theater of operations that most slaves got their first taste of freedom and where Union armies devastated the heart of the plantation economy. The process of emancipation played out in a far more comprehensive way in the western theater than in the eastern. Western commanders and officers were forced to deal with huge numbers of slaves across a vast region and implement appropriate policies and programs to carry out emancipation. Besides the sheer numbers, Union officers had to also handle questions of whether and how to liberate slaves across very different regions of the West. They confronted slaves in the Lower South, the Upper South, and the Border South, regions that were all distinct from one another politically and socially. In particular, the Border South proved especially difficult in managing the legal and political questions surrounding emancipation. So the West's diversity and size provide critical insights into the emancipation process. Undoubtedly, what happened in the East in Virginia was vital for pushing the country in an emancipationist direction, but once emancipation was adopted, it would have to implemented on the ground in the West on a grand scale. And it was the Union army and its officers there that ultimately had to carry out this crucial policy.[2]

At the war's end, slaves clearly understood the army's key role in their deliverance. They enthusiastically cheered Union armies as long as they were in the field. Surgeon Elijah Burton of the Twelfth Illinois noted that in May 1865, "the darkies all seemed pleased to see us & *shouted* for 'Sherman.'" Some black people went further. In June 1865, former slaves in Macon, Mississippi, invited Federal soldiers to a public dinner of thanks. The freed slaves told the soldiers that they were "grateful for the many perils and privations undergone by you in our behalf, and realizing fully the extent of our indebtedness to the Government of the United States."[3] These black men and women knew who was responsible for making them free.

The destruction of slavery had seemed remote at the war's beginning. The government in Washington had clearly stated that its goal was to preserve the Union and not free the slaves, a view shared by many western officers. During the initial stages of the war many of the West's top commanders wanted nothing to do with liberating slaves and, in fact, explicitly barred them from Union camps. Some officers even returned slaves to their owners. There were officers who were willing to take in slaves early in the war, but they often found themselves rebuked by their superiors. If anything, policy toward fugitive slaves could be best characterized as inconsistent.

But as the war dragged on into its second year, the armies and the government became more emancipationist. In July 1862, Congress passed the Second Confiscation Act and western armies started to allow significant numbers of slaves into their lines. This process accelerated after the final Emancipation Proclamation went into effect in January 1863, and it continued until the end of the war. The army became the key instrument for bringing freedom to Southern slaves. Many officers also came to support emancipation and even the use of black troops. The army had been transformed on the emancipation question.

Yet this transformation was not nearly as revolutionary as it seemed. Most officers only embraced emancipation because they believed it was necessary to win the war and save the Union. Many officers agreed with the sentiments of Illinois assistant surgeon Thomas Winston: "I have made up my mind that this war will not end until slavery has been destroyed."[4] Slaves were sustaining the Confederacy and needed to be taken away and used instead to benefit the Union if the rebellion was to be crushed. Similarly, the officers who supported the use of black troops (and plenty of officers actually opposed this new policy until the end of the war) did so mainly for practical reasons. Black soldiers could provide valuable manpower to Union forces and certainly could take a musket ball like any white soldier, or so ran the logic. Far from viewing emancipation and the enlistment of black troops as moral policies that would uplift an oppressed race, most Union officers instead saw these measures merely as ways to defeat the Confederacy.

If officers' attitudes lacked moral idealism, so did their emancipation policies. Throughout the various western armies, officers of all ranks liberated slaves for the army's benefit. They brought in thousands of slaves and put them to work building fortifications, driving teams, and performing menial tasks around camp. Military priorities thus dictated emancipation policy and practice. Capt. William Ferry of the Fourteenth Michigan captured this well when he wrote his wife, "Well negroes come into our lines + so far as they can be made to work they are carried along by whoever feels inclined to have a 'servant' + feed + clothed by Uncle Sam or if a 'yellow gal' happens in that suits she follows + is attached to some officers mess as convenient *for incidentals.*"[5] Slaves were freed to labor for the Union army, and any slave who could not help the military in some way was usually sent to a contraband camp.

Reinforcing this lack of sympathy for slaves were the racial attitudes of most western officers. These attitudes changed little as a result of the war. Officers consistently characterized black people as ignorant, childlike, pitiful, and animalistic. Indeed, some officers did not even want to be around black people. There were plenty of instances where the army abused former slaves even during the war's final campaigns. The war might have ended slavery, but it had surprisingly little effect on the racial prejudices of white Americans. The officers who had liberated so many slaves were hardly ready to accept black people on an equal basis as citizens.

So in the end, the war represented no watershed moment for these officers when it came to race. The Union had been saved and that was most important. As emancipation had been seen by most officers as just a practical tool to win the war, there was no great moral outcry for racial justice. It was good enough that slavery was abolished and that the former slaves could enjoy the benefits of free labor.

The officers in fact reflected broader Northern attitudes. As Reconstruction began, many in the North supported a speedy reunification of the country and were not very concerned about securing political equality for former slaves. Only after President Andrew Johnson's lenient policies toward the defeated rebels seemed to jeopardize the fruits of victory did many Northerners embrace harsher Reconstruction measures. Under Johnson's plan, white Southerners elected some former Confederates to political office. Moreover, Southern legislatures enacted the infamous Black Codes to control the labor of black men and women and curtail their freedom. It seemed to many Northerners that the rebels were trying to restore the old antebellum political and social order. This pushed many in the North to support the measures of congressional Reconstruction, including the Fourteenth and Fifteenth Amendments, which granted citizenship rights and suffrage to black men. Northerners' support for these radical measures, which would have resounding consequences for the future of the country, stemmed more from the desire to punish treasonous Southerners than from any benevolent impulse to aid freed slaves.[6]

The commander of all Federal armies confirmed this evolution of Northern attitudes. Lt. Gen. Ulysses S. Grant asserted that at the war's close, "the great majority of the Northern people, and the soldiers unanimously, would have been in favor of a speedy reconstruction on terms that would be the least humiliating to the people who had rebelled against their government. They believed, I have no doubt, as I did, that besides being the mildest, it was also the wisest, policy.... They [the Rebels] surely would not make good citizens if they felt that they had a yoke around their necks." Grant added that he thought that a majority of the North was not "at that time ... in favor of negro suffrage." But after President Johnson decided to be so lenient on the rebels, and the rebels tried to reassert their political power, Northerners "became more radical in their views." Black suffrage had seemingly become a necessity "because of the foolhardiness of the President and the blindness of the Southern people to their own interest," Grant maintained.[7] So Northerners were most concerned about subduing the former Confederates.

Working for the Freedmen's Bureau in Arkansas, James Davidson, a Union army officer, asserted that he and his comrades supported congressional Reconstruction primarily out of the desire to crush the rebellious sentiment in the South. "I hope . . . that Military Governors will be put over them [the rebels] and kept over them until they are thoroughly reconstructed which in my opinion will be several years," wrote Davidson. He had been in the South for almost a year and was growing frustrated with the defiant attitudes of Southern civilians: "It behooves the supporters of the government to hang together and work with all their might to . . . exterminate the whole Rebel race." Nowhere did Davidson mention the benefits that black people would gain from Congress's policies; it was rather all about how they would hurt the rebels.[8]

Given that many Northerners lacked a strong commitment to racial equality after the war, it is hardly shocking that they eventually abandoned

Radical Reconstruction and black Southerners. Of course, there were many reasons that Reconstruction came to an end, including the changing nature of the Republican Party, the business interests of the North, and the intense violence perpetrated by the Ku Klux Klan and other groups in the South, but Northern racism certainly played an instrumental role. This vividly demonstrates the limits of the war as a transformative moment for the North. While it had pushed Northerners to emancipate the slaves, it did not make them into racial egalitarians. No group better illustrates the limits of revolutionary change than the Union officers who fought in the western theater.[9]

ACKNOWLEDGMENTS

I would like to thank the staff at the University of North Carolina Press for all their patience and assistance. I could not have asked for a more encouraging editor than Mark Simpson-Vos. He patiently offered great advice throughout the whole revision process and helped guide this project to publication. I would also like to especially thank Caroline Janney. She read numerous drafts of this book and offered great suggestions each time, which have immeasurably improved the final product. Jessica Newman and Mary Carley Caviness were instrumental in helping me prepare the final manuscript. Iza Wojciechowska was a superb copy editor whose careful attention to detail prevented me from making numerous mistakes.

Several libraries and archives provided grants and fellowships for this project. The Filson Historical Society in Louisville, Kentucky, awarded me a very nice fellowship which enabled me to spend a productive week working with its great collections. I especially want to thank Mark Wetherington, A. Glenn Crothers, Mike Veach, and Jacob Lee for all their assistance at the Filson. I also received the Mark C. Stevens Fellowship at the Bentley Historical Library of the University of Michigan. This generous fellowship allowed me to extensively mine the Bentley's voluminous collections of Civil War letters, which proved invaluable for this project. I am very grateful for the help of the Bentley's excellent library staff, particularly that of William Wallach, the associate director. Lastly, I was very privileged to receive the General and Mrs. Matthew B. Ridgway Research Grant at the United States Army Military History Institute (USAMHI) in Carlisle, Pennsylvania. As all Civil War historians know, the collections of soldiers' letters and diaries at the USAMHI are extremely rich and extensive, and I was able to find loads of good material for my project during my two lengthy visits to the institute. I would like to thank the institute's great staff for rolling out cart after cart of excellent archival collections. I would especially like to thank Richard Sommers for his excellent advice on what collections to examine. Additionally, Sommers kindly put me in contact with Mark Grimsley and even drove me to Harrisburg, Pennsylvania, to hear Grimsley give a great presentation. The morning after the presentation Grimsley graciously agreed to have breakfast with me in Carlisle, and we had an excellent discussion about academics and my topic. His insights have helped me to greatly improve this work. I would also like to give a special thanks to Nan Card of the Rutherford B. Hayes Presidential Center. Her knowledge and assistance helped make my time at the Hayes Center very productive. I also very much appreciate Ron and Mary Vanke's kindness in allowing me to stay at their home while I researched at the Ohio Historical Society.

I would also like to thank a few other historians who aided me with invaluable information and insight. Both Kari Frederickson and Andrew Huebner offered great support, encouraging me with this project and providing constructive and useful feedback. Two of my early mentors, James Ramage and Michael C. C. Adams, were always willing to discuss my ideas and never ceased offering their sage advice on complicated questions. I am also very thankful for the many conversations I had with one of my former colleagues and a good friend, Kathleen Quinn, on this project. Some historians provided me with crucial insights on the geography of Civil War campaigns. The chief historian of the Chickamauga and Chattanooga National Military Park, Jim Ogden, helped me identify the counties Gen. William S. Rosecrans's troops moved through during the Tullahoma campaign and the Chickamauga and Chattanooga campaign. David Slay, who holds a PhD and is a National Park Service ranger at the Vicksburg National Military Park, helped me do the same thing for Gen. Ulysses S. Grant's army and the Vicksburg campaign. At the Atlanta History Center, Erica Hague, a collections and reference assistant, and Bill Dyer, a Civil War expert there, aided me in determining the counties Gen. William T. Sherman's army went through during the Atlanta campaign and subsequent March to the Sea.

My friends were a constant source of support and encouragement throughout this process. I especially want to thank my friends at the University of Alabama. I spent countless evenings enjoying good discussion and entertainment with Glenn Brasher, Jon Hooks, Kevin Windham, Christian and Corrin McWhirter, Michael and Heather Hoekstra, Joe Danielson, Lauren Gill, and Justin and Brooke Turner. They all offered valuable moral support and advice during this project. I will always treasure their great friendship and all the memorable trips we have taken together. In particular, Glenn Brasher, who has completed an excellent book on the Peninsula campaign's important influence on the emancipation debate in the North, spent hours discussing this project with me and never ceased to offer significant insights. He especially helped me with the intricacies of the Second Confiscation Act and ideas for the introduction. I will also always fondly remember the great times I spent in the TA office with John Mitcham, Jared Galloway, Colin Chapell, Megan Bever, Becky Bruce, Daniel Menestres, Charles Roberts, Christopher Swindle, Ryan Floyd, Matthew Downs, Charity Rakestraw, and Scott Suarez. Jared Galloway even kindly read drafts of some of the early chapters and offered feedback. Charity Rakestraw and I reconnected after graduate school, and she offered me great advice as I put the final touches on the book. I greatly value our friendship. Thank you to Foster Hays for her hard work and careful attention to detail in preparing the index in this book. In addition to my friends in Alabama, I would like to thank Chris Sevier, Tammy Sevier, and Katie Ditchen for their enduring friendship and support. I would also like to thank my friend David Kimling, who took an excellent photograph of me for the book.

This book would not have been possible without the help of two people. First, George Rable provided invaluable support and insight at every stage of this project. His great advice, careful editing, and probing questions greatly improved every aspect of this book. I feel very privileged to have worked with such a great scholar and good person. Lawrence Kohl also proved vital in the completion of this work. He pushed me to reconsider some issues early on in this project and consistently helped make this book a better product. He was always kindly willing to discuss my ideas about the project.

This project would have never been completed without the unwavering support of my family. I am very pleased that my ninety-four-year-old grandmother, Edith Jacobs, who was always so proud of me, has lived to see this project come to fruition. I only wish that my grandfather Lawrence Jacobs, who was just as proud, had lived to see this day. My parents, Kenneth and Kathleen Teters, never lost faith in me or this project, and I cannot express how grateful I am for all their love, support, and encouragement. Their sacrifices enabled me to complete this book.

NOTES ON METHODOLOGY

This study relies heavily on the letters, diaries, and memoirs of western officers. As much as possible, it is based on letters and diaries written during the war itself, especially those discussing officers' views on emancipation and slavery. These letters and diaries come from many of the major archives for Civil War letters in the Midwest. Moreover, this work extensively uses the orders and correspondence from the official records. The sample for this study consists of 410 western Union officers. When looking at the characteristics of all these officers, including age, rank, branch of service, nativity, marital status, and prewar occupation, the sample is fairly representative in those categories that can be determined from the available data. It should be noted that there are many problems with ascertaining whether any sample of Civil War soldiers is representative of the whole army, or even of specific armies operating in certain theaters of war. Without scientific polling data from the period, and with only the soldiers' letters and diaries that have survived to the present, any historian is left building a quasi-representative sample that approximates the characteristics of all the soldiers. The other problem, specifically regarding my sample and its representativeness, is that raw data for all western officers is not available for all these categories. Sometimes, it was thus necessary to extrapolate data from that which is available.[1]

This was true when it came to the officers' nativity and branch of service. In this sample, 77.7 percent of officers were from the Midwest, which included the states of Ohio, Illinois, Indiana, Michigan, Wisconsin, Minnesota, Kansas, and Iowa. Officers from Ohio, Illinois, and Indiana make up the greatest portion of this midwestern group, representing 25.3 percent, 16.2 percent, and 10.5 percent of the sample, respectively. Officers hailing from the border states comprise 10.5 percent of the sample, with a heavy preponderance of them coming from Kentucky and Missouri. The remaining officers were almost all from the New England or Middle Atlantic states. Two officers were from the Confederate states. Looking at the numbers of all Union soldiers by state, the figures for the midwestern and border state officers are generally proportionate and representative with some slight over- and underrepresentation. Thus, the sample of officers fairly represents the geographic origins of the western armies. Similarly, the sample is generally representative when it comes to officers' branch of service, with some slight overrepresentation for the infantry and underrepresentation for the cavalry and artillery. In the sample, 85 percent of officers served in the infantry. Only 11.1 percent were part of the cavalry, and 3 percent were part of the artillery. The rest were engineers.[2]

With rank, there is no data on all western officers. The goal of this project was to obtain a good balance between senior and junior officers, which was accomplished in the sample. While line officers represent 41.7 percent of the total sample, field and staff officers account for 26.3 percent. General officers make up about 22 percent of the sample. This way overrepresents generals, as they did not constitute such a high percentage of the whole western officer corps. But this overrepresentation was necessary for this study because a high number of general officers were required to properly determine and analyze army policy. In addition to these combat officers, a number of chaplains and surgeons appear in the sample. While 7.3 percent of the officers were surgeons, 2.2 percent were chaplains.[3]

Surgeons and chaplains played very different roles in the army from those of other officers. While surgeons were in charge of the physical well-being of the soldiers, chaplains were trusted with the spiritual welfare of the troops. Many chaplains and surgeons were overworked with the many duties they were expected to perform. For example, chaplains had to lead prayer meetings, Sunday schools, and funerals, among many other responsibilities. Surgeons had to help the sick and wounded in the most difficult of circumstances and without the medical knowledge to administer proper treatment in many cases. Some surgeons and chaplains got very near or even in battles, and soldiers and officers respected their courage. So while they did not have the same responsibilities as other officers, they did share the same hardships and hazards of a military life. On the issues of emancipation and black troops, their opinions reflected those of other officers. After all, many chaplains and surgeons came from similar backgrounds as many of the combat officers.[4]

Most of the officers in the sample had professional or white-collar occupations before the war. It was possible to find prewar occupations for 332 officers. Out of that number, 168 officers held professional jobs and 85 had white-collar jobs. Combined, these two occupational categories represent over 76 percent of the sample. Among the professional occupations of officers, the most predominant were lawyers and professional soldiers. In the sample, sixty-three officers were lawyers and forty-eight officers were professional soldiers. Well after professional and white-collar occupations, farming and various skilled trades were the next most common occupations for officers. Farmers constitute 12.7 percent of the sample and officers with skilled-labor jobs 9.3 percent. Relatively few officers engaged in unskilled labor: less than 2 percent of the total sample. These numbers for officers' occupations are relatively consistent with the findings of other studies and their samples. This includes very large samples of Union officers. The average age of the officers in this sample is also pretty representative of officers' average age as a whole. The officers in this study had an average age of 32.1, and the average age for all officers was 30.4. Unlike with age and occupation, it is impossible to tell whether the marital status of the officers is representative. No data exists on the marital status of officers specifically. Nevertheless, out of the 340 officers for which marital status could be determined, around 60 percent of them were married and about 40 percent of them were single when they enlisted.[5]

Some of the officers in the sample were West Point graduates and had combat experience in the Mexican War. Officers with West Point training make up about 11 percent of the sample, and almost all of these officers were generals. Out of all the generals in the sample, 45.6 percent were West Point graduates. Slightly fewer officers in the sample, about 9 percent, were Mexican War veterans, and like the West Point graduates, they were nearly all generals. Among the officers in the sample, 4.6 percent went to West Point and served in the Mexican War. Finally, 6.1 percent of the officers in the sample spent at least part of their time, or their whole time, as officers leading regiments of black soldiers.[6]

So, in the end, this study relies on a sample of western Union officers that is generally representative in many categories. Given the limitations discussed above and the absence of data, this sample is about as representative as can be gleaned from the available sources. This study's conclusions are thus drawn from a balanced and illustrative source base.

NOTES

ABBREVIATIONS

ALPL Abraham Lincoln Presidential Library, Springfield, Illinois
BGU Bowling Green State University, Bowling Green, Ohio
BHL Bentley Historical Library, University of Michigan, Ann Arbor, Michigan
CHICAGO HS Chicago Historical Society, Chicago, Illinois
CINCINNATI HS Cincinnati Historical Society, Cincinnati, Ohio
CWMC Civil War Miscellaneous Collection
CWTIC *Civil War Times Illustrated* Collection
FHS Filson Historical Society, Louisville, Kentucky
IHS Indiana Historical Society, Indianapolis, Indiana
OHS Ohio Historical Society, Columbus, Ohio
OR *The War of the Rebellion: Official Records of the Union and Confederate Armies.* 128 vols. Washington, D.C.: Government Printing Office, 1881–1901.
RBHPC Rutherford B. Hayes Presidential Center, Fremont, Ohio
USAMHI United States Army Military History Institute, Carlisle Barracks, Pennsylvania
WHS Wisconsin Historical Society, Madison, Wisconsin
WRHS Western Reserve Historical Society, Cleveland, Ohio

INTRODUCTION

1. Scene 8, *Gettysburg*. See Gary W. Gallagher, *Causes Won, Lost, and Forgotten*, 92–104, for a discussion of emancipation themes in modern Civil War movies. Gallagher argues that since the late 1980s emancipation has become an increasingly popular theme in Civil War film. Chamberlain shows an idealistic commitment to emancipation in both *Gettysburg* and its prequel, *Gods and Generals*.

2. For works looking at the attitudes of the Union army toward emancipation, see Bell Irvin Wiley, *Life of Billy Yank*, 40–44; Mitchell, *Civil War Soldiers*, 126–31; McPherson, *For Cause and Comrades*, 117–30; Gary W. Gallagher, *Union War*, 75–118; and Manning, *What This Cruel War Was Over*, 43–51, 72–80, 83–102, 114–25, 148–57, 182–93. Wiley's *Life of Billy Yank* was the pioneering work on Union soldiers. Regarding emancipation, Wiley

emphasizes that many soldiers opposed the measure and very few were ever fighting to primarily free the slaves. "It seems doubtful that one soldier in ten at any time during the conflict had any real interest in emancipation per se," Wiley asserts. Wiley does stress that many soldiers came to support emancipation because they believed it was necessary to win the war. Since Wiley, historians have reached varying conclusions on the extent of the opposition to emancipation in the army and when, why, and how much soldiers embraced freeing the slaves. The works of Gallagher and Manning represent the two extremes of this argument. While Manning maintains that moral arguments and enthusiasm for emancipation appeared even early in the war, Gallagher argues that the army mainly supported emancipation as just a practical tool to win the war and that its overriding objective was always preserving the Union. McPherson's conclusions fall in between those of Gallagher and Manning. McPherson implies more parity between the soldiers who supported emancipation for moral reasons and those who supported it for pragmatic reasons. This project's conclusions are closer to those of Gallagher, and they directly challenge Manning's arguments that the army saw emancipation in moral terms and supported it so early in the war. This work also challenges James Oakes's more recent book, *Freedom National*. Oakes argues that the war from the beginning had an emancipationist purpose. He points out that the Lincoln administration, Republicans in Congress, and the armies in the field worked actively to undermine slavery from the very start. This argument is not supported by the policies of western armies or the attitudes of most western officers. See Oakes, *Freedom National*, xi–xix, 78–83, 93–105, 136–44, 181–89, 218–23, 245–55.

One of the only other major works that deals with the army's emancipation policies is Gerteis's *From Contraband to Freedman*, and Gerteis mainly concentrates on the plantation labor systems adopted by the army to employ black Southerners. Significantly, Gerteis argues that "federal policy toward Southern blacks pursued two major objectives: the mobilization of black laborers and soldiers, and the prevention of violent change" (5). His study also finds pragmatism at the heart of the army's emancipation policy. In *Hard Hand of War*, Mark Grimsley provides a valuable overview of army policy toward fugitive slaves, especially during the period before the Emancipation Proclamation. Ultimately, he argues that emancipation was indispensable "as a symbol of Northern resolve, a touchstone of its intention to smash the slaveholding aristocracy that had spawned secession" (120–41). See Ash, *When the Yankees Came*, 149–69, for a brief treatment of the emancipation process on the ground in the South. Ash discusses the role the army played in destroying slavery and mentions some of its policies, but focuses more on the responses of white Southerners and black Southerners to the invading Federal army.

3. Many historians have emphasized that the slaves themselves helped push the cause of emancipation onto the federal government's agenda. Through their actions, particularly their willingness to serve the Union war effort, slaves forced the army and the government in a more emancipationist direction. This argument undoubtedly has a lot of validity. But those historians who focus on slave agency in bringing about emancipation have in the process slighted the army's role in freeing the slaves; see the five volumes of the *Freedom* series, edited by Berlin and others, for an exhaustively documented work that advances this idea. Also see Hahn, *Nation under Our Feet*, 13–15, 65–115; and Mohr, *On the Threshold of Freedom*, 68–96. Recently some historians have started to point to the Union army's key role in freeing the slaves; see Gary W. Gallagher, *Union War*, 141–47.

4. Hess, *Civil War in the West*, xi; Wagner, Gallagher, and Finkelman, *Library of Congress Civil War Desk Reference*, 236–39.

5. Kolchin, *American Slavery*, 242; University of Virginia Library, "Historical Census Browser (1860)"; Freehling, *Road to Disunion*, 499–500, 504, 529–31; McPherson, *Battle Cry of Freedom*, 255, 282–84, 290–97; William C. Harris, *Lincoln and the Border States*, 1–2. Harris provides an excellent analysis of Lincoln's difficulties with the border states on emancipation; see 196–200, 223–45, 308–33.

6. Kolchin, *American Slavery*, 242; University of Virginia Library, "Historical Census Browser (1860)"; Cooper and Terrill, *American South*, 189–91; Freehling, *Road to Disunion*, 530; McPherson, *Battle Cry of Freedom*, 234–35, 255.

7. Kolchin, *American Slavery*, 242.

CHAPTER 1

1. *OR*, ser. 1, 3:466–67; ser. 2, 1:766–68; Grimsley, *Hard Hand of War*, 123–24; McPherson, *Battle Cry of Freedom*, 350, 352–53; Warner, *Generals in Blue*, 160–61.

2. Fellman, *Inside War*, 5, 11, 51, 65–66; Astor, *Rebels on the Border*, 33–50, 75–78, 83–84, 87, 94–97; Phillips, *Missouri's Confederate*, 75, 77–80, 231–33, 236–41; Gerteis, *Civil War in Missouri*, 8–9; McPherson, *Battle Cry of Freedom*, 293. McPherson asserts, "Nearly three-quarters of the white men in Missouri . . . who fought in the Civil War did so on the side of the Union."

3. Astor, *Rebels on the Border*, 11–13, 15, 19–24, 28–32; William C. Harris, *Lincoln and the Border States*, 2; Library of Congress, "Map showing the distribution of the slave population"; University of Virginia Library, "Historical Census Browser (1860)."

4. *OR*, ser. 2, 1:771, 775–76; Dodge, *Battle of Atlanta*, 11.

5. Robert H. Carnahan to his wife, October 25, 1861, Carnahan Letters, USAMHI; George W. Gordon Diary, September 22, 1861, USAMHI; Gilbert, *Colonel A. W. Gilbert*, 55.

6. Marszalek, *Sherman*, 6–17, 39–51, 59, 61–68, 119, 120–39; Warner, *Generals in Blue*, 441–42.

7. William T. Sherman, *Sherman's Civil War*, 16, 65; William T. Sherman, *Sherman Letters*, 113; see Marszalek, *Sherman*, 126, 142–43, for some of Sherman's views on slavery on the eve of the war. Marszalek points out that Sherman's views on the issue were closer to those of Southerners than to those of his own brother, Republican senator John Sherman.

8. *OR*, ser. 2, 1:774, 776, 777.

9. Marszalek, *Sherman*, 160–63; Marszalek, *Commander of All Lincoln's Armies*, 104.

10. Marszalek, *Commander of All Lincoln's Armies*, 15–47, 52–74, 104–7; Warner, *Generals in Blue*, 195–96.

11. *OR*, ser. 2, 1:778; Marszalek, *Commander of All Lincoln's Armies*, 111.

12. Grant, *Papers of Ulysses S. Grant*, 2:3–4; 3:227; see ibid., 5:264, for a very clear statement of Grant's subordination to his superiors on questions involving emancipation.

13. Waugh, *U. S. Grant*, 20–24, 26–33, 45; Simpson, *Ulysses S. Grant*, 30–47, 74–75.

14. Grant, *Papers of Ulysses S. Grant*, 3:203; *OR*, ser. 2, 1:794–95.

15. Grant, *Papers of Ulysses S. Grant*, 4:471–72.

16. Berlin et al., *Freedom*, ser. 1, 1:417–19; *OR*, ser. 2, 1:781.

17. *OR*, ser. 2, 1:789–90, 796, 799.

18. *OR*, ser. 2, 1:803, 804.

19. *OR*, ser. 2, 1:784; Cong. Globe, 37th Cong., 2d Sess. 76 (1861). See Marszalek, *Commander of All Lincoln's Armies*, 111–12; and Tap, *Over Lincoln's Shoulder*, 40–41, for discussions of the political fallout over General Orders No. 3.

20. Cimprich, *Slavery's End in Tennessee*, 2, 7, 8–9; Library of Congress, "Map showing the distribution of the slave population"; University of Virginia Library, "Historical Census Browser (1860)"; Tennessee State Library and Archives, "Tennessee Civil War GIS Project." These numbers for slaves, as future numbers will also be, are based on the 1860 census data. The Union army launched its campaign into Tennessee in 1862, so the numbers of slaves undoubtedly changed some during this time interval. For details on Union movements into West and Middle Tennessee, see Symonds and Clipson, *Battlefield Atlas*, 16; Woodworth, *Nothing but Victory*, 65–139; and Daniel, *Days of Glory*, 69–81.

21. Crofts, *Reluctant Confederates*, 130–31, 340, 341–45; Ash, *Middle Tennessee Society Transformed*, 2–4, 10–11, 69–73. While Middle Tennessee supported secession 58,063 to 8,143, West Tennessee endorsed leaving the Union 30,626 to 6,717. On Unionism in the Tennessee River valley, see Woodworth, *Nothing but Victory*, 135; Grimsley, *Hard Hand of War*, 51; Ash, *When the Yankees Came*, 115–16; and Frisby, "'Homemade Yankees,'" 62–63, 74. On the Union army's difficulty in occupying Middle and West Tennessee among a generally hostile white population, see Hess, *Civil War in the West*, 41–42, 62–70.

22. *OR*, ser. 1, 8:555–56, 563–64; ser. 2, 1:808.

23. Grant, *Papers of Ulysses S. Grant*, 4:384, 437–38; John Steele to his brother, March 18, 1862, Steele-Boyd Family Papers, USAMHI.

24. Grant, *Papers of Ulysses S. Grant*, 4:453–55; *U.S. Statutes at Large*, 12:354; McPherson, *Tried by War*, 85; Foner, *Fiery Trial*, 195.

25. Channing Richards Diary, March 28, 1862, Cincinnati HS.

26. Heg, *Civil War Letters*, 66–67; William Collin Stevens to his father, April 8, 1862, Stevens Papers, BHL; Wills, *Army Life of an Illinois Soldier*, 83; Gilbert, *Colonel A. W. Gilbert*, 91.

27. Jackson, *Colonel's Diary*, 53–54, 55; *Racine Journal*, February 22, 1922, copy in WHS.

28. Engle, *Don Carlos Buell*, 1–18, 31–42, 45, 47–48, 66–67.

29. *OR*, ser. 2, 1:809; ser. 1, 10(2):31; Berlin et al., *Freedom*, ser. 1, 1:274–75; Engle, *Don Carlos Buell*, 111; Mitchel, *Ormsby MacKnight Mitchel*, 44–45, 47–57.

30. Shanklin, *"Dearest Lizzie,"* 130–31.

31. Danielson, *War's Desolating Scourge*, 10–11, 25–30, 37; Library of Congress, "Map showing the distribution of the slave population"; University of Virginia Library, "Historical Census Browser (1860)."

32. Danielson, *War's Desolating Scourge*, 5–9, 12, 17–23, 37–46. Danielson provides an excellent examination of the nature and evolution of Mitchel's policies toward Confederate civilians in north Alabama; see ibid., 46–77.

33. Beatty, *Citizen-Soldier*, 124, 132, 140; George W. Landrum to his sister, March 28, April 15, 1862, Landrum Letters, OHS.

34. *OR*, ser. 1, 10(2):115, 162–63, 165, 195.

35. George W. Landrum to Obed J. Wilson, June 1, 1862, Landrum Letters, OHS; Alfred Pirtle to Henry Pirtle, May 31, 1862, Pirtle Papers, FHS.

36. *OR*, ser. 1, 16(2):44; Garfield, *Wild Life of the Army*, 116–17; Millard, *Destiny of the Republic*, 29–30.

37. William P. Moore Diary, June 26, 1862, WHS; John Gibson McMynn to his wife, June 28, 1862, McMynn Papers, WHS. All of the officers in the Twenty-Fourth Illinois did offer their resignations, but apparently only that of Maj. Julius Standan was accepted; see Wagner, *History of the 24th Illinois*, 11.

38. Wisconsin officer to his wife, July 25, 1862, enclosed in James R. Doolittle to Abraham Lincoln, August 4, 1862, Lincoln Papers, Library of Congress, Washington, D.C.

39. Beatty, *Citizen-Soldier*, 152–53; William A. Brown to his mother, July 13, 1862, Brown Family Papers, OHS; John H. Bolton Diary, July 16, 1862, OHS.

40. Grant, *Papers of Ulysses S. Grant*, 5:51; *OR*, ser. 1, 17(2):21.

41. *OR*, ser. 1, 17(2):15–16.

42. Lew Wallace, *Lew Wallace*, 2:583–84.

43. *OR*, ser. 1, 17(2):53–54, 66–67; Berlin et al., *Freedom*, ser. 1, 1:276–78; Josephy, *Civil War in the American West*, 350. See Starr, *Jennison's Jayhawkers*, 11–14, for Lane; and ibid., 170–85, for more on the controversies between the Seventh Kansas and their superiors over confiscation. Starr argues that the Kansans helped push the war into a struggle for emancipation.

44. Trefousse, *Ben Butler*, 28, 29–31, 37–38, 47–64, 75–76; Hearn, *When the Devil Came Down to Dixie*, 13–14, 18–24, 29.

45. Trefousse, *Ben Butler*, 78–79, 82–83, 102–4.

46. Capers, *Occupied City*, 1–2, 5, 19–24; Hearn, *When the Devil Came Down to Dixie*, 77, 78–80; Trefousse, *Ben Butler*, 107. See Roland, "Louisiana and Secession," 389–99, for an excellent examination of how secession unfolded in Louisiana.

47. Ash, *When the Yankees Came*, 117; Capers, *Occupied City*, 24, 90–92; Capers, "Confederates and Yankees," 411–12; Hunter, "Politics of Resentment," 186–87; Penn, "Geographical Variation of Unionism," 409–12; *OR*, ser. 1, 15:439–42; Hess, *Civil War in the West*, 83–91.

48. *OR*, ser. 1, 15:439–42; McDonald, "Independent Economic Production by Slaves," 486–87; Library of Congress, "Map showing the distribution of the slave population"; University of Virginia Library, "Historical Census Browser (1860)."

49. Berlin et al., *Freedom*, ser. 1, 1:199–201; *OR*, ser. 1, 6:679–80.

50. *OR*, ser. 1, 15:439–42; for more information on Hunter's pro-emancipationist policies in his department, see Edward A. Miller, *Lincoln's Abolitionist General*, 99–106.

51. *OR*, ser. 1, 15:442–43, 444, 445; Butler, *Private and Official Correspondence*, 1:177; Gerteis, *From Contraband to Freedman*, 68.

52. *OR*, ser. 1, 15:446–47; Butler, *Private and Official Correspondence*, 1:553–54; Gerteis, *From Contraband to Freedman*, 69–70.

53. *OR*, ser. 1, 15:486–91; Grimsley, *Hard Hand of War*, 128–29. Grimsley astutely points out that Phelps's letter never addressed the military advantages that could be gained from emancipation.

54. *OR*, ser. 1, 15:485–86.

55. Berlin et al., *Freedom*, ser. 1, 1:192, 216; Butler, *Private and Official Correspondence*, 1:632–34; Gerteis, *From Contraband to Freedman*, 70–71. Gerteis provides an excellent overview of the Butler-Phelps controversy. He rightly concludes that the incident

demonstrated "the shallowness of Butler's reputation as a Radical." But it is worth noting that Butler did become more emancipationist later on when Washington shifted in that direction.

56. Warner, *Generals in Blue*, 563; Paine, *Wisconsin Yankee*, 70, 75; "A Shameful History—Further in Regard to Col. Paine of the 4th Wisconsin," unattributed newspaper clipping, July 1862, originally printed in the *Kenosha Telegraph*, in a scrapbook at WHS.

57. Paine, *Wisconsin Yankee*, 77–80.

58. Cong. Globe, 37th Cong., 2d Sess. 3341–42 (1862); Paine, *Wisconsin Yankee*, 80–83.

59. Eli Augustus Griffin Diary, June 5, 1862, Griffin Papers, BHL; Paine, *Wisconsin Yankee*, 94; Harrison Soule to father and mother, June 11, 1862, Soule Papers, BHL.

60. William H. White to Phineas A. Hager, June 22, 1862, and White to "Brother John," July 11, 1862, Hager Family Papers, BHL; Charles Henry Moulton to brother and sister, December 9, 1861, and Moulton to brother and sister, June 15, 1862, Moulton Papers, BHL.

61. Paine, *Wisconsin Yankee*, 94–95.

62. Ibid., 93, 95–97.

CHAPTER 2

1. See Siddali, *From Property to Person*, 227–43; Blair, "Friend or Foe," 27–51; and Brasher, *Peninsula Campaign*, 206–7, for interpretations that emphasize that slaves might have had to obtain their freedom from a court rather than from the army or government. See Foner, *Fiery Trial*, 215, for the view that slaves were free when they came into Union lines.

2. Hess, "Confiscation," 60–61; *OR*, ser. 1, 13:756; on Curtis's background and career, see Ruth A. Gallagher, "Samuel Ryan Curtis," 331–58. For a clear expression of Curtis's intense desire to preserve the Union, see Curtis, "Irrepressible Conflict of 1861," 57–58.

3. *OR*, ser. 1, 13:524–25; Berlin et al., *Freedom*, ser. 1, 1:259; Shea and Hess, *Pea Ridge*, 301–2; see McPherson, *Battle Cry of Freedom*, 355–56, on the First Confiscation Act.

4. Nathan Paine to brother George, July 18, 1862, Paine Family Papers, WHS; Henry S. Eggleston to wife, July 31, 1862, and Eggleston undated and unaddressed letter, Eggleston Papers, WHS.

5. Curtis's General Orders No. 40, August 25, 1862, and N. P. Chipman to Abraham Lincoln, November 10, 1863, Curtis Papers, ALPL; *OR*, ser. 1, 13:546, 684; Hess, "Confiscation," 63.

6. N. P. Chipman to Abraham Lincoln, November 10, 1863, Curtis Papers, ALPL; *OR*, ser. 1, 13:783; Hess, "Confiscation," 62–64.

7. *New York Daily Tribune*, September 26, October 13, 1862, January 1, 1863; Warner, *Generals in Blue*, 474; Hess, "Confiscation," 65–66.

8. Statement of J. G. Forman regarding "Genl Steele's Orders Returning Fugitive Slaves at Helena, Sept 1862," Curtis Papers, ALPL; *New York Daily Tribune*, January 1, 1863; Hess, "Confiscation," 66.

9. Lincoln, *Collected Works*, 6:72–73; Grant, *Papers of Ulysses S. Grant*, 7:332–33; Hess, "Confiscation," 68. Hess provides a brief overview of the Craig incident but relies on Steele's account of the episode, which claims the slaves were in a brothel. The Forman

document cited above presents reliable evidence that the slaves were employed instead in the hospital. It is possible that Craig told Steele they were in the brothel.

10. Berlin et al., *Freedom*, ser. 1, 1:433–34; *OR*, ser. 1, 13:642–43.

11. *OR*, ser. 1, 22(1):796–98, 841–51.

12. *OR*, ser. 1, 13:772–73; 22(1):868–71.

13. *OR*, ser. 1, 15:162; Butler, *Private and Official Correspondence*, 2:450, 556–57. See Horowitz, "Ben Butler and the Negro," 159–86, for an insightful look at Butler's changing policies and attitudes toward slavery during the war. Horowitz argues that Butler moved toward a more emancipationist position as a result of political concerns and his experiences on the ground. Ultimately, Horowitz concludes that Butler was convinced of the justice of emancipation.

14. *OR*, ser. 1, 15:534–37; Butler, *Private and Official Correspondence*, 2:145–46, 154.

15. Frank Wells to his brother, August 7, 1862, and Wells to his brother, September 23, 1862, Wells Letters, Northwest Corner Civil War Round Table Collection, USAMHI; *New York Daily Tribune*, September 26, 1862.

16. *OR*, ser. 1, 15:553–54, 588; Kinsley, *Diary of a Christian Soldier*, 23, 107, 109–10; Butler, *Private and Official Correspondence*, 2:448.

17. *OR*, ser. 1, 15:441, 555–56; Westwood, "Benjamin Butler's Enlistment of Black Troops," 13, 20–21; Butler, *Private and Official Correspondence*, 2:186. Historians debate the extent to which Butler was following Phelps's policies. See Westwood, "Benjamin Butler's Enlistment of Black Troops," 1, 18–22; and Horowitz, "Ben Butler and the Negro," 178–79, for varying interpretations of the issue. From the evidence, it is clear that Butler was pursuing a similar course to Phelps but with some important differences. Whereas Phelps was willing to arm any slave who came into his camp, Butler was only willing to arm and organize those that were eligible to be confiscated. Moreover, many of the black men Butler did arm were free before the war.

18. *OR*, ser. 1, 15:164–66, 171–72; Butler, *Autobiography and Personal Reminiscences*, 498. In the correspondence, Butler was referring to Gen. Braxton Bragg's invasion of Kentucky in September–October 1862. It is important to note that Weitzel gave Butler only two examples of the supposed rebelliousness among the slaves in the region; see Butler, *Autobiography and Personal Reminiscences*, 497.

19. Paine, *Wisconsin Yankee*, 102 3, 114; Eli Augustus Griffin to his father, July 17, 1862, Griffin Papers, BHL.

20. Hoffman, *Camp, Court and Siege*, 59–60; Joseph Bailey to Perry G. Stroud, December 5, 1862, Bailey-Stroud Papers, USAMHI.

21. *OR*, ser. 1, 15:592–95, 610; Butler, *Private and Official Correspondence*, 2:447–49; for the repressive characteristics of Gen. Nathaniel Banks's labor system in Louisiana, see Gerteis, *From Contraband to Freedman*, 73–82.

22. Grant, *Papers of Ulysses S. Grant*, 5:273–74; Simpson, *Ulysses S. Grant*, 146, 147–48. Both Simpson and John Simon, editor of Grant's papers, point out the change in Grant's policies during this period.

23. Grant, *Papers of Ulysses S. Grant*, 5:273–74, 264, 311.

24. Grant, *Papers of Ulysses S. Grant*, 5:226. On Washburne and Grant, see Lewis, *Captain Sam Grant*, 394–410; and Catton, *Grant Moves South*, 16–17, 260–61.

25. *OR*, ser. 1, 17(2):15–16, 158–60, 169–70; William T. Sherman, *Sherman's Civil War*, 263–64, 272–73.

26. William T. Sherman, *Sherman's Civil War*, 302–4; 292–93; *OR*, ser. 1, 17(2):159, 172.

27. William T. Sherman, *Sherman's Civil War*, 272–73, 279–80, 285–86, 302–3; on Sherman's desire for order, see Marszalek, *Sherman*, xvii-xviii, 193. Also see Marszalek, 191–93, for a useful overview of Sherman's attitudes and policies in Memphis.

28. William T. Sherman, *Sherman's Civil War*, 311–12, 260, 292–93; on this last point, see Marszalek, *Sherman*, 193, for a similar conclusion.

29. Gilbert, *Colonel A. W. Gilbert*, 106–8; Jackson, *Colonel's Diary*, 62; "Journal of Captain George H. Palmer," 11, Palmer Biography, ALPL.

30. William B. Britton to the editors of the *Janesville Gazette*, July 29, August 26, September 11, 1862, Britton Letters, WRHS; James Lawrence unaddressed letter, August 23, 1862, Lawrence Papers, Chicago HS; Channing Richards Diary, September 2, 1862, Cincinnati HS. While confiscation was occurring at all levels of command, there were virtually no officers still willing to return fugitive slaves to their masters in Grant's army. A rare exception was Capt. John W. Rigby, provost marshal in Jackson, Tennessee. Rigby ordered several slaves working in the hospital there returned to their owners. Upon learning of this, Grant immediately directed that Rigby be placed under arrest for violating the law and his orders. The army was now in the business of seizing slaves, not returning them. White Southerners also found that it was dangerous for them to try to recover slave property from Union lines. At Fort Pickering in Memphis, a man tried to lure a slave toward his carriage to capture him. Understanding his purpose, the slave assaulted the man. The man soon found himself the target of all the slaves at the fort. William Caldwell, a surgeon in the Seventy-Second Ohio, observed "a thousand and one negroes yelling like so many ebony demons" chasing the man with stones and clubs until he was arrested by the guards. Caldwell thought the slaves "manifested a strong disposition to eat the gentleman on the spot." The slaves confiscated the man's carriage and horses, pronouncing them "contraband." All of this amused the soldiers at the fort. See Grant, *Papers of Ulysses S. Grant*, 6:426; and William C. Caldwell to his sister, October 24, 1862, Caldwell Family Papers, RBHPC.

31. Grant, *Papers of Ulysses S. Grant*, 6:315–17, 329–30; Grant, *Personal Memoirs*, 424–26; Eaton, *Grant, Lincoln, and the Freedmen*, 11–15; Simpson, *Ulysses S. Grant*, 162–63; see Downs, *Sick from Freedom*, 21–41, for an examination of the devastating toll illness took on African Americans in Union lines during the war. Downs shows how unprepared the government and doctors were to combat the extensive outbreak of disease.

32. Engle, *Don Carlos Buell*, 317–18; Daniel, *Days of Glory*, 175–76; Don Carlos Buell to Almon F. Rockwell, July 10, 1864, Buell Papers, FHS.

33. *OR*, ser. 1, 16(1):351; ser. 1, 16(2):332; Berlin et al., *Freedom*, ser. 1, 1:287–89; Don Carlos Buell to Charles E. Bliven, December 20, 1880, Buell Papers, FHS.

34. Ormsby M. Mitchel to "my dear Ripley," July 21, 1862, Mitchel Papers, Cincinnati HS; *OR*, ser. 1, 16(2):583–86; Berlin et al., *Freedom*, ser. 1, 1:282–84; Daniel, *Days of Glory*, 94–95, 97–100.

35. *OR*, ser. 1, 16(2):264, 268, 269, 287; ser. 1, 16(1):355, 617; Noe, *Perryville*, 59. Buell actually ordered Harker to return two more slaves to their master two days later for a similar reason; see *OR*, ser. 1, 16(2):303.

36. William H. Kemper Diary and Papers, August 8, 11, 1862, OHS; Ephraim S. Holloway to his wife, August 4, September 4, 1862, Holloway Papers, OHS.

37. William W. Blair to his wife, August 31, September 2, 1862, Blair Letters, IHS.

38. Daniel, *Days of Glory*, 6–7, 194; Alfred Pirtle Journal, September 2, 1862, Pirtle Papers, FHS; George W. Landrum to his sister, August 11, 1862, Landrum Letters, OHS. Rousseau did report to the Buell Court of Inquiry that he employed slaves as teamsters and on fortifications, so he did confiscate some; see *OR*, ser. 1, 16(1):351.

39. Otto, *Memoirs of a Dutch Mudsill*, 34–38; Fitch, *Echoes of the Civil War*, 55–56; Henry Clay Taylor to his father and mother, October 13, 1862, Taylor Papers, WHS. For another example of conflict between officers in Buell's army over fugitive slaves in Kentucky, see Tourgée, *Story of a Thousand*, 106; also see examples below of conflict in the Army of Kentucky.

40. Leander Stem to his sister, October 24, 1862, and Stem to his wife, October 26, 1862, Stem Family Collection, RBHPC; Thomas E. Smith to "Moss" (?), November 6, 1862, and Smith to "Will," November 16, 1862, Smith Family Papers, Cincinnati HS.

41. Ramage and Watkins, *Kentucky Rising*, 236–39, 257, 276, 325; Harrison, *Civil War in Kentucky*, 1–3; Noe, *Perryville*, 3; Williams and Harris, "Kentucky in 1860," 751; Astor, *Rebels on the Border*, 11–13, 15, 19–25, 33–36; Wallace B. Turner, "Kentucky Slavery," 291–94; Library of Congress, "Map showing the distribution of the slave population."

42. Harrison, *Civil War in Kentucky*, 3–5, 8–13; Potter and Fehrenbacher, *Impending Crisis*, 416–17; Wallace B. Turner, "Secession Movement in Kentucky," 260–61, 270–78; Ramage and Watkins, *Kentucky Rising*, 277–78, 289; Noe, *Perryville*, 3–9; Williams and Harris, "Kentucky in 1860," 756–59, 759–64. Williams and Harris provide an excellent discussion of the number of Kentuckians who served in the Union and Confederate armies. These numbers help gauge the relative strength of Unionist or secessionist feelings among Kentuckians. While reaching exact numbers is impossible, Williams and Harris show that between 25,000 and 40,000 Kentuckians served the Confederacy, and between 76,335 and 95,978 served the Union. The strength of Unionism in Kentucky is quite clear.

43. Berlin et al., *Freedom*, ser. 1, 1:534; *OR*, ser. 1, 20(2):160–63; Warner, *Generals in Blue*, 176, 181; Stephen G. Burbridge to "Uncle Harry," October 29, 1862, Burbridge Papers, FHS.

44. Bentley, *History of the 77th Illinois*, 103–4; William Wiley, *Civil War Diary*, 22; Victor B. Howard, *Black Liberation in Kentucky*, 17, 20, 25–26; Berlin et al., *Freedom*, ser. 1, 1:546–47.

45. Victor B. Howard, *Black Liberation in Kentucky*, 23–24; Berlin et al., *Freedom*, ser. 1, 1:528–38; Thomas Winston to his wife, October 30, November 1, 17, December 4, 1862, Winston Papers, USAMHI.

46. Bradley, *Star Corps*, 63–67; Berlin et al., *Freedom*, ser. 1, 1:539; Fliss, "Wisconsin's 'Abolition Regiment,'" 4, 6–8; Benjamin Franklin Heuston to his wife, October 23, 1862, and Heuston Journal of the same date, Heuston Papers, WHS; William N. Peak to "Henrie," October 27, 1862, Moxley-Offutt Family Papers, FHS.

47. Fliss, "Wisconsin's 'Abolition Regiment,'" 3, 8, 9–12; Bradley, *Star Corps*, 68–79; Berlin et al., *Freedom*, ser. 1, 1:539–44; for Lincoln's offer see Lincoln, *Collected Works*, 5:512. Before he made the offer to Robertson, Lincoln penned a much harsher response to the judge, asking him, "Do you not know that I may as well surrender this contest,

directly, as to make any order, the obvious purpose of which would be to return fugitive slaves?" This letter was apparently not sent; see Lincoln, *Collected Works*, 5:502–3. The feud between Judge Robertson and Colonel Utley over Adam continued long after the war. Finally, in 1871, Robertson was able to get a judgment against Utley in federal court for $934.46. Congress ended up paying this for Utley.

CHAPTER 3

1. There is an extensive literature on Union soldiers' attitudes toward emancipation and black soldiers. See McPherson, *For Cause and Comrades*, 117–30; Gary W. Gallagher, *Union War*, 75–118; and Manning, *What This Cruel War Was Over*, 43–51, 72–80, 83–102, 114–25, 148–57, 182–93, for some important treatments of the subject. McPherson's and Gallagher's conclusions are much more consistent with the findings of this study, especially Gallagher's emphasis on practical motives for supporting emancipation. Manning argues that there was a great deal of pro-emancipation sentiment among Union soldiers early in the war, but I have found this to be less true for officers. She also downplays the extent of opposition to emancipation. Manning studies enlisted men and, at one point, admits that they were ahead of at least high-ranking officers when it came to favoring emancipation.

2. Isabel Wallace, *Life & Letters*, 106; Sparks, "Memoirs and Letters of David Rhodes Sparks (unpublished)," 96, in Curtis J. Herrick Papers, USAMHI; George Smith Avery to Lizzie Little Avery, April 29, May 6, 1861, January 12, 26, February 25, 1862, Avery Papers, Chicago HS. See McPherson, *For Cause and Comrades*, 17–19, 98–100, 110–14; and Gary W. Gallagher, *Union War*, 33–74, for important studies that emphasize the importance of the Union in Northern soldiers' motivations.

3. John Beatty, *Citizen-Soldier*, 157–58; McPherson, *For Cause and Comrades*, 120; Bowler and Bowler, *Go If You Think It Your Duty*, 112.

4. William P. Moore Diary, ca. May 1862, WHS; Brackett, *Surgeon on Horseback*, 95, 97, 142; George W. Landrum to his sister, May 13, 1862, Landrum Letters, OHS.

5. George W. Landrum to Obed J. Wilson, June 1, 1862, Landrum Letters, OHS; Sparks, "Memoirs and Letters of David Rhodes Sparks (unpublished)," 111–12, in Curtis J. Herrick Papers, USAMHI; William H. Kemper Diary and Papers, July 2, 1862, OHS. Not every officer was moved toward abolition by seeing slavery firsthand. Lt. Robert S. Dilworth of the Twenty-First Ohio wrote: "I have not seen a negro since I have come out but loves their master and are much better treated than they would treat themselves.... They are all comfortable. Some are anxious to be free but I do not believe they would stay in the north 2 years if they were free." See Dilworth to Lois A. Blakeman, May 12, 1862, Dilworth Papers, BGU. On Northern racial beliefs and practices before the war, see Litwack, *North of Slavery*, 64–186; and Berwanger, *Frontier against Slavery*, 30–59.

6. Opdycke, *To Battle for God*, 37; John B. Rice to his brother, August 11, 1862, Rice Papers, RBHPC.

7. Heg, *Civil War Letters*, 110; Lyon and Lyon, *Reminiscences of the Civil War*, 50–51; William C. Caldwell to his father, July 15, 1862, Caldwell Family Papers, RBHPC. Historians have emphasized the importance of the Union defeat at Richmond in pushing the North to adopt harsher measures, including emancipation, to suppress the rebellion;

see McPherson, *Battle Cry of Freedom*, 489–94, 499–510; Grimsley, *Hard Hand of War*, 74–78, 94–95; and Brasher, *Peninsula Campaign*.

8. Lucius Dwight Hinkley to his mother, July 24, 1862, Hinkley Papers, WHS; Gilbert, *Colonel A. W. Gilbert*, 108.

9. John R. Ziegler to "Nelly," April 22, 1862, Ziegler Papers, ALPL; Alfred Pirtle to Henry Pirtle, May 31, 1862, Pirtle Papers, FHS.

10. Alfred Pirtle to his mother, June 1, August 18, 1862, Pirtle Papers, FHS; Harrison Soule to his wife, June 16, 1862, Soule Papers, BHL; for more discontent, see Frank Wells to "Ginnie," August 11, 1862, and Wells to his brother, August 7, 1862, Wells Letters, Northwest Corner Civil War Round Table Collection, USAMHI; see Cong. Globe, 37th Cong., 2d Sess. 162–227 (1862), for some of the extensive debates over confiscation at the end of May 1862. From the evidence, it appears that Pirtle was referring to the Fifteenth Kentucky.

11. Wills, *Army Life of an Illinois Soldier*, 106, 127; Moss, *History of the Civil War*, 2:61. I am very grateful to James W. Moss Sr. for pointing out this excellent primary source to me and kindly sending me letters that related to my topic.

12. Albert G. Hart to his mother, December 5, 1861, and Hart unaddressed letter, June 16, 1862, Hart Papers, WRHS; Frederick A. Boardman to Josiah A. Noonan, June 11, 1862, Noonan Papers, WHS; William M. Ferry to his wife, May 1, 1862, Ferry Family Papers, BHL.

13. Jackson, *Colonel's Diary*, 27–35, 53–55, 88, 90, 244–45.

14. Seneca B. Thrall to his wife, November 15, 1862, in Thrall, "Seneca B. Thrall Union Letters"; Channing Richards Diary, November 10, 1862, Cincinnati HS; Richards to his sister, March 22, 1863, Richards Papers, FHS; also see Thomas Winston to his wife, December 21, 1862, Winston Papers, USAMHI.

15. George W. Landrum to his sister, February 6, 1863, Landrum Letters, OHS; George W. Lawrence to his uncle, February 2, 1863, Nina L. Ness Papers, BHL; Robert B. Latham to his wife, January 22, 1863, Latham Papers, ALPL.

16. On Copperheads and their rise in the North, see McPherson, *Battle Cry of Freedom*, 591–600; and Weber, *Copperheads*, 63–102.

17. Henry F. Hole to his sister, October 13, 1862, Hole Papers, ALPL; Luther H. Cowan to Kingsley Olds, February 25, 1863, Cowan Letters and Diary, WHS; Orville T. Chamberlain unaddressed letters, January 29, 1863, April 12, 1863, and Chamberlain to "Friends," May 31, 1863, Chamberlain Papers, IHS; for another example of officer anger at the Copperheads over their denunciations of the proclamation, see Jonathan F. Harrington to his nephew, April 17, 1863, Harrington Papers, RBHPC. Lieutenant Harrington of the Seventy-Second Ohio wrote, "If those Copper Pates open their heads to Slander the Presidents Procamation they will hang the first one to the nearest Tree and keep Doing So untill they know enough to keep a civil tongue this is my wishes and the Sympathy I have for the Trators at home I think less of them than I do of the Rebs here in the army for if it were not for them this uncalled for war would have ben Settled long a go it is them that has incouraged the South So long." See McPherson, *For Cause and Comrades*, 124–25, for a good discussion of how Copperheads helped convert Union soldiers who were at first opposed to support emancipation. This was undoubtedly the case, but it is important to note that Copperheads also played an important role in motivating some soldiers to *initially* embrace emancipation as well.

18. Grant, *Papers of Ulysses S. Grant*, 9: 196–97, 218; Schofield, *Forty-Six Years in the Army*, 74–75; Bickham, *Rosecrans' Campaign*, 85, 143–44.

19. Garfield, *Wild Life of the Army*, 140, 145, 207; John G. Crawford to James Packard, January 11, 1863, Wiley Sword Papers, USAMHI; Beatty, *Citizen-Soldier*, 193–94, 313.

20. Vermilion and Vermilion, *Love Amid the Turmoil*, 14, 15, 23, 29, 44, 211; Francis Trowbridge Sherman, *Quest for a Star*, 36–37.

21. John Quincy Adams Campbell, *Union Must Stand*, 61; Kamphoefner and Helbich, *Germans in the Civil War*, 351, 352, 353–54; also see Julius C. Burrows to William H. Withington, May 3, 1863, Withington Papers, BHL.

22. Humphrey H. Hood to his wife, January 6, 1863, Hood Papers, ALPL; Stevens, "Dear Carrie," 62; Alexander Varian to his sister, October 5, 1862, Varian Letters, WRHS.

23. George C. Burmeister Diary, November 20, 1862, January 22, 1863, CWMC, USAMHI; John Robert Dow to "Ann," December 14, 1862, Dow Family Papers, FHS. See Morris E. Fitch to "folks at home," January 25, 1863, Fitch Papers, BHL; Spiegel, *Your True Marcus*, 226–27, 230; and Hedley, *Marching through Georgia*, 53–54, for additional examples of discontent in the army.

24. John Robert Dow to his sister, February 7, 1863, Dow Family Papers, FHS; John Grey McDermott to his wife, March 6, 1863, McDermott Letters, WHS; Grant, *Papers of Ulysses S. Grant*, 7:536–37, 8:94; Victor B. Howard, *Black Liberation in Kentucky*, 32–34; Daniel, *Days of Glory*, 250; Beatty, *Citizen-Soldier*, 223–24; Stevenson, *Letters from the Army*, 190–91.

25. William M. Ferry to his wife, October 31, December 9, 1862, Ferry Family Papers, BHL.

26. Oliver L. Spaulding Diary, December 25, 1862, Spaulding Papers, BHL; Henry Clay Taylor unaddressed letter, November 28, 1862, Taylor Papers, WHS; John Grey McDermott to "Isabella," January 25, 1863, McDermott Letters, WHS. Interestingly, Spaulding remembered himself as an abolitionist in his memoirs; see "Military Memoirs of Brigadier General Oliver L. Spaulding," 13, Spaulding Papers, BHL.

27. John G. McMynn Diary, November 30, 1862, McMynn Papers, WHS; Spiegel, *Your True Marcus*, 204, 226–27, 230.

28. Downs, *Sick from Freedom*, 22–24.

29. Spiegel, *Your True Marcus*, 261; William W. Van Antwerp to his wife, February 16, March 5, 1863, Van Antwerp Papers, BHL; Culver and Culver, *"Your Affectionate Husband,"* 72.

30. Hughes and Whitney, *Jefferson Davis in Blue*, 157; Heg, *Civil War Letters*, 178.

31. Voegeli, *Free but Not Equal*, 1–9, 13–14; Donald, *Lincoln*, 380, 417–18.

32. Opdycke, *To Battle for God*, 112; Culver and Culver, *"Your Affectionate Husband,"* 202, 203, 245–46.

33. Connolly, *Three Years in the Army*, 146; Alfred Pirtle to his sister, September 8, 1863, Pirtle Papers, FHS; William W. Van Antwerp to his wife, August 28, 1863, Van Antwerp Papers, BHL.

34. Spiegel, *Your True Marcus*, 315–16, 320–21; Fitch, *Echoes of the Civil War*, 268–69.

35. Ritner and Ritner, *Love and Valor*, 304–5; Clifford Stickney to "Rose," August 5, 1864, Stickney Collection, Chicago HS. For other late-war expressions of support see Bradley, *Star Corps*, 150–51; Opdycke, *To Battle for God*, 161, 203; Burton, *Diary*

of E. P. Burton, 5, 17; Thomas Winston to his wife, February 3, 1864, Winston Papers, USAMHI; and "The Reminiscences of General Andrew Hickenlooper, 1861–1865," 130, *CWTIC,* USAMHI.

36. William H. White to "Mr. Hager," December 18, 1861, and White to his mother, October 3, 1862, Hager Family Papers, BHL; Seneca B. Thrall to his wife, January 20, 1863, in Thrall, "Seneca B. Thrall Union Letters"; Channing Richards to his sister, March 1, 22, 1863, Richards Papers, FHS.

37. Harrison Soule to his wife, April 5, 12, 1863, Soule Papers, BHL.

38. Charles Dana Miller, *Struggle for the Life,* 91; John H. Ferree to Dr. Laughlin Oneal, May 9, 1863, Ferree Papers, IHS; Stevens, *"Dear Carrie,"* 90; Henry Albert Potter to his sister, April 20, 1863, Potter Papers, BHL.

39. Cornish, *Sable Arm,* 110–14; Glatthaar, *Forged in Battle,* 37.

40. Vermilion and Vermilion, *Love Amid the Turmoil,* 76; Edward S. Redington to his wife, April 10, 1863, Redington Papers, WHS; Underhill, *Helena to Vicksburg,* 65–66; Cornish, *Sable Arm,* 116.

41. Cornish, *Sable Arm,* 116–19; Woodworth, *Nothing but Victory,* 311; William B. Britton to the editors of the *Janesville Gazette,* April 21, 1863, Britton Letters, WRHS; James Harrison Wilson, *Under the Old Flag,* 1:165; Cornwell, "Dan. Caverno," 117–18, Cornwell Memoirs, CWMC, USAMHI.

42. Dwight, "Four Year's Relics," 60, 62, in Dwight Papers, OHS; Jordan C. Harris to his parents (?), April 11, 1863, in Harris, "Jordan C. Harris Letters"; Woodworth, *Nothing but Victory,* 311; Ritner and Ritner, *Love and Valor,* 159–60; Asa A. Lawrence to his wife, April 22, 1863, Lawrence Papers, WRHS.

43. George Throop to his sister, April 19, 1863, Throop-Vaughan Family Papers, Chicago HS; Edward P. Stanfield to his father, April 8, 1863, Stanfield Papers, IHS; William B. Britton to the editors of the *Janesville Gazette,* April 21, 1863, Britton Letters, WRHS; Luther H. Cowan to M. P. Rindlaub, April 21, 1863, Cowan Letters and Diary, WHS.

44. Jacob Bruner to his wife, October 14, 1862, January 3, April 9, 1863, Bruner Papers, OHS.

45. Grant, *Papers of Ulysses S. Grant,* 8:328; William B. Britton to the editors of the *Janesville Gazette,* June 13, 1863, Britton Letters, WRHS; Currie, *Warfare along the Mississippi,* 120–21; Irwin Eckels to his family, March 29, 1864, Eckels Papers, WHS.

46. Connolly, *Three Years in the Army,* 191–92; Grierson, *Just and Righteous Cause,* 231–32; Kinsley, *Diary of a Christian Soldier,* 146; John B. Wilson to his wife, February 13, 1865, Wilson Letters, CWMC, USAMHI.

47. Grant, *Papers of Ulysses S. Grant,* 8:106; William T. Sherman, *Sherman's Civil War,* 454, 657–58, 677–78, 699–700; Marszalek, *Sherman,* 270–71.

48. Hosea Smith to his sister, December 18, 1862, July 12, 1863, Hosea Smith Letters, CWMC, USAMHI; John Henry Hammond Diary, June 8, 1863, Hammond Papers, FHS.

49. Lucius Dwight Hinkley to his mother, undated (probably summer 1863 from content), Hinkley Papers, WHS; Harrison Soule to his wife, July 24, 1863, Soule Papers, BHL; William M. Ferry to his aunt, February 29, 1864, Ferry Family Papers, BHL. Black soldiers did not rescue Gen. Halbert Paine from the Port Hudson battlefield, but the fact that Soule had such an angry reaction to the claim demonstrates his hostility toward black troops; see Cunningham, *Port Hudson Campaign,* 92; and Paine, *Wisconsin Yankee,* 151.

50. Morgan, *Reminiscences of Service*, 20–21; Robert Winn to his sister, December 11, 1863, Winn-Cook Papers, FHS.

51. Lee, *Kentuckian in Blue*, 132–34; William T. Ward to John H. Ward, February 6, 1864, and enclosed letter from Lovell Rousseau, Speed Family Papers, FHS; Grant, *Papers of Ulysses S. Grant*, 10:548; Robert Winn to his sister, March 15, 1864, Winn-Cook Papers, FHS; Tapp, "Incidents in the Life of Frank Wolford," 91–95; see Victor B. Howard, *Black Liberation in Kentucky*, 56–71, for an extensive discussion of the opposition of Kentuckians to black troops.

CHAPTER 4

1. See Fox-Genovese, *Within the Plantation Household*, 22–23, 139, 165; and Oakes, *Ruling Race*, 113, 167, for some examples of white Southerners calling their slaves "servants."

2. Voegeli, *Free but Not Equal*, 1–2; Litwack, *North of Slavery*, 64–103, 113–17, 131–35; Berwanger, *Frontier against Slavery*, 34.

3. Edward Gee Miller, *Captain Edward Gee Miller*, 15–16; Jonathan F. Harrington to his parents, June 23, 1862, Harrington Papers, RBHPC; Bennet Grigsby to his wife and children, May 18, 1863, Grigsby-McDonald Papers, IHS; Stevens, *"Dear Carrie,"* 66.

4. Stevens, *"Dear Carrie,"* 114; Asa Slayton Journal, reprinted in *Grand Rapids Weekly Eagle*, October 1, 1863, Slayton Family Papers, BHL; Wills, *Army Life of an Illinois Soldier*, 122–23.

5. Paine, *Wisconsin Yankee*, 59; William W. McCarty to "George and Ellie," October 25, [1862,] McCarty Papers, CWMC, USAMHI; Luther H. Cowan to Josephine J. Cowan, August 3, 1862, Cowan Letters and Diary, WHS; Joseph Bailey to Perry G. Stroud, December 24, 1862, Bailey-Stroud Papers, USAMHI; Thomas Winston to his wife, October 30, November 1, 26, 1862, Winston Papers, USAMHI.

6. Connolly, *Three Years in the Army*, 332–33, 312–13. See Mitchell, *Civil War Soldiers*, 118–19, for a similar conclusion about what Union soldiers thought of black people dancing.

7. Greene, *Camp Ford Prison; And How I Escaped*, 44–49, in Greene Reminiscences, CWTIC, USAMHI; Paine, *Wisconsin Yankee*, 92; David D. Porter, *Incidents and Anecdotes*, 243–44.

8. Brackett, *Surgeon on Horseback*, 213; Burton, *Diary of E. P. Burton*, 6, 8; George C. Burmeister Diary, April 24, 1864, CWMC, USAMHI.

9. George C. Burmeister Diary, March 14, 1864, CWMC, USAMHI; Bennitt, *"I Hope to Do My Country Service,"* 265.

10. John Grey McDermott to "Isabella," January 25, 1863, McDermott Letters, WHS; Luther H. Cowan Diary, February 23, 1863, Cowan Letters and Diary, WHS; Wills, *Army Life of an Illinois Soldier*, 127.

11. William T. Sherman, *Sherman's Civil War*, 537; James Harrison Wilson, *Under the Old Flag*, 1:189; David D. Porter, *Incidents and Anecdotes*, 155.

12. Hosea Smith to his sister, June 3, 1864, Hosea Smith Letters, CWMC, USAMHI; Samuel T. Wells to Lizzie Wells, April 21, 1862, Wells Papers, FHS; Ephraim Brown to Drusilla Brown, December 19, 1862, Brown Papers, OHS.

13. Thomas Thomson Taylor, *Tom Taylor's Civil War*, 78–79; Harrison Soule to his wife, July 24, 1862, Soule Papers, BHL; George Throop to friends, November 17, 1862, Throop-Vaughan Family Papers, Chicago HS; George T. Shaffer to his wife, November 27, December 23, 1863, Shaffer Papers, BHL; Grierson, *Just and Righteous Cause*, 222–24.

14. Alfred Pirtle to his mother, December 16, 21, 1862, Pirtle Papers, FHS; Eli A. Griffin to his wife, February 19, 1863, Griffin Papers, BHL; Elisha Mix to his wife and children, February 17, 1864, Mix Papers, BHL; Frank J. Jones to his mother, June 17, 1862, Jones Letters, Cincinnati HS.

15. Humphrey H. Hood to his wife, December 16, 1862, Hood Papers, ALPL; Charles Dana Miller, *Struggle for the Life*, 66; Hartzell, *Ohio Volunteer*, 94.

16. Joseph Bailey to "captain," July 12, 1864, Bailey-Stroud Papers, USAMHI; Robert Winn to his sister, February 25, 1864, Winn-Cook Papers, FHS; Henry Albert Potter Diary, February 20, 1864, Potter Papers, BHL; William M. Ferry to his aunt, February 29, 1864, Ferry Family Papers, BHL.

17. Brackett, *Surgeon on Horseback*, 202, 206–7; George C. Burmeister Diary, March 11, 30, 1864, CWMC, USAMHI; Wills, *Army Life of an Illinois Soldier*, 135–36. For more on the abuse of black people and officer sympathy see Jackson, *Colonel's Diary*, 192–94; James E. Graham Diary, August 22, 1863, OHS; and Jesse B. Connelly Diary, July 1862, IHS.

18. See Mitchell, *Civil War Soldiers*, 123–25, for a discussion of the positive reaction of Union soldiers to heroic black people. Mitchell astutely notes how Union soldiers could react favorably to individual black Southerners, but does not say anything about officers' servants, probably the most important group of black Southerners that officers came to respect.

19. James R. Stillwell to his wife and children, January 16, 1865, Stillwell Papers, OHS; George C. Burmeister Diary, March 24, 1864, CWMC, USAMHI; Thomas Winston to his wife, December 14, 1862, Winston Papers, USAMHI.

20. Vermilion and Vermilion, *Love Amid the Turmoil*, 251.

21. Bowler and Bowler, *Go If You Think It Your Duty*, 194–95; Bradley, *Star Corps*, 265, 243–44; David D. Porter, *Incidents and Anecdotes*, 154–55.

22. Charles Dana Miller, *Struggle for the Life*, 47; George W. Landrum to his sister, June 16, 1863, Landrum Letters, OHS; Dwight, "Four Year's Relics," 44, in Dwight Papers, OHS.

23. Byers, *With Fire and Sword*, 148, 163–67, 173; McCreery, *My Experience as a Prisoner of War and Escape from Libby Prison*, 33–35, in McCreery-Fenton Family Papers, BHL; Johnston, *Four Months in Libby*, 105–7, 112.

24. Edward E. Dickerson Diary, October 30, November 1, 2, 3, 14, 26, 1864, WHS. For more on black Southerners helping officers escape from prison, see Greene, *Camp Ford Prison; And How I Escaped*, 44–49, 77–81, in Greene Reminiscences, *CWTIC*, USAMHI; and Fulton, "Personal Reminiscences of Military Prison Life," 6, 7, 9, in Fulton-Lenz Collection, *CWTIC*, USAMHI.

25. Samson Jack North to his wife, October 1, 1863, North Papers, BHL; Henry S. Eggleston to his wife, July 4, 1862, Eggleston Papers, WHS; Heg, *Civil War Letters*, 57, 60; also see Jerome Spilman to his wife, February 25, 1862, Spilman Letters, *CWTIC*, USAMHI.

26. Stevens, *"Dear Carrie,"* 138, 173; Edward P. Stanfield to his father, March 2, December 8, 1862, January 28, 1863, Stanfield Papers, IHS.

27. Stevens, *"Dear Carrie,"* 204; William Ward Diary, February 1864, IHS; Lyman Daniel Ames Diary, June 9, 1864, *CWTIC*, USAMHI; Edgar N. Wilcox to unknown, February 9, 1862, Wilcox Letters, CWMC, USAMHI; Evangelist J. Gillmore to his wife, July 14, 1863, Gillmore Papers, ALPL; Newell and Shrader, *Of Duty Well and Faithfully Done*, 48; Vermilion and Vermilion, *Love Amid the Turmoil*, 138–39; Ephraim Brown to Drusilla Brown, January 25, 1863, Brown Papers, OHS; Samson Jack North to his wife, October 1, 1863, North Papers, BHL.

28. Nathan Paine to his sister, August 30, 1862, Paine Family Papers, WHS; Jackson, *Colonel's Diary*, 244–45; Eli A. Griffin to his wife, June 27, 1863, Griffin Papers, BHL; Kircher, *German in the Yankee Fatherland*, 149, 152.

29. *Racine Journal*, February 22, 1922, copy in WHS; Brackett, *Surgeon on Horseback*, 163–64. Brackett was referring to the efforts of Senator James Lane to recruit and organize black troops in Kansas in late summer 1862.

30. Luther H. Cowan to his wife, November 27, 1862, Cowan Letters and Diary, WHS; Wills, *Army Life of an Illinois Soldier*, 106, 31–32; Thomas Winston to his wife, February 23, March 16, 1863, March 11, 1864, Winston Papers, USAMHI.

31. Horace Porter, *Campaigning with Grant*, 129–31; Hazen, *Narrative of Military Service*, 268–69.

32. Garfield, *Wild Life of the Army*, 102; Henry S. Clubb to his wife, January 4, 1863, Clubb Papers, BHL; O. O. Howard, *Autobiography of Oliver Otis Howard*, 1:496.

33. Humphrey H. Hood to his wife, December 4, 1862, Hood Papers, ALPL; Arthur L. Conger Diary, January 19, 1863, Conger Papers, USAMHI; Thomas Winston to his wife, November 4, 1862, Winston Papers, USAMHI.

34. Thomas E. Smith to "Moss" (?), November 6, 1862, Smith to "Will," November 16, 1862, and Smith to "Maria," March 29, July 9, 1863, Smith Family Papers, Cincinnati HS.

35. See Genovese, *Roll, Jordan, Roll*, 347–49, 367–68, 369, 374–77, for some useful evidence of how masters described their choice slaves.

36. William B. Britton to the editors of the *Janesville Gazette*, August 8, 1862, Britton Letters, WRHS; John Gibson McMynn to his wife, June 28, 1862, McMynn Papers, WHS; Heg, *Civil War Letters*, 106; Horace Porter, *Campaigning with Grant*, 130–31.

37. John B. Wilson to his wife, February 3, 1865, Wilson Letters, CWMC, USAMHI; William W. McCarty to "George and Ellie," October 25, [1862,] McCarty Papers, CWMC, USAMHI; Culver and Culver, *"Your Affectionate Husband,"* 209, 361–62, 366.

38. John Corden to his wife, November 2, 1862, Corden Papers, BHL; George T. Shaffer to his wife, January 7, 1863, Shaffer Papers, BHL. Also see Wills, *Army Life of an Illinois Soldier*, 142.

39. Albert J. Rockwell to Eva Rockwell, November 15, 1862, Rockwell Letters, WHS; Orville T. Chamberlain to his father, April 21, 1865, Chamberlain Papers, IHS.

40. Ralph P. Buckland to Horace Buckland, June 7, 1862, Buckland Papers, RBHPC; Lennard, "Give Yourself No Trouble," 35–37, 46.

41. Heg, *Civil War Letters*, 170, 172; Nelson B. Sisson Diary, February 6, 8, 1864, Sisson Collection, OHS; Garfield, *Wild Life of the Army*, 212, 243, 258, 267.

42. Scribner, *How Soldiers Were Made*, 201–4; Carlin, *Memoirs of Brigadier General*, 266; Humphrey H. Hood to his wife, December 6, 1862, Hood Papers, ALPL; Brackett, *Surgeon on Horseback*, 176–77.

43. Paine, *Wisconsin Yankee*, 92; Hartzell, *Ohio Volunteer*, 108–9; Robert H. Carnahan to his wife, January 9, 1862, Carnahan Papers, USAMHI; Lucius D. Hinkley to his mother, February 15, 1863, Hinkley Papers, WHS. Also see George C. Burmeister Diary, October 3, 1863, CWMC, USAMHI; and Harvey S. Wood to his wife, December 15, 1862, Wood Family Papers, Cincinnati HS. Wood described his young servant as a dirty "Little Cub."

44. Alfred Pirtle to his father, February 25, 1862, January 30, 1863, Pirtle to his mother, April 15, May 4, 13, June 1, 27, July 20, 24, August 10, December 16, 21, 1862, January 8, 14, February 17, March 26, April 5, 1863, and Pirtle to his sister, July 21, 1862, Pirtle Papers, FHS.

45. Bradley, *Star Corps*, 195; Alvah Stone Skilton Diary, September 18, 1864, Skilton Papers, RBHPC; Connolly, *Three Years in the Army*, 359, 360; Thomas E. Smith to his brother, December 27, 1864, Smith Family Papers, Cincinnati HS; Seymour Howell to John Corden, December 29, 1864, Corden Papers, BHL.

46. Jackson, *Colonel's Diary*, 192–94; Charles W. Felker to his wife, April 5, May 2, 1865, Felker Letters, WHS; Daniel R. Sheiler to his sister, March 20, 1865, Fitch Papers, BHL.

47. William P. Moore Diary, ca. May 1862, WHS; Albert G. Hart to "Mary," July 24, 1862, Hart Papers, WRHS; Channing Richards to his sister, March 22, 1863, Richards Papers, FHS.

48. Kircher, *German in the Yankee Fatherland*, 91–92; William M. Ferry to his wife, December 9, 1862, Ferry Family Papers, BHL; Joseph Bailey to "captain," September 17, 1864, Bailey-Stroud Papers, USAMHI. There were a few exceptions to the general trend of officers disapproving of racial equality; see Daniels, *Thank God My Regiment*, 68–69, 127–28; and Bennitt, *"I Hope to Do My Country Service,"* 365–66, 368–69.

49. William T. Sherman, *Sherman's Civil War*, 740–41, 888–89; William T. Sherman, *Sherman Letters*, 252, 261–62.

50. William T. Sherman, *Sherman Letters*, 248; William T. Sherman, *Sherman's Civil War*, 897, 899–901; Schofield, *Forty-Six Years in the Army*, 373–77; James Harrison Wilson, *Under the Old Flag*, 2:557–62, 563, 566–67, 549–50.

51. Squier, *This Wilderness of War*, 119–21; Engs and Brooks, *Their Patriotic Duty*, 357–58. See Manning, *What This Cruel War Was Over*, 191–93, for a differing interpretation of Union soldiers and their commitment to black equality and rights. Manning maintains that although the army was divided in sentiment on the issue of black rights, "in the final months of the Civil War, a critical mass of white Union troops supported expanded rights for African Americans, and believed that the U.S. government had a duty to work toward equality for black citizens." This study finds that this was not the case when it came to western Union officers. Most of them were against black equality and political rights.

CHAPTER 5

1. Lamers, *Edge of Glory*, 12–15, 18, 180–83, 245–47; Bickham, *Rosecrans' Campaign*, 85, 143–44; Warner, *Generals in Blue*, 410–11.

2. *OR*, ser. 1, 23(2):17–18. On the difficulty of compensating loyal masters of slaves, see Berlin et al., *Freedom*, ser. 1, 2:392–94, 408–10.

3. George W. Landrum to Christiana Wilson, February 19, 1863, Landrum Letters, OHS; Thomas E. Smith to "Skip," April 1, 1863, Smith Family Papers, Cincinnati HS; Berlin et al., *Freedom*, ser. 1, 2:398; *OR*, ser. 1, 23(1):269–70; also see William A. Brown to his mother, April 9, 1863, Brown Family Papers, OHS. Brown wrote that "great droves of them [black people] have been coming in all winter; we have used many of them in policing the town—scraping and sweaping the streets, and the post Quartermaster finds employment for a number in various capacities of teamsters and scavaging about hospitals &c. Hundreds have been sent south, to Nashville and Murfreesboro for police duty, and I presume will be worked in trenches, also, and on fortifications to save the soldiers." Some officers took advantage of the situation to find servants. Lt. Alfred Pirtle of the Tenth Ohio employed a good groom to care for his beloved horse that had been badly neglected by his other servant. "He makes 'Old Starry' shine like a dollar," Pirtle happily commented. After one servant failed to return from foraging, Lt. Orville Chamberlain's Seventy-Fourth Indiana acquired two others who provided much in the way of entertainment. The two black men, however, did not want to move away from the region with the army because they would have to leave behind their families. See Alfred Pirtle to his father, January 30, 1863, and Pirtle to his mother, March 26, April 5, 1863, Pirtle Papers, FHS; Orville T. Chamberlain to his brother, March 22, 1863, and Chamberlain to "Friends," March 24, May 31, 1863, Chamberlain Papers, IHS.

4. Berlin et al., *Freedom*, ser. 1, 2:396–97; Cimprich, *Slavery's End in Tennessee*, 38, 46–48, 50–59; Garfield, *Wild Life of the Army*, 257; Ash, *Middle Tennessee Society Transformed*, 135–40; Downs, *Sick from Freedom*, 25.

5. Crofts, *Reluctant Confederates*, 45–46, 54, 63–64, 81–82, 85, 341–45; Cimprich, *Slavery's End in Tennessee*, 2; Woodworth, *Six Armies in Tennessee*, 61–62. See Woodworth, *Six Armies in Tennessee*, 19–78; and Daniel, *Days of Glory*, 265–76, 285–313, for detailed descriptions of Rosecrans's movements in the Tullahoma and Chickamauga and Chattanooga campaigns. The author would especially like to thank Jim Ogden, the chief historian of the Chickamauga and Chattanooga National Military Park, for helping to identify the counties the Union army marched through during these campaigns. The people of East Tennessee voted against secession 32,323 to 15,782, and many East Tennesseans joined the Union cause. Although exact numbers are impossible to know, official reports at the end of the war included over 31,000 white Tennesseans who fought for the Union. A heavy majority of them came from East Tennessee; see Crofts, *Reluctant Confederates*, 341–42; and Current, *Lincoln's Loyalists*, 59–60, 133, 214–15. For some detailed discussions of East Tennessee Unionists, see Martha L. Turner, "The Cause of the Union," 366–80; Sheeler, "The Development of Unionism," 166–75; and Hess, *Civil War in the West*, 22–26. On north Alabama's loyalty, see Danielson, *War's Desolating Scourge*, 2–3, 44, 90–91, 127, 131–32, 141. On Georgia, see Bryan, *Confederate Georgia*, 14, 32, 137; and Inscoe, "Unionists."

6. Library of Congress, "Map showing the distribution of the slave population"; University of Virginia Library, "Historical Census Browser (1860)"; Ash, *Middle Tennessee Society Transformed*, 3–11. For a valuable discussion of Buell's Chattanooga campaign, see Prokopowicz, "Last Chance for a Short War," 36–59.

7. *OR*, ser. 1, 23(2):526–27; 23(1):826; excerpt taken from "History of the Ninety-Second Illinois," 91–92, found in Thomas Winston Papers, USAMHI.

8. Stanley, *Personal Memoirs*, 151–52. Some of Stanley's men had to deal with citizens coming into their lines trying to reclaim their slaves; they apparently refused to return them. See William E. Crane Diary, July 18, 21, 22, 26, 1863, Cincinnati HS.

9. Beatty, *Citizen-Soldier*, 303; William W. Van Antwerp to his wife, July 20, 1863, Van Antwerp Papers, BHL.

10. *OR*, ser. 1, 30(1):687–89; Opdycke, *To Battle for God*, 94–95.

11. James Harrison Wilson, *Under the Old Flag*, 1:189–90; also see John Quincy Adams Campbell, *Union Must Stand*, 216–18.

12. Kolchin, *American Slavery*, 242; Moore, *Agriculture in Ante-bellum Mississippi*, 115; Cooper and Terrill, *American South*, 193; Library of Congress, "Map showing the distribution of the slave population"; University of Virginia Library, "Historical Census Browser (1860)." The author would like to especially thank David Slay, PhD, a National Park Service ranger at the Vicksburg National Military Park, for his assistance in identifying the counties that Grant's army campaigned in during his extensive operations against Vicksburg. For detailed descriptions and maps of the Vicksburg campaign, see Ballard, *Vicksburg*, 191–318; Shea and Winschel, *Vicksburg Is the Key*, 3, 19, 40, 66, 97, 106–39; and Grabau, *Ninety-Eight Days*, 535–602. On Adm. David Farragut's naval operation against Vicksburg in the summer of 1862, see Ballard, *Civil War in Mississippi*, 37–54.

13. McCrary, Miller, and Baum, "Class and Party in the Secession Crisis," 436–38; Woolley and Peters, "Election of 1860"; Rainwater, *Mississippi*, 5, 15, 193–95, 198–201, 207–17; Barney, *Secessionist Impulse*, 54–55, 77–78, 95–96, 101–5, 108–9, 126–27, 130, 132–33, 144–47, 198–99, 201, 231, 263, 265, 272, 285–92, 306–8, 319–20. Vicksburg was located in Warren County, which voted for John Bell during the 1860 presidential election and voted heavily for cooperationist delegates for the secession convention. Despite the county's strong opposition to at least immediate secession and its pro-Union sentiment, its citizens became more pro-Confederate once Mississippi left the Union and they knew they could be attacked by the Union army. See Rainwater, *Mississippi*, 199; and Ballard, *Vicksburg*, 5–8, 11. On Mississippi Unionists, see Cockrell, "Patriots or Traitors," 31–54; and Timothy B. Smith, *Mississippi in the Civil War*, 2, 125–42. On difficulties with the white population of Mississippi, see Hess, *Civil War in the West*, 166–67. On the beginning of Grant's hard war strategy during the Vicksburg campaign, see Grimsley, *Hard Hand of War*, 142–44, 151–58; and Dossman, "The 'Stealing Tour,'" 194–213.

14. Grant, *Papers of Ulysses S. Grant*, 7:278–80; *OR*, ser. 1, 24(1):15; Vermilion and Vermilion, *Love Amid the Turmoil*, 50; also see Kircher, *German in the Yankee Fatherland*, 61.

15. Stevens, *"Dear Carrie,"* 40; Ephraim Brown to Drusilla Brown, January 25, 1863, Brown Papers, OHS; Seneca B. Thrall to his wife, February 25, 1863, in Thrall, "Seneca B. Thrall Union Letters."

16. *OR*, ser. 1, 24(3):46–47, 156–57; 24(1):18; Grimsley, *Hard Hand of War*, 140–41; Simpson, *Ulysses S. Grant*, 179–80.

17. Berlin et al., *Freedom*, ser. 1, 3:630–41, 699–702. For the problems black laborers faced on the leased plantations, see Gerteis, *From Contraband to Freedman*, 122–33.

18. *OR*, ser. 1, 24(3):186–87; 24(1):73–74; Ritner and Ritner, *Love and Valor*, 157–58, 159–60; Charles Dana Miller, *Struggle for the Life*, 91, 259; Asa A. Lawrence to his wife,

April 22, 1863, Lawrence Papers, WRHS; Grimsley, *Hard Hand of War*, 151–52. The slaves who became soldiers during the expedition were more than willing. "It is becoming a perfect mania with the colored population to become yankees; and most of the men express their willingness to fight for their freedom," Steele wrote to Sherman; see Grant, *Papers of Ulysses S. Grant*, 8:51. At this time, Grant faced significant pressure from Washington to enlist black men in the service. Adj. Gen. Lorenzo Thomas was just then visiting the army to encourage the soldiers to embrace the enlistment of black troops. Grant endorsed this policy and made sure that his officers carried it out; see Simpson, *Ulysses S. Grant*, 186–87; and Catton, *Grant Moves South*, 401–5.

19. Grant, *Papers of Ulysses S. Grant*, 8:262; Ballard, *Vicksburg*, 286; Bennet Grigsby to his wife and children, May 18, 1863, Grigsby-McDonald Papers, IHS; OR, ser. 1, 24(1):734–36.

20. Grant, *Papers of Ulysses S. Grant*, 7:415, 417; 8:370; OR, ser. 1, 24(2):176–78; Samuel Calvin Jones, *Reminiscences of the Twenty-Second Iowa*, 40.

21. OR, ser. 1, 24(3):351, 362; 24(2):435–36; Grant, *Papers of Ulysses S. Grant*, 8:278.

22. OR, ser. 1, 24(3):470, 483, 484, 487; Catton, *Grant Moves South*, 480–81.

23. OR, ser. 1, 24(3):330, 400; 24(2):427–28; Engs and Brooks, *Their Patriotic Duty*, 139, 141–42; Rankin P. McPheeters to Annie M. McPheeters, May 17, 1863, McPheeters Family Papers, USAMHI.

24. Berlin et al., *Freedom*, ser. 1, 1:302–3; Grant, *Papers of Ulysses S. Grant*, 8:173, 177, 197, 512, 341, 351, 406, 416; OR, ser. 1, 24(3):292. Sometimes, information from black people could help officers on the ground escape perilous situations. An officer in the Twelfth Missouri, Henry Kircher, mentioned how a black man prevented the Twenty-Fourth Indiana from being flanked by three Confederate regiments. "So the Negroes are good for something," Kircher remarked. "The Black will probably soon become a major general, as he already knows what flanking is"; see Kircher, *German in the Yankee Fatherland*, 85. Slaves also greatly assisted the Union army in the eastern theater with information about the enemy and the local geography; see Brasher, *Peninsula Campaign*, for a detailed exploration of the ways black Southerners helped the army during that campaign. Brasher persuasively argues that this help was an important factor in pushing the Northern public to embrace emancipation.

25. Grierson, *Just and Righteous Cause*, 161–62, 177–78; George C. Burmeister Diary, May 11, 1863, CWMC, USAMHI; Sparks, "Memoirs and Letters of David Rhodes Sparks (unpublished)," 70, in Herrick Papers, USAMHI. Also see Dwight, "Four Year's Relics," 59, in Dwight Papers, OHS; and Ayling, *Yankee at Arms*, 151.

26. Grant, *Papers of Ulysses S. Grant*, 9:218; OR, ser. 1, 30(3):694–700.

27. Grant, *Papers of Ulysses S. Grant*, 9:135–37; OR, ser. 1, 24(3):585.

28. Grant, *Papers of Ulysses S. Grant*, 9:112; OR, ser. 1, 30(3):26, 476.

29. Robert F. Braden to his mother, July 22, 1863, Beach Family Histories, IHS; Albert J. Rockwell to Anna P. Rockwell, July 23, 1863, Rockwell Letters, WHS. A few months before black men were being used to fortify Vicksburg, Capt. Thomas Stevens of the Twenty-Eighth Wisconsin wrote how fortifications were being built in Helena, Arkansas, with the help of black labor: "The negro brigade is being made useful with the spade & pickaxe (the drill is 'hard-ee' instead of Scott!) building forts &c., &c. 'Long may they wave' while they help us"; see Stevens, *"Dear Carrie,"* 96.

30. Downs, *Sick from Freedom*, 26–27; Berlin and Rowland, *Families and Freedom*, 59–62.

31. *OR*, ser. 1, 24(3):570–71; 30(3):212–13, 401–4; Grant, *Papers of Ulysses S. Grant*, 9:133–34.

32. Grant, *Papers of Ulysses S. Grant*, 9:207–9; *OR*, ser. 1, 30(4):233–34. When slaves were seized from known Unionists, it could cause much turmoil. Large plantation owners, Mr. and Mrs. Henry Duncan, were strong Unionists who had hired their slaves. Despite this, a Union officer pressed nearly all their black males into the army. Mrs. Duncan appealed directly to Washington, and Grant ordered a full investigation and wanted responsible parties arrested. The officer who had taken the slaves, however, had already been killed in combat. With this the matter was laid to rest. See *OR*, ser. 1, 24(3):500–501; and Grant, *Papers of Ulysses S. Grant*, 9:23–26 39–40. On Grant's efforts to promote Unionism, see Simpson, *Ulysses S. Grant*, 223–25; and Catton, *Grant Takes Command*, 19–21. On the disaffection among some white Mississippians following the Vicksburg campaign, see Timothy B. Smith, *Mississippi in the Civil War*, 2–3, 119–24; and Hess, *Civil War in the West*, 165–66.

33. Hollandsworth, *Pretense of Glory*, 7–9, 11–12, 20–21, 23–35, 38, 43, 44–46, 50–69, 72–82, 84–85; Warner, *Generals in Blue*, 17–18.

34. Grimsley, *Hard Hand of War*, 139; Gerteis, *From Contraband to Freedman*, 73–75; Foner, *The Fiery Trial*, 242. Banks himself noted how slaves from exempted parishes were "slaves *de jure*" but "not *de facto*"; see McCrary, *Abraham Lincoln and Reconstruction*, 114.

35. Winters, *Civil War in Louisiana*, 207–8; Bosson, *History of the Forty-Second Regiment Infantry*, 334–42; John Grey McDermott to "Isabella," January 1, 25, 1863, McDermott Letters, WHS. The black laborers lived in squalid conditions; see McCrary, *Abraham Lincoln and Reconstruction*, 114–15.

36. *OR*, ser. 1, 15:666–67; 34(2):227–31; McPherson, *Battle Cry of Freedom*, 71; Grimsley, *Hard Hand of War*, 139–40; Gerteis, *From Contraband to Freedman*, 73–82. See Hollandsworth, *Pretense of Glory*, 94–95, for some of the more positive aspects of Banks's system. Under Banks's system, abandoned and confiscated plantations were worked by black Southerners for the benefit of the government.

37. Cunningham, *Port Hudson Campaign*, 34; Hollandsworth, *Pretense of Glory*, 115; George G. Smith, *Leaves from a Soldier's Diary*, 50–51; Hepworth, *Whip, Hoe and Sword*, 139–43, 146–48. Hollandsworth states that 6,000 slaves were reportedly liberated by Banks in the Teche country.

38. Cornish, *Sable Arm*, 126–27. The Louisiana regiments of black troops that Butler had previously organized were absorbed into Banks's African Corps. The black officers in Butler's regiments were replaced with white ones. See Kinsley, *Diary of a Christian Soldier*, 34, 36–37; and Daniels, *Thank God My Regiment*, 36, 110. Banks did not believe that the black officers were competent and did not think the white soldiers were ready to accept them.

39. Ripley, *Slaves and Freedmen*, 109; Berlin et al., *Freedom*, ser. 2, 1:151–52. Some of the forced enlistment was done under the authority of Brig. Gen. Daniel Ullmann, who had orders from the War Department to recruit a black brigade in the Gulf. Banks did not like Ullmann and did not want his recruiting efforts to interfere with his contract labor system. But Banks had a hard time controlling Ullmann, whose

authority came directly from Washington. In June 1863, Banks absorbed Ullmann's troops into his African Corps. Heavy-handed recruitment, however, continued. On Ullmann and other instances of forced enlistment, see Ripley, *Slaves and Freedmen*, 106–14; Berlin et al., *Freedom*, ser. 2 1:116, 118–19, 144–46, 150–52, 157–61; and *OR*, ser. 1, 26(1):736–38.

40. *OR*, ser. 1, 26(1):497, 649–50, 688–89. By the time Banks left the Department of the Gulf, he had enlisted more black troops than any other Union commander. More than twenty-eight regiments of black soldiers served under him at that time; see Hollandsworth, *Pretense of Glory*, 153.

41. Hollandsworth, *Pretense of Glory*, 152–53; Harrison Soule to his wife, September 24, 1863, Soule Papers, BHL.

42. *OR*, ser. 1, 26(1):775, 780; John C. Dinsmore to his wife, November 5, 1863, Dinsmore Papers, ALPL; Harrison Soule to his wife, July 24, 1863, Soule Papers, BHL.

43. See William C. Harris, *Lincoln and the Border States*, 159–93, for Lincoln's efforts to enact compensated emancipation in the border states.

44. *OR*, ser. 1, 22(2):88–89, 134–37; Berlin et al., *Freedom*, ser. 1, 1:444–45, 449–50. Despite Curtis's orders, slaves of loyal Missourians did make their way into Federal lines; see Berlin et al., *Freedom*, ser. 1, 1:450–53, 454–56.

45. William C. Harris, *Lincoln and the Border States*, 308–18; Connelly, *John M. Schofield*, 63–66.

46. Connelly, *John M. Schofield*, 19, 21–22, 25–26, 33–35, 41–57; McDonough, *Schofield*, 9–10, 13, 29; Warner, *Generals in Blue*, 425–26.

47. Schofield, *Forty-Six Years in the Army*, 56–58, 74–75; Connelly, *John M. Schofield*, 63–64; Berlin et al., *Freedom*, ser. 1, 1:408–9. Interestingly, Schofield asked the War Department about whether the military or the courts were empowered to give the slaves freedom under the confiscation acts. The judge advocate general told Schofield that, at least under the Second Confiscation Act, slaves should be protected by the army and given certificates declaring them to be captives of war. Despite these instructions, Schofield did not change his previous orders that put the courts in charge of confiscation; see Berlin et al., *Freedom*, ser. 1, 1:461–65.

48. William C. Harris, *Lincoln and the Border States*, 321–25; Foner, *Fiery Trial*, 277–78; *OR*, ser. 1, 22(2):301, 330, 331–32; Schofield, *Forty-Six Years in the Army*, 75–76.

49. Berlin et al., *Freedom*, ser. 2, 1:187–88, 230–32; *OR*, ser. 3, 3:860–61, 1034–36. Before the fall of 1863 there was some limited recruitment of black men in Missouri, but most of the time it involved taking black men out of state to be made soldiers. In particular, in August 1863, Brig. Gen. Thomas Ewing took slaves from rebel masters in a few western Missouri counties and escorted them to Kansas, where they were enlisted; see *OR*, ser. 1, 22(2):450, 460–61, 482–84. At the same time Lincoln ordered Schofield to recruit black men in Missouri, he ordered their recruitment in Maryland and Tennessee. Only Kentucky was still exempt from black recruitment. In the summer of 1863, a Federal army of white men, black men, and Native Americans operated in the Indian Territory in present-day Oklahoma and won some significant victories together. This force, however, was unique in its composition and led by prominent abolitionist officers. It certainly did not represent the dominant attitudes

or policies of the Union army. This diverse army was very much the product of the circumstances on the western frontier. See Lause, *Race and Radicalism*, for an excellent study of these troops.

50. *OR*, ser. 1, 34(2):160–61, 551–53; Berlin et al., *Freedom*, ser. 1, 1:410–12; ser. 2, 1:188–90. In January 1865, Missouri officially abolished slavery.

51. Berlin et al., *Freedom*, ser. 1, 1:548–49, 506; *OR*, ser. 1, 23(2):287.

52. Warner, *Generals in Blue*, 57–58; McPherson, *Battle Cry of Freedom*, 372–73, 543, 571–72; Marvel, *Burnside*, 12, 20, 90–91, 97, 422.

53. Byron M. Cutcheon, "Autobiography," 96–98, in Cutcheon Papers, BHL; Morris S. Hall, "Autobiographical Sketch and Reminiscences," 78–79, in Hall Papers, BHL; Oliver L. Spaulding, "Military Memoirs," 21, in Spaulding Papers, BHL; N. G. Markham to his family, April 13, 1863, Markham Papers, FHS. Spaulding said the orders to expel the slaves came directly from Boyle. Undoubtedly, Manson was carrying out Boyle's policy regarding slaves.

54. Oliver L. Spaulding Diary, January 13, February 19, March 7, 1863, and Spaulding, "Military Memoirs," 20–21, Spaulding Papers, BHL.

55. Berlin et al., *Freedom*, ser. 1, 1:577–79, 503–6, 572–74; Moore, "A Copy of the Original Military Records written by Colonel Orlando Hurley Moore United States Army," 5–6, in Moore Papers, BHL; *OR*, ser. 1, 23(2):291, 287. In early January 1863, two Kentucky captains in the Union army actually bid for a slave being auctioned off in Louisville. A Michigan officer was horrified by the whole affair; see Asa Slayton Journal, January 5, 1863, reprinted in *Grand Rapids Weekly Eagle*, Slayton Family Papers, BHL.

56. Berlin et al., *Freedom*, ser. 1, 1:574–76, 507.

57. Berlin et al., *Freedom*, ser. 1, 1:585–87, 508–9; *OR*, ser. 1, 30(3):92–93, 786–87; Cox, *Military Reminiscences of the Civil War*, 2:21–22. There was some limited impressment of Kentucky slaves by the army before the summer of 1863; see Victor B. Howard, *Black Liberation in Kentucky*, 45–47.

58. William C. Harris, *Lincoln and the Border States*, 223–24, 226–29, 237–38; Victor B. Howard, *Black Liberation in Kentucky*, 47–57; Berlin et al., *Freedom*, ser. 2, 1:191–92. In February 1864, Congress amended the Enrollment Act of March 1863 to explicitly include black men. The original had not excluded them, but it had not specifically mentioned them either.

59. Thomas Bramlette to Stephen Burbridge, March 14, 1864, Burbridge Papers, FHS; William C. Harris, *Lincoln and the Border States*, 238–40; Victor B. Howard, *Black Liberation in Kentucky*, 59–61.

60. *OR*, ser. 3, 4:233–34; Thomas Brooks Fairleigh Diary, April 18, 1864, FHS. When Governor Bramlette challenged Burbridge, saying that he had no authority to recruit black troops, Burbridge responded by citing the Second Confiscation Act and the February 1864 Enrollment Act. See Stephen Burbridge to Thomas Bramlette, June 16, 1864, Burbridge Papers, FHS; and *OR*, ser. 1, 39(2):76–77.

61. *OR*, ser. 1, 39(2):81, 212–15; William C. Harris, *Lincoln and the Border States*, 242. This number for Kentucky black soldiers is low because, as Harris notes, it does not account for the black men who enlisted in regiments being raised in adjoining states before Kentucky began recruiting. Slavery did not officially end in Kentucky

until December 1865 with the ratification of the Thirteenth Amendment to the Constitution.

CHAPTER 6

1. William T. Sherman, *Sherman's Civil War*, 613. Sherman's comments tie in well with the recent arguments of Gary W. Gallagher in *Union War*. Gallagher emphasizes that the North fought primarily to save the Union, and emancipation was mainly seen as a practical measure to achieve that objective; see Gallagher, *Union War*, 1–6, 34–35, 76–77.

2. William T. Sherman, *Sherman's Civil War*, 311–12, 537, 574, 582, 688; William T. Sherman, *Sherman Letters*, 221–22; Marszalek, *Sherman*, 45–46, 126, 191–93, 271; Mohr, *On the Threshold of Freedom*, 90.

3. Marszalek, *Sherman*, 256–59. On hard war and Grant's strategy for the spring 1864 Union offensive, see Grimsley, *Hard Hand of War*, 165–66.

4. *OR*, ser. 1, 32(2):267–70; Bennitt, *"I Hope to Do My Country Service,"* 244, 258–59. Around the same time, Brig. Gen. Ralph Buckland contended that "slavery is dead beyond the possibility of resurrection"; see Buckland to his son, March 9, 1864, Buckland Papers, RBHPC.

5. Wills, *Army Life of an Illinois Soldier*, 237, 246; *OR*, ser. 1, 39(2):132; Mohr, "The Atlanta Campaign," 272, 273–75; also see *OR*, ser. 1, 32(2):476–77.

6. Library of Congress, "Map showing the distribution of the slave population"; University of Virginia Library, "Historical Census Browser (1860)"; Weitz, *Higher Duty*, 11–13, 18–26. The author would like to especially thank Erica Hague, a collections and reference assistant at the Atlanta History Center, for her invaluable assistance in identifying the counties Sherman's army went through during the Atlanta campaign and the subsequent March to the Sea. Additionally, the author would like to thank Bill Dyer, a Civil War expert at the same location, for his help with this same issue. For some maps on the Atlanta campaign, see Castel, *Decision in the West*, 13, 122, 187, 210, 337. Castel offers an exhaustive account of the campaign.

7. Carey, *Parties, Slavery, and the Union*, xvii, 229, 230–31; Burnham, *Presidential Ballots*, 172–75, 332–62; Michael P. Johnson, *Toward a Patriarchal Republic*, 60–61, 65–70, 120–23; Bryan, *Confederate Georgia*, 4–5, 8–10, 137, 145–46, 159; Weitz, *Higher Duty*, 14–15. See Hebert, "'The Bottomless Pit of Hell,'" 127–49, for a discussion of Cass (Bartow) County's rebel sympathies and its resistance to Union occupation. Federal forces devastated the county. In *Higher Duty*, Mark Weitz points out that north Georgia, along with other regions of the state, contributed a number of troops proportional to its overall population. But in the latter part of the war, as Weitz brilliantly demonstrates, Sherman's campaign increased Confederate desertion rates among north Georgia soldiers. Soldiers felt they needed to protect hearth and home from the invaders and thus abandoned the Confederacy; see Weitz, *Higher Duty*, 30–31, 78–81. Also on disaffection in north Georgia, see Bryan, *Confederate Georgia*, 139–44, 150–51.

8. William T. Sherman, *Memoirs*, 2:54–56; *OR*, ser. 3, 4:433–34. The organization of pioneers was never as uniform as Sherman indicated. They were organized into different-sized units at different times; see Mohr, "Atlanta Campaign," 281.

9. *OR*, ser. 1, 38(4):400, 542–43, 571–72; 39(2):132; 38(5):305–6; William T. Sherman, *Sherman's Civil War*, 657–58. Sherman's candid letter to the Massachusetts recruiter, detailing his opposition to black troops and his racial prejudice, was published and got him into trouble with the administration. At the beginning of September 1864, Sherman wrote Henry Halleck: "I hope anything I may have said or done will not be construed unfriendly to Mr. Lincoln or Stanton. That negro letter of mine I never designed for publication, but I am honest in my belief that it is not fair to our men to count negroes as equals." See William T. Sherman, *Sherman's Civil War*, 699–700; and Marszalek, *Sherman*, 270–71.

10. *OR*, ser. 1, 38(5):120–21; Heber S. Thompson Diary, May 29, 1864, Harrisburg Civil War Round Table Collection, USAMHI; Castel, *Decision in the West*, 436–42; Mohr, "Atlanta Campaign," 284.

11. *OR*, ser. 1, 38(5):248, 250–51, 433–34; 38(1):174–75; 38(2):809, 925–29; George W. Gallup to his wife, July 24, 1864, and Gallup Diary, July 25, 1864, Gallup Papers, FHS.

12. Mohr, "Atlanta Campaign," 287; *OR*, ser. 1, 39(1):653–54; Lyman Daniel Ames Diary, July 9, October 11, 1864, *CWTIC*, USAMHI.

13. Williams, *From the Cannon's Mouth*, 351, 378–79.

14. *OR*, ser. 1, 38(5):791–94; William W. Van Antwerp to his wife, August 26, September 8, 1864, Van Antwerp Papers, BHL.

15. Henry Albert Potter to his father, September 29, 1864, Potter Papers, BHL.

16. Grimsley, *Hard Hand of War*, 190–91; Marszalek, *Sherman*, 293–97; Glatthaar, *March to the Sea and Beyond*, 6–7.

17. Mohr, *On the Threshold of Freedom*, 68; Bryan, *Confederate Georgia*, 75–77; Weitz, *Higher Duty*, 3, 12–16, 30–31; Michael P. Johnson, *Toward a Patriarchal Republic*, 60–61, 70–78, 120–21, 197–98, 200–201, 206–8; Burnham, *Presidential Ballots*, 172–75, 332–62. On the rebellious white Georgia population during the march, see Trudeau, *Southern Storm*, 126, 140; Rubin, *Through the Heart of Dixie*, 47, 48–49, 57–59, 61–63; and Glatthaar, *March to the Sea and Beyond*, 69, 71–72. On disenchantment, see Glatthaar, *March to the Sea and Beyond*, 70; and Kennett, *Marching through Georgia*, 312–13. For some useful maps on the march, see Bell and Rubin, "Sherman's March and America."

18. Library of Congress, "Map showing the distribution of the slave population"; University of Virginia Library, "Historical Census Browser (1860)"; Weitz, *Higher Duty*, 15–18, 27. For a good discussion of the cotton culture of central Georgia, see Reidy, *From Slavery to Agrarian Capitalism*, 31–81. For a useful examination of the Georgia Lowcountry and the war's effect on the area, see Jacqueline Jones, "Georgia Lowcountry Battlegrounds," 67–93. It is important to note that, as in other areas, these figures for slaves are for 1860. This campaign took place in 1864, so the numbers, of course, are not completely accurate. While central Georgia was spared Union invasion until Sherman's army arrived, coastal Georgia, as mentioned, was significantly disrupted by Union naval and army operations. As a result, some planters decided to evacuate their slaves from the area. On these specific operations and their effect on the enslaved people of the region, see Mohr, *On the Threshold of Freedom*, 68–86, 99–119.

19. *OR*, ser. 1, 39(2):713–14, 701.

20. William T. Sherman, *Memoirs*, 2:180–81; Hitchcock, *Marching with Sherman*, 70–72, 127–28; Marszalek, *Sherman*, 312.

21. Hitchcock, *Marching with Sherman*, 122–23, 126–27, 65; Nichols, *Story of the Great March*, 71–72.

22. *OR*, ser. 1, 44:166–67, 756, 768–69, 481–82; Hazen, *Narrative of Military Service*, 325, 328.

23. *OR*, ser. 1, 44:170–71, 179, 261; Wills, *Army Life of an Illinois Soldier*, 330.

24. Connolly, *Three Years in the Army*, 313.

25. Fitch, *Echoes of the Civil War*, 336–37; Alfred H. Trego Diary, November 29, 1864, Chicago HS; "The Reminiscences of General Andrew Hickenlooper, 1861–1865," 88, Hickenlooper Reminiscences, *CWTIC*, USAMHI.

26. Hedley, *Marching through Georgia*, 311–12; William T. Sherman, *Sherman's Civil War*, 778; William T. Sherman, *Memoirs*, 2:185–87; Bonner, "Sherman at Milledgeville," 276–77. In Savannah, Maj. Henry Hitchcock observed Sherman shaking hands with black people. The black people hailed Sherman as their deliverer, saying things to him like, "Been prayin' for you all long time, Sir, prayin' day and night for you, and now, bless God, you is come"; see Hitchcock, *Marching with Sherman*, 202–3.

27. "The Reminiscences of General Andrew Hickenlooper, 1861–1865," 88, Hickenlooper Reminiscences, *CWTIC*, USAMHI; *OR*, ser. 1, 44:648–49, 683–84; also see Hedley, *Marching through Georgia*, 312–13.

28. Bradley, *Star Corps*, 188; Wills, *Army Life of an Illinois Soldier*, 331–32; Jackson, *Colonel's Diary*, 164–65.

29. Otto, *Memoirs of a Dutch Mudsill*, 300, 306; William Henry Pittenger Diary, December 4, 1864, OHS.

30. Carlin, *Memoirs of Brigadier General*, 145; *OR*, ser. 1, 44:502. In *When Sherman Marched*, Jacqueline Glass Campbell argues that the men in the ranks also viewed the slaves following the army as an "encumbrance" (17).

31. Marszalek, *Sherman*, 312–13; Hughes and Whitney, *Jefferson Davis in Blue*, 305–9; Carlin, *Memoirs of Brigadier General*, 157–58. Hughes and Whitney note that no evidence exists of Confederate cavalry killing the black people abandoned at Ebenezer Creek, and it was unlikely that it happened, since the commander of the cavalry, Maj. Gen. Joseph Wheeler, usually returned captured slaves to their owners.

32. Hughes and Whitney, *Jefferson Davis in Blue*, 309–14; Connolly, *Three Years in the Army*, 354–55. See Fitch, *Echoes of the Civil War*, 236, for more officer dismay over Davis's actions. Connolly followed up his protest at the creek with a letter to the U.S. Senate detailing Davis's treatment of the black refugees. He hoped to influence the pending confirmation of Davis as a major general, which he very well might have as Davis was never confirmed; see Connolly, *Three Years in the Army*, 367, 389.

33. *OR*, ser. 1, 44:211–12.

34. Connolly, *Three Years in the Army*, 339–40, 362–63. Baird only reported having 668 slaves with him when he reached Savannah, but this is probably far from the actual number he brought into his lines during the march. His division was one of those that crossed Ebenezer Creek and undoubtedly lost many slaves there; see *OR*, ser. 1, 44:205. Ironically, Baird wrote a very positive letter about Sherman's dealings with black people to his uncle, Gerrit Smith. He had just witnessed Sherman's kind treatment of individual black people who came to speak with him in Savannah. This inspired Baird to think that Sherman was "not simply a great man but a good man as well." Baird obviously did not

know the extent of Sherman's antiblack attitudes; see William T. Sherman, *Memoirs*, 2:570–71.

35. *OR*, ser. 1, 44:700–701; William T. Sherman, *Sherman's Civil War*, 794.

36. Chase, *Salmon P. Chase Papers*, 4:3–4, 6–7; William T. Sherman, *Sherman's Civil War*, 794–95; *OR*, ser. 1, 44:836–37; 47(2):36–37; Marszalek, *Sherman*, 313–14.

37. William T. Sherman, *Memoirs*, 2:244–47; *OR*, ser. 1, 47(2):37–41; Marszalek, *Sherman*, 314; James, "Sherman at Savannah," 127–33. Sherman was deeply offended by Stanton's actions. "It certainly was a strange fact that the great War Secretary should have catechized negroes concerning the character of a general who had commanded a hundred thousand men in battle, had captured cities conducted sixty-five thousand men successfully across four hundred miles of hostile territory, and had just brought tens of thousands of freedmen to a place of security; but because I had not loaded down my army by other hundreds of thousands of poor negroes, I was construed by others as hostile to the black race," Sherman wrote in *Memoirs* (2:247).

38. William T. Sherman, *Memoirs*, 2:249–50; *OR*, ser. 1, 47(2):60–62; William T. Sherman, *Sherman's Civil War*, 760; Otto, *Memoirs of a Dutch Mudsill*, 318–19; O. O. Howard, *Autobiography of Oliver Otis Howard*, 2:191–92; Westwood, "Sherman Marched," 39- 41, 46; Marszalek, *Sherman*, 314–15. Marszalek astutely notes that the Sea Island order "was Stanton's more than it was Sherman's." Westwood agrees with this but also argues that Sherman understood that some plan needed to be adopted to help the black refugees. Westwood, however, goes on to convincingly show that Sherman was complicit in the return of the Sea Island land to white Southerners after the war; see Westwood, "Sherman Marched," 41, 46–47. For a very detailed examination of what happened on the Sea Islands in the postwar period, see Rose, *Rehearsal for Reconstruction*, 346–408. In his biography of Sherman, Michael Fellman argues that the Sea Island order was the result of Sherman's desire to get rid of all the black people encumbering his army and, at the same time, silence his critics in Washington. The general also wanted to punish Confederates through land redistribution; see Fellman, *Citizen Sherman*, 165–70.

39. Barrett, *Sherman's March through the Carolinas*, 26; McPherson, *Battle Cry of Freedom*, 825–26.

40. *OR*, ser. 1, 47(2):99; Hazen, *Narrative of Military Service*, 340.

41. Cyrus M. Roberts Diary, March 9, 1865, CWMC, USAMHI; Osborn, *Fiery Trail*, 121, 92.

42. Cyrus M. Roberts Diary, February 10, 1865, CWMC, USAMHI; Henry Hurter Diary, March 2, 1865, CWTIC, USAMHI; also see *OR*, ser. 1, 47(1):613.

43. *OR*, ser. 1, 47(2):105–6, 365, 608–9; 47(1):269–70. For more on black Southerners helping Sherman's army with information, see *OR*, ser. 1, 47(2):585; 47(1):223–24, 255; and Bradley, *Star Corps*, 265. As they had done during the Savannah campaign, slaves also showed the army where their masters' valuable possessions were hidden; see Bradley, *Star Corps*, 258; Cyrus M. Roberts Diary, March 19, 1865, CWMC, USAMHI; and "The Reminiscences of General Andrew Hickenlooper, 1861–1865," 109, Hickenlooper Reminiscences, CWTIC, USAMHI. Hickenlooper asserted that in "a spirit of friendship," slaves "disclose[d] the hiding places of household treasures."

44. *OR*, ser. 1, 47(2):184–85, 331; Jacqueline Glass Campbell, *When Sherman Marched North*, 45–46, 65–66; Sosnowski, "Burning of Columbia," 195, 203.

45. Cyrus M. Roberts Diary, March 21, 1865, CWMC, USAMHI; Bradley, *Star Corps*, 258.

46. O. O. Howard, *Autobiography of Oliver Otis Howard*, 2:127; Burton, *Diary of E. P. Burton*, 64. On efforts to stop black people from following the army, see Hazen, *Narrative of Military Service*, 339–40; *OR*, ser. 1, 47(2):479; and Dunkelman, *Marching with Sherman*, 126.

47. Wills, *Army Life of an Illinois Soldier*, 360; Jacqueline Glass Campbell, *When Sherman Marched North*, 86–87. Campbell argues that "the majority of Sherman's men regarded the slave population as a tool with which to strike at the economic foundation of Southern society, thus ignoring the humanity of individual African Americans" (45). This study finds the same to be largely true of western Union officers.

48. *OR*, ser. 1, 47(2):816–17, 803, 779, 790–91, 794–95, 798, 830–31; O. O. Howard, *Autobiography of Oliver Otis Howard*, 2:140; Barrett, *Sherman's March through the Carolinas*, 137.

49. Hedley, *Marching through Georgia*, 401–2, 405; Hazen, *Narrative of Military Service*, 358–59; Jackson, *Colonel's Diary*, 192–94. Also see Burton, *Diary of E. P. Burton*, 69; and O. O. Howard, *Autobiography of Oliver Otis Howard*, 2:140.

50. William T. Sherman, *Sherman's Civil War*, 832–33.

51. William T. Sherman, *Memoirs*, 2:482–83. In *On the Threshold of Freedom*, Clarence Mohr notes the military priorities and lack of idealism of Sherman's emancipation policy. He correctly points out that neither the general nor his army "behaved like messianic figures." They could be downright hostile to black Southerners. But what Mohr fails to mention is how much black people still regarded Sherman and his men as their liberators; see Mohr, *On the Threshold of Freedom*, 90–96.

CONCLUSION

1. William T. Sherman, *Sherman's Civil War*, 797–98.

2. See Brasher, *Peninsula Campaign*, for a deep analysis of how the events and eventual failure of the Peninsula campaign persuaded the government and many people in the North to embrace emancipation. Like this study, Brasher emphasizes the importance of military necessity in convincing Northerners to support the idea of freeing the slaves.

3. Burton, *Diary of E. P. Burton*, 76; invitation "To Lt. Col. W. T. Pepper, Officers and Enlisted Men of the Army of the United States at this Post," found in Edward F. Reid Papers, IHS.

4. Thomas Winston to his wife, December 21, 1862, Winston Papers, USAMHI.

5. William M. Ferry to his wife, December 9, 1862, Ferry Family Papers, BHL.

6. Gary W. Gallagher, *Union War*, 151–53; Foner, *Reconstruction*, 176–227, 251–61, 446.

7. Grant, *Personal Memoirs of U. S. Grant*, 2:510–12; Gary W. Gallagher, *Union War*, 155–56.

8. James W. Davidson to his wife, February 24, 1867, Davidson Papers, BGU.

9. On racism as an important factor in the North's retreat from Reconstruction, see Gary W. Gallagher, *Union War*, 152–53; Gillette, *Retreat from Reconstruction*, 366–67; Franklin, *Reconstruction*, 200–201; and Stampp, *Era of Reconstruction*, 193–95. See

Blight, *Race and Reunion*, for a detailed look at how Northerners and Southerners after Reconstruction reconciled under a white supremacist memory of the Civil War that emphasized their common sacrifices and excluded African Americans and emancipation. This form of reconciliation, Blight contends, helped lead to the eventual segregation and disfranchisement of black people in the South. In *Won Cause*, Barbara Gannon challenges the extent of Northern racism after the war by exploring the interracial nature of the Grand Army of the Republic (GAR). She argues that black and white veterans bonded in this organization over their common cause and sacrifices. But it is important to note that her findings are focused just on black veterans, not black people in general. Indeed, Gannon demonstrates that the GAR was often unsympathetic to the civil rights of black Southerners who were not veterans; see Gannon, *Won Cause*, 1–11, 117–77.

NOTES ON METHODOLOGY

1. See McPherson, *For Cause and Comrades*, vii–viii, for a discussion of the difficulty in building a representative sample of Civil War soldiers.

2. Considering that most troops from the Midwest and the Border South served in the western armies, the numbers of overall troops from these regions are useful in very roughly computing the total number of western officers by state, at least in these areas. Around 10 percent of all soldiers served as officers. This does not lead to exact numbers by any means as some midwestern regiments, particularly from Ohio, Indiana, and Michigan, served in the Army of the Potomac, but lacking precise raw data on the nativity of all western officers, it is a useful method for estimating it. See McPherson, *For Cause and Comrades*, ix, for the 10 percent figure for officers; see Gould, *Investigations in the Military*, 15–29, for a discussion of the nativity of all Union soldiers. Gould provides some especially useful tables presenting this information. On army branch of service, see Guelzo, *Fateful Lightning*, 249. Guelzo notes that in the Union army, 80 percent of all soldiers were part of the infantry, 14 percent part of the cavalry, and 6 percent part of the artillery. These percentages would also roughly apply to western officers and their branches of service.

3. Civil War officers were often promoted during the course of the war. When determining an officer's rank, I used the rank that he held for most, or at least a majority, of the war. There were only 583 generals in the Union service, and many of these served in the eastern theater. This is how it is easy to determine that my sample overrepresents general officers; see Warner, *Generals in Blue*, xviii.

4. On chaplains, see Rable, *God's Almost Chosen Peoples*, 113–16. On surgeons, see Freemon, *Gangrene and Glory*, 35–36, 41, 43–46, 48–50; and Schroeder-Lein, *Encyclopedia of Civil War Medicine*, 294, 296. Almost all the chaplains and surgeons in my sample whose prewar occupations could be found had professional jobs.

5. For another sample of Union officers and their corresponding occupations, see McPherson, *For Cause and Comrades*, 182. McPherson's officers were also primarily engaged in professional or white-collar occupations during the antebellum period. McPherson does have many more officers in the white-collar category and far fewer in the professional category. The disparity here probably has a lot to do with the number

of general officers used in this study. Also see Gould, *Investigations in the Military*, 208–9. Gould claims that out of a sample of 3,330 commissioned officers, around four-fifths were probably from the professional class. On officers' average age, see Gould, *Investigations in the Military*, 57–58. For age, I used the officer's age when he entered the service, or if he was not an officer upon enlistment, I used the age when he became an officer.

6. Generals who graduated from West Point are probably a bit overrepresented in the sample; 37.2 percent of all Union generals were West Point graduates. Given that Union generals were pretty evenly distributed between the major theaters of war, this percentage is probably fairly accurate for all western generals; see Warner, *Generals in Blue*, xx.

BIBLIOGRAPHY

PRIMARY SOURCES

Manuscript Collections

Abraham Lincoln Presidential Library, Springfield, Illinois
Samuel Ryan Curtis Papers
John C. Dinsmore Papers
Evangelist J. Gillmore Papers
Isham Nicholas Haynie Papers
Henry F. Hole Papers
Humphrey H. Hood Papers
Robert B. Latham Papers
John A. McClernand Papers
Moore Family Papers
E. H. Owen Letter
George H. Palmer Biography
G. W. Roberts Letters
Harley Wayne Correspondence
Lysander R. Webb Letter
Philip Welshimer Papers
Thomas Winston Papers
John R. Ziegler Papers

Bowling Green State University, Bowling Green, Ohio
James Wilson Davidson Papers
Robert S. Dilworth Papers

Chicago Historical Society Research Center, Chicago, Illinois
A. Achen Letter
George Smith Avery Papers
David Cleland Bradley Papers
Mason Brayman Papers
Alfred Clark Hills Papers
James Lawrence Papers
Clifford Stickney Collection
Throop-Vaughan Family Papers
Alfred H. Trego Diary

Cincinnati Historical Society, Cincinnati, Ohio
William E. Crane Diary
Frank Johnston Jones Letters
Henry A. Langdon Letters
Stanley Matthews Letters
Ormsby Mitchel Papers
Channing Richards Diary
Thomas E. Smith Family Papers
Harvey Scribner Wood Family Papers

Filson Historical Society, Louisville, Kentucky
Theodore F. Allen Civil War Diaries
Don Carlos Buell Papers
Stephen Gano Burbridge Papers
Corlis-Respess Family Papers
Dow Family Papers
Thomas Brooks Fairleigh Diary
George W. Gallup Papers
John Henry Hammond Papers
N. G. Markham Papers
Edward Irvine McDowell Papers
Moxley-Offutt Family Papers
Alfred Pirtle Papers
James H. Pratt Papers
Channing Richards Papers
Thomas Speed Letter Book
Speed Family Papers
Julius Caesar Stedman Letters
Luther Thayer Thustin Papers

J. H. Tilford Diary
Samuel T. Wells Papers
Winn-Cook Papers

Indiana Historical Society, Indianapolis, Indiana
Sue Beach Family Histories
William W. Blair Letters
Joseph W. and Orville T. Chamberlain Papers
Jesse B. Connelly Diary
Robert H. Crowder Papers
Jefferson C. Davis Papers
John H. Ferree Papers
Walter Quintin Gresham Collection
Grigsby-McDonald Papers
Alfred Heath Civil War Materials
James Leeper Papers
Caleb Mills Papers
Col. Bernard F. Mullen Family Materials
George W. Parsons Papers
Edward F. Reid Papers
Edward P. Stanfield Papers
Lew Wallace Collection
William Ward Diary

Library of Congress, Washington, D.C.
Abraham Lincoln Papers

Ohio Historical Society, Columbus, Ohio
John H. Bolton Diary
Ephraim Brown Papers
Brown Family Papers
Jacob Bruner Papers
Walter Carpenter Diary
Henry Otis Dwight Papers
Oscar Lumas Russell French Papers
James E. Graham Diary
William McKindree Heath Diary
Ephraim Holloway Papers
John D. Inskeep Diary
James Family Papers
William H. Kemper Papers
George W. Landrum Letters
William Henry Pittenger Diary
Nelson Banks Sisson Collection
James R. Stillwell Papers
Sturges Family Papers

Rutherford B. Hayes Presidential Center, Fremont, Ohio
Ralph P. Buckland Papers
Caldwell Family Papers
Orin O. England Papers
Wilfred Forester Papers
Jonathan F. Harrington Papers
James B. McPherson Papers
John B. Rice Papers
Alvah Stone Skilton Papers
Leander Stem Papers
Victor J. Zahm Papers

University of Michigan, Bentley Historical Library, Ann Arbor, Michigan
John Sidney Andrews Papers
Orlando Carpenter Papers
Henry S. Clubb Papers
John Corden Papers
Byron M. Cutcheon Papers
DeLand Family Papers
Ferry Family Papers
Morris E. Fitch Papers
Eli Augustus Griffin Papers
Hager Family Papers
Morris Stuart Hall Papers
Henry Mortimer Hempstead Papers
Rosanna Covey Hulbert Papers
McCreery-Fenton Family Papers
Elisha Mix Papers
Orlando Moore Papers
Charles Henry Moulton Papers
Nina L. Ness Papers
S. Jack North Papers
Jessie Phelps Papers
Henry Albert Potter Papers
Curtis Z. Pratt Papers
George T. Shaffer Papers
Slayton Family Papers
Sligh Family Papers
Harrison Soule Papers
Oliver Lyman Spaulding Papers
William Collin Stevens Papers
Nellie Swift Papers
William W. Van Antwerp Papers

William Herbert Withington Papers

U.S. Army Military History Institute, Carlisle Barracks, Pennsylvania

Leslie Anders Collection
Bailey-Stroud Papers
Robert H. Carnahan Papers
Eugene Carr Papers
Arthur L. Conger Papers
James E. Edmonds Papers
Perrin V. Fox Papers
George W. Gordon Papers
Hawkins-Canby-Speed Family Papers
Curtis J. Herrick Papers
Earl M. Hess Collection
August Valentine Kautz Papers
McPheeters Family Papers
Charles B. Smith Papers
Steele-Boyd Family Papers
Wiley Sword Papers
Henry Van Aernum Papers
Thomas Winston Papers
William M. Woodard Papers
Civil War Miscellaneous Collection
   Robert M. Addison Diary
   Anderson-Capehart-McCowan Family Collection
   George C. Burmeister Diary
   David Cornwell Memoirs
   John M. Eaton Letter
   John N. Eggleston Diary
   Jonas D. Elliot Papers
   Lucien A. Foote Letter
   Charles Foster Papers
   John Scott Lyle Papers
   William W. McCarty Papers
   C. C. Morrey Letters
   Joseph K. Nelson Memoirs
   Cyrus M. Roberts Diary
   Hosea Smith Letters
   Thomas K. Smith Letters
   Richard H. Watson Letters
   Edgar N. Wilcox Letters
   John B. Wilson Letters
Civil War Times Illustrated Collection
   Lyman Daniel Ames Diary
   George Bargus Diary
   Timothy Blaisdell Papers
   Eleazer B. Doane Letters
   Featherstone Collection
   Fulton-Lenz Collection
   John W. Greene Reminiscences
   John E. Hart Letters
   Andrew Hickenlooper Reminiscences
   Henry Hurter Diary
   Joseph J. Scroggs Diary
   Jerome Spilman Letters
   Eben P. Sturgis Papers
Harrisburg Civil War Round Table Collection
   George Shuman Letters
   Heber S. Thompson Diary
Lewis Leigh Collection
   William McAdams Letters
Northwest Corner Civil War Round Table Collection
   Frank Wells Letters

Western Reserve Historical Society, Cleveland, Ohio

William B. Britton Letters
Albert Gaillard Hart Papers
George Hurlbut Diary
Asa A. Lawrence Papers
Carlos Parsons Lyman Papers
Alexander Varian Letters
Edward A. Webb Papers

Wisconsin Historical Society, Madison, Wisconsin

Kelsey M. Adams Letters
Luther H. Cowan Letters and Diary
Henry Miller Culbertson Papers
Edward E. Dickerson Diary
Irwin Eckels Papers
Henry S. Eggleston Papers
Charles W. Felker Letters
Jerry E. Flint Papers
Frank D. Harding Papers
Benjamin Franklin Heuston Papers
Carlisle V. Hibbard Papers
Lucius Dwight Hinkley Papers
John Grey McDermott Letters

John Gibson McMynn Papers
William P. Moore Diary
"The Negro in the War,"
    Milwaukee Sunday Telegraph
Josiah A. Noonan Papers
Paine Family Papers
James Peet Diaries
Herbert S. Perry, "Prize Story"

Edward S. Redington Papers
Albert J. Rockwell Letters
Henry Clay Taylor Papers
Unattributed Newspaper Clippings—
    June and July 1862—
    from Scrapbook
"Veteran of Civil War," *Racine Journal*
D. S. Whyte Letter

Newspapers

New York Daily Tribune

New York Times

Government Documents

Congressional Globe. 46 vols. Washington, D.C.: Blair and Rives, 1834–73.

United States. *United States Statutes at Large*. Washington, D.C.: Government Printing Office, 1937.

United States War Department. *The War of the Rebellion: Official Records of the Union and Confederate Armies*. 128 vols. Washington, D.C.: Government Printing Office, 1881–1901.

Published Primary Sources

Addeman, J. M. *Reminiscences of Two Years with the Colored Troops*. Providence: N. Bangs Williams, 1880.

Anderson, Nicholas Longworth. *The Letters and Journals of General Nicholas Longworth Anderson: Harvard, Civil War, Washington, 1854–1892*. Edited by Isabel Anderson. New York: F. H. Revell, 1942.

Andrew, A. Piatt. *Some Civil War Letters*. Gloucester, Mass.: privately printed, 1925.

Ayers, James T. *The Diary of James T. Ayers, Civil War Recruiter*. Edited by John Hope Franklin. Springfield: Printed by authority of the State of Illinois, 1947.

Ayling, Augustus D. *A Yankee at Arms: The Diary of Lieutenant Augustus D. Ayling, 29th Massachusetts Volunteers*. Edited by Charles F. Herberger. Knoxville: University of Tennessee Press, 1999.

Beatty, John. *The Citizen-Soldier: Memoirs of a Volunteer*. Cincinnati: Wilstach, Baldwin, 1879.

Bennitt, John. *"I Hope to Do My Country Service": The Civil War Letters of John Bennitt, MD, Surgeon, 19th Michigan Infantry*. Edited by Robert Beasecker. Detroit: Wayne State University Press, 2005.

Bentley, William H. *History of the 77th Illinois Volunteer Infantry, Sept. 2, 1862–July 10, 1865*. Peoria, Ill.: E. Hine, 1883.

Berlin, Ira, Barbara J. Fields, Thavolia Glymph, Joseph P. Reidy, and Leslie S. Rowland, eds. *Freedom: A Documentary History of Emancipation, 1861–1867*. Selected from the Holdings of the National Archives of the United States. Ser. I, vol. 1: *The Destruction of Slavery*. Cambridge: Cambridge University Press, 1985. Ser. I, vol. 2: *The Wartime Genesis of Free Labor: The Upper South*. Cambridge: Cambridge University Press, 1993. Ser. I, vol. 3: *The Wartime Genesis of Free Labor: The Lower South*. Cambridge: Cambridge University Press, 1990. Ser. II: *The Black Military Experience*. Cambridge: Cambridge University Press, 1982.

Berlin, Ira, and Leslie S. Rowland. *Families and Freedom: A Documentary History of African-American Kinship in the Civil War Era*. New York: New Press, 1997.

Bickham, William Denison. *Rosecrans' Campaign with the Fourteenth Army Corps, or the Army of the Cumberland: A Narrative of Personal Observations with ... Official Reports of the Battle of Stone River*. Cincinnati: Moore, Wilstach, Keys, 1863.

Bosson, Charles P. *History of the Forty-Second Regiment Infantry, Massachusetts Volunteers, 1862, 1863, 1864*. Boston: Mills, Knight, 1886.

Bowler, James Madison, and Elizabeth Caleff Bowler. *Go If You Think It Your Duty: A Minnesota Couple's Civil War Letters*. Edited by Andrea R. Foroughi. St. Paul: Minnesota Historical Society Press, 2008.

Brackett, Charles. *Surgeon on Horseback: The Missouri and Arkansas Journal and Letters of Dr. Charles Brackett of Rochester, Indiana, 1861–1863*. Compiled by James W. Wheaton. Carmel: Guild Press of Indiana, 1998.

Bradley, George S. *The Star Corps; or, Notes of an Army Chaplain, during Sherman's Famous "March to the Sea."* Milwaukee: Jermain & Brightman, 1865.

Brinton, John H. *Personal Memoirs of John H. Brinton, Major and Surgeon U. S. V., 1861–1865*. New York: Neale, 1914.

Burbank, Jerome. *Jerome: To My Beloved Absent Companion; Letters of a Civil War Surgeon to His Wife at Home Caring for Their Family*. Edited by Sylvia B. Morris. Cullman, Ala.: S. Morris, 1996.

Burton, Elijah P. *Diary of E. P. Burton, Surgeon, 7th Reg. Ill., 3rd Brig., 2nd Div. 16 A. C.* Des Moines, Iowa: Historical records survey, 1939.

Butler, Benjamin F. *Autobiography and Personal Reminiscences of Major-General Benj. F. Butler: Butler's Book; A Review of His Legal, Political, and Military Career*. Boston: A. M. Thayer, 1892.

———. *Private and Official Correspondence of Gen. Benjamin F. Butler during the Period of the Civil War*. Compiled by Jessie Ames Marshall. 5 vols. Norwood, Mass.: Plimpton Press, 1917.

Byers, S. H. M. *With Fire and Sword*. New York: Neale, 1911.

Cadwallader, Sylvanus. *Three Years with Grant: As Recalled by War Correspondent Sylvanus Cadwallader*. Edited by Benjamin P. Thomas. Lincoln: University of Nebraska Press, 1996.

Campbell, John Quincy Adams. *The Union Must Stand: The Civil War Diary of John Quincy Adams Campbell, Fifth Iowa Volunteer Infantry*. Edited by Mark Grimsley and Todd D. Miller. Knoxville: University of Tennessee Press, 2000.

Carlin, William Passmore. *The Memoirs of Brigadier General William Passmore Carlin, U.S.A.* Edited by Robert I. Girardi and Nathaniel Cheairs Hughes. Lincoln: University of Nebraska Press, 1999.

Chase, Salmon P. *The Salmon P. Chase Papers*. Edited by John Niven. 5 vols. Kent, Ohio: Kent State University Press, 1993–98.

Chetlain, Augustus L. *Recollections of Seventy Years*. Galena, Ill.: Gazette, 1899.

Connolly, James Austin. *Three Years in the Army of the Cumberland: The Letters and Diary of Major James A. Connolly*. Edited by Paul M. Angle. Bloomington: Indiana University Press, 1959.

Cox, Jacob D. *Military Reminiscences of the Civil War*. 2 vols. New York: C. Scribner's Sons, 1900.

———. *Sherman's March to the Sea: Hood's Tennessee Campaign & the Carolina Campaigns of 1865*. New York: Da Capo Press, 1994.
Culver, Joseph Franklin, and Mary Culver. *"Your Affectionate Husband, J. F. Culver": Letters Written during the Civil War*. Edited by Leslie W. Dunlap. Iowa City: Friends of the University of Iowa Libraries, 1978.
Currie, George E. *Warfare along the Mississippi: The Letters of Lieutenant Colonel George E. Currie*. Edited by Norman E. Clarke, Sr. Mount Pleasant: Central Michigan University, 1961.
Curtis, Samuel Ryan. "'The Irrepressible Conflict of 1861': The Letters of Samuel Ryan Curtis." Edited by Kenneth E. Colton. *Annals of Iowa* 24 (July 1942): 14–58.
Daniels, Nathan W. *Thank God My Regiment an African One: The Civil War Diary of Colonel Nathan W. Daniels*. Edited by C. P. Weaver. Baton Rouge: Louisiana State University Press, 1998.
Demuth, Albert. *The Civil War Letters of Albert Demuth, and, Roster, Eighth Missouri Volunteer Cavalry*. Edited by Leo E. Huff. Springfield, Mo.: Greene County Historical Society, 1997.
Dodge, Grenville Mellen. *The Battle of Atlanta and Other Campaigns, Addresses, Etc.* Council Bluffs, Iowa: Monarch, 1911.
———. *Personal Recollections of President Abraham Lincoln, General Ulysses S. Grant and General William T. Sherman*. Council Bluffs, Iowa: Monarch, 1914.
Eaton, John, in collaboration with Ethel Osgood Mason. *Grant, Lincoln, and the Freedmen: Reminiscences of the Civil War with Special Reference to the Work for the Contrabands and Freedmen of the Mississippi Valley*. New York: Longmans, Green, 1907.
Engs, Robert F., and Corey M. Brooks, eds. *Their Patriotic Duty: The Civil War Letters of the Evans Family of Brown County, Ohio*. New York: Fordham University Press, 2007.
Fitch, Michael Hendrick. *Echoes of the Civil War as I Hear Them*. New York: R. F. Fenno, 1905.
Garfield, James A. *The Wild Life of the Army: Civil War Letters of James A. Garfield*. Edited by Frederick D. Williams. East Lansing: Michigan State University Press, 1964.
Geary, John White. *A Politician Goes to War: The Civil War Letters of John White Geary*. Edited by William Alan Blair and Bell Irvin Wiley. University Park: Pennsylvania State University Press, 1995.
Gilbert, A. W. *Colonel A. W. Gilbert: Citizen-Soldier of Cincinnati*. Edited by William E. Smith and Ophia D. Smith. Cincinnati: Historical and Philosophical Society of Ohio, 1934.
Grant, Ulysses S. *General Grant's Letters to a Friend, 1861–1880*. Edited by James Grant Wilson. New York: T. Y. Crowell, 1897.
———. *The Papers of Ulysses S. Grant*. Edited by John Y. Simon. 31 vols. Carbondale: Southern Illinois University Press, 1967–2009.
———. *Personal Memoirs of U. S. Grant*. 2 vols. New York: C. L. Webster, 1885.
Grierson, Benjamin Henry. *A Just and Righteous Cause: Benjamin H. Grierson's Civil War Memoir*. Edited by Bruce J. Dinges and Shirley A. Leckie. Carbondale: Southern Illinois University Press, 2008.
Grose, William. *The Story of the Marches, Battles and Incidents of the 36th Regiment Indiana Volunteer Infantry*. New Castle, Ind.: Courier, 1891.

Hartzell, John Calvin. *Ohio Volunteer: The Childhood & Civil War Memoirs of Captain John Calvin Hartzell, OVI.* Edited by Charles I. Switzer. Athens: Ohio University Press, 2005.

Hazen, William Babcock. *A Narrative of Military Service.* Boston: Ticknor, 1885.

Hedley, Fenwick Y. *Marching through Georgia: Pen-Pictures of Every-Day Life in General Sherman's Army, from the Beginning of the Atlanta Campaign until the Close of the War.* Chicago: Donohue, 1884.

Heg, Hans Christian. *The Civil War Letters of Colonel Hans Christian Heg.* Edited by Theodore Christian Blegen. Northfield, Minn.: Norwegian-American Historical Association, 1936.

Hepworth, George H. *The Whip, Hoe, and Sword; or, the Gulf-Department in '63.* Boston: Walker, Wise, 1864.

Hinkley, Julian Wisner. *A Narrative of Service with the Third Wisconsin Infantry.* Madison: Wisconsin History Commission, 1912.

Hitchcock, Henry. *Marching with Sherman: Passages from the Letters and Campaign Diaries of Henry Hitchcock, Major and Assistant Adjutant General of Volunteers, November 1864–May 1865.* Edited by M. A. De Wolfe Howe. New Haven: Yale University Press, 1927.

Hoffman, Wickham. *Camp, Court and Siege: A Narrative of Personal Adventure and Observation during Two Wars: 1861–1865; 1870–1871.* New York: Harper & Brothers, 1877.

Howard, O. O. *Autobiography of Oliver Otis Howard, Major General, United States Army.* 2 vols. New York: Baker & Taylor, 1907.

Jackson, Oscar L. *The Colonel's Diary: Journals Kept before and during the Civil War by the Late Colonel Oscar L. Jackson . . . Sometime Commander of the 63rd Regiment O. V. I.* Edited by David Prentice Jackson. Sharon (?), Pa.: privately printed, 1922.

Johnson, Richard W. *A Soldier's Reminiscences in Peace and War.* Philadelphia: J. B. Lippincott, 1886.

Johnston, Isaac N. *Four Months in Libby, and the Campaign against Atlanta.* Cincinnati: Methodist Book Concern, 1864.

Jones, Samuel Calvin. *Reminiscences of the Twenty-Second Iowa Volunteer Infantry.* Iowa City: Camp Pope Book Shop, 1907.

Kamphoefner, Walter D., and Wolfgang Helbich, eds. *Germans in the Civil War: The Letters They Wrote Home.* Chapel Hill: University of North Carolina Press, 2006.

Kinsley, Rufus. *Diary of a Christian Soldier: Rufus Kinsley and the Civil War.* Edited by David C. Rankin. Cambridge: Cambridge University Press, 2004.

Kircher, Henry A. *A German in the Yankee Fatherland: The Civil War Letters of Henry A. Kircher.* Edited by Earl J. Hess. Kent, Ohio: Kent State University Press, 1983.

Lennard, George W. "Give Yourself No Trouble about Me: The Shiloh Letters of George W. Lennard." Edited by Paul Hubbard and Christine Lewis. *Indiana Magazine of History* 76 (March 1980): 21–53.

Lincoln, Abraham. *The Collected Works of Abraham Lincoln.* 9 vols. Edited by Roy P. Basler. New Brunswick, N.J.: Rutgers University Press, 1953–55.

Logan, John Alexander. *The Volunteer Soldier of America: With Memoir of the Author and Military Reminiscences from General Logan's Private Journal.* Chicago: R. S. Peale, 1887.

Lyon, William P., and Adelia Caroline Duncotabe Lyon. *Reminiscences of the Civil War: Comp. from the War Correspondence of Colonel William P. Lyon and from Personal Letters and Diary by Mrs. Adelia C. Lyon.* San Jose, Calif.: Press of Muirson & Wright, 1907.

Lytle, William Haines. *For Honor, Glory & Union: The Mexican and Civil War Letters of Brig. Gen. William Haines Lytle.* Edited by Ruth C. Carter. Lexington: University Press of Kentucky, 1999.

Miller, Charles Dana. *The Struggle for the Life of the Republic: A Civil War Narrative by Brevet Major Charles Dana Miller, 76th Ohio Volunteer Infantry.* Edited by Stewart Bennett and Barbara Tillery. Kent, Ohio: Kent State University Press, 2004.

Miller, Edward Gee. *Captain Edward Gee Miller of the 20th Wisconsin: His War, 1862–1865.* Edited by W. J. Lemke. Fayetteville, Ark.: Washington County Historical Society, 1960.

Mitchel, F. A. *Ormsby MacKnight Mitchel, Astronomer and General.* Boston: Houghton Mifflin, 1887.

Morgan, T. J. *Reminiscences of Service with Colored Troops in the Army of the Cumberland, 1863–65.* Providence, R.I.: The Society, 1885.

Mosman, Chesley A. *The Rough Side of War: The Civil War Journal of Chesley A. Mosman, 1st Lieutenant, Company D, 59th Illinois Volunteer Infantry Regiment.* Edited by Arnold Gates. Garden City, N.Y.: Basin, 1987.

Moss, James W., ed. *A History of the Civil War as Presented by the Church Advocate.* 4 vols. Harrisburg, Pa.: Jim Moss, 2009–12.

Nichols, George Ward. *The Story of the Great March from the Diary of a Staff Officer.* New York: Harper & Brothers, 1865.

Opdycke, Emerson. *To Battle for God and the Right: The Civil War Letterbooks of Emerson Opdycke.* Edited by Glenn Longacre and John E. Haas. Urbana: University of Illinois Press, 2003.

Orendorff, H. H., et al. *Reminiscences of the Civil War from Diaries of Members of the 103rd Illinois Volunteer Infantry.* N.p., 1904.

Osborn, Thomas Ward. *The Fiery Trail: A Union Officer's Account of Sherman's Last Campaigns.* Edited by Richard Barksdale Harwell and Philip N. Racine. Knoxville: University of Tennessee Press, 1986.

Otto, John Henry. *Memoirs of a Dutch Mudsill: The "War Memories" of John Henry Otto, Captain, Company D, 21st Regiment Wisconsin Volunteer Infantry.* Edited by David Gould and James B. Kennedy. Kent, Ohio: Kent State University Press, 2004.

Paine, Halbert E. *A Wisconsin Yankee in Confederate Bayou Country: The Civil War Reminiscences of a Union General.* Edited by Samuel C. Hyde. Baton Rouge: Louisiana State University Press, 2009.

Palmer, John M. *Personal Recollections of John M. Palmer: The Story of an Earnest Life.* Cincinnati: R. Clarke, 1901.

Pope, John. *The Military Memoirs of General John Pope.* Edited by Peter Cozzens and Robert I. Girardi. Chapel Hill: University of North Carolina Press, 1998.

Porter, David D. *Incidents and Anecdotes of the Civil War.* New York: D. Appleton, 1886.

Porter, Horace. *Campaigning with Grant.* New York: Century, 1897.

Reinhart, Joseph R., ed. *August Willich's Gallant Dutchmen: Civil War Letters from the 32nd Indiana Infantry.* Kent, Ohio: Kent State University Press, 2006.

Richards, Henry. *Letters of Captain Henry Richards of the Ninety-Third Ohio Infantry*. Cincinnati: Press of Wrightson, 1883.

Ritner, Jacob B., and Emeline Ramsey Ritner. *Love and Valor: The Intimate Civil War Letters between Captain Jacob and Emeline Ritner*. Edited by Charles F. Larimer. Western Spring, Ill.: Sigourney Press, 2000.

Schofield, John M. *Forty-Six Years in the Army*. New York: Century, 1897.

Schurz, Carl. *The Reminiscences of Carl Schurz*. Edited by Frederic Bancroft and William Archibald Dunning. 3 vols. New York: McClure, 1907.

Scribner, B. F. *How Soldiers Were Made; or, the War as I Saw It under Buell, Rosecrans, Thomas, Grant, and Sherman*. New Albany, Ind.: Donohue & Henneberry, 1887.

Shanklin, James Maynard. *"Dearest Lizzie": The Civil War as Seen through the Eyes of Lieutenant Colonel James Maynard Shanklin of Southwest Indiana's Own 42nd Regiment, Indiana Volunteer Infantry*. Edited by Kenneth P. McCutchan. Evansville, Ind.: Friends of Willard Library Press, 1988.

Sheridan, Philip H. *Personal Memoirs of P. H. Sheridan*. 2 vols. New York: Charles L. Webster, 1888.

Sherman, Francis Trowbridge. *Quest for a Star: The Civil War Letters and Diaries of Colonel Francis T. Sherman of the 88th Illinois*. Edited by C. Knight Aldrich. Knoxville: University of Tennessee Press, 1999.

Sherman, William T. *Memoirs of General W. T. Sherman*. Edited by James G. Blaine. 4th ed. 2 vols. New York: Charles L. Webster, 1892.

———. *The Sherman Letters: Correspondence between General and Senator Sherman from 1837 to 1891*. Edited by Rachel Sherman Thorndike. New York: Charles Scribner's Sons, 1894.

———. *Sherman's Civil War: Selected Correspondence of William T. Sherman, 1860–1865*. Edited by Brooks D. Simpson and Jean V. Berlin. Chapel Hill: University of North Carolina Press, 1999.

Smith, George G. *Leaves from a Soldier's Diary: The Personal Record of Lieutenant George G. Smith, Co. C, 1st Louisiana Regiment Infantry Volunteers [White] during the War of the Rebellion; also a Partial History of the Operations of the Army and Navy in the Department of the Gulf from the Capture of New Orleans to the Close of the War*. Putnam, Conn.: George G. Smith, 1906.

Sosnowski, Madame S. "Burning of Columbia." *Georgia Historical Quarterly* 13 (September 1924): 195–214.

Spiegel, Marcus M. *Your True Marcus: The Civil War Letters of a Jewish Colonel*. Edited by Frank L. Byrne and Jean Powers Soman. Kent, Ohio: Kent State University Press, 1985.

Squier, George W. *This Wilderness of War: The Civil War Letters of George W. Squier, Hoosier Volunteer*. Edited by Julie A. Doyle, John David Smith, and Richard M. McMurry. Knoxville: University of Tennessee Press, 1998.

Stanley, David Sloane. *Personal Memoirs of Major-General D. S. Stanley, U.S.A.* Cambridge, Mass.: Harvard University Press, 1917.

Stevens, Thomas N. *"Dear Carrie—": The Civil War Letters of Thomas N. Stevens*. Edited by George M. Blackburn. Mount Pleasant: Clarke Historical Library, Central Michigan University, 1984.

Stevenson, B. F. *Letters from the Army*. Cincinnati: W. E. Dibble, 1884.

Taylor, John Thomas. *Reminiscences of Services as an Aide-de-Camp with General William Tecumseh Sherman: A Paper Prepared and Read before the Kansas Commandery of the M.O.L.L.U.S., April 6th, 1892.* Leavenworth, Kan., 1892.

Taylor, Thomas Thomson. *Tom Taylor's Civil War.* Edited by Albert E. Castel. Lawrence: University Press of Kansas, 2000.

Thompson, William G. *The Civil War Letters of Major William G. Thompson of the 20th Iowa Infantry Regiment.* Edited by Edwin C. Bearss. Fayetteville, Ark.: Washington County Historical Society, 1966.

Tourgée, Albion Winegar. *The Story of a Thousand: Being a History of the Service of the 105th Ohio Volunteer Infantry, in the War for the Union from August 21, 1862 to June 6, 1865.* Buffalo, N.Y.: S. McGerald & Son, 1896.

Tuttle, John W. *The Union, the Civil War, and John W. Tuttle: A Kentucky Captain's Account.* Edited by Hambleton Tapp and James C. Klotter. Frankfort: Kentucky Historical Society, 1980.

Underhill, Joshua Whittington. *Helena to Vicksburg: A Civil War Odyssey: The Personal Diary of Joshua Whittington Underhill, Surgeon, 46th Regiment, Indiana Volunteer Infantry, 23 October 1862–21 July 1863.* Edited by Christopher Morss. Lincoln Center, Mass.: Heritage House, 2000.

Vermilion, William, and Mary Vermilion. *Love Amid the Turmoil: The Civil War Letters of William and Mary Vermilion.* Edited by Donald C. Elder. Iowa City: University of Iowa Press, 2003.

Waddle, Angus L. *Three Years with the Armies of the Ohio, and the Cumberland.* Chillicothe, Ohio: Scioto Gazette Book and Job Office, 1889.

Wagner, William. *History of the 24th Illinois Volunteer Infantry Regiment (Old Hecker Regiment).* Chicago, 1864.

Wallace, Isabel. *Life & Letters of General W. H. L. Wallace.* Chicago: R. R. Donnelley, 1909.

Wallace, Lew. *Lew Wallace: An Autobiography.* 2 vols. New York: Harper & Brothers, 1906.

———. *Smoke, Sound & Fury: The Civil War Memoirs of Major-General Lew Wallace, U.S. Volunteers.* Edited by Jim Leeke. Portland, Ore.: Strawberry Hill Press, 1998.

Weller, Edwin. *A Civil War Courtship: The Letters of Edwin Weller from Antietam to Atlanta.* Edited by William Walton. Garden City, N.Y.: Doubleday, 1980.

Wiley, William. *The Civil War Diary of a Common Soldier: William Wiley of the 77th Illinois Infantry.* Edited by Terrence J. Winschel. Baton Rouge: Louisiana State University Press, 2001.

Williams, Alpheus S. *From the Cannon's Mouth: The Civil War Letters of General Alpheus S. Williams.* Edited by Milo M. Quaife. Lincoln: University of Nebraska Press, 1995.

Wills, Charles Wright. *Army Life of an Illinois Soldier Including a Day-by-Day Record of Sherman's March to the Sea: Letters and Diary of Charles W. Wills.* Edited by Mary E. Kellogg. Washington, D.C.: Globe, 1906.

Wilson, James Harrison. *Under the Old Flag: Recollections of Military Operations in the War for the Union, the Spanish War, the Boxer Rebellion, Etc.* 2 vols. New York: D. Appleton, 1912.

Online Primary Sources

Harris, Jordan Carroll. "Jordan C. Harris Letters." Civil War Voices, Soldier Studies. http://www.Soldierstudies.org (accessed February 13, 2012).

Library of Congress. "Map showing the distribution of the slave population of the southern states of the United States. Compiled from the census of 1860." http://www.loc.gov/resource/g3861e.cw0013200/ (accessed December 14, 2015).

Thrall, Seneca B. "Seneca B. Thrall: Union Letters." The Civil War Archive. http://www.civilwararchive.com (accessed May 8, 2012).

University of Virginia Library. "Historical Census Browser (1860)." http://mapserver.lib.virginia.edu/php/county.php (accessed December 14, 2015).

SECONDARY SOURCES

Books

Adams, George Worthington. *Doctors in Blue: The Medical History of the Union Army in the Civil War*. New York: Collier Books, 1961.

Ash, Stephen V. *Middle Tennessee Society Transformed, 1860–1870: War and Peace in the Upper South*. Baton Rouge: Louisiana State University Press, 1988.

———. *When the Yankees Came: Conflict and Chaos in the Occupied South, 1861–1865*. Chapel Hill: University of North Carolina Press, 1995.

Astor, Aaron. *Rebels on the Border: Civil War, Emancipation, and the Reconstruction of Kentucky and Missouri*. Baton Rouge: Louisiana State University Press, 2012.

Ballard, Michael B. *The Civil War in Mississippi: Major Campaigns and Battles*. Jackson: University Press of Mississippi for the Mississippi Historical Society and the Mississippi Dept. of Archives and History, 2011.

———. *Vicksburg: The Campaign That Opened the Mississippi*. Chapel Hill: University of North Carolina Press, 2004.

Barney, William L. *The Secessionist Impulse: Alabama and Mississippi in 1860*. Princeton, N.J.: Princeton University Press, 1974.

Barrett, John Gilchrist. *Sherman's March through the Carolinas*. Chapel Hill: University of North Carolina Press, 1956.

Berwanger, Eugene H. *The Frontier against Slavery: Western Anti-Negro Prejudice and the Slavery Extension Controversy*. Urbana: University of Illinois Press, 1967.

Bettersworth, John K. *Confederate Mississippi: The People and Policies of a Cotton State in Wartime*. Baton Rouge: Louisiana State University Press, 1943.

Blight, David W. *Race and Reunion: The Civil War in American Memory*. Cambridge, Mass.: Harvard University Press, 2002.

Boatner, Mark Mayo. *The Civil War Dictionary*. New York: McKay, 1988.

Brasher, Glenn David. *The Peninsula Campaign and the Necessity of Emancipation: African Americans and the Fight for Freedom*. Chapel Hill: University of North Carolina Press, 2012.

Bryan, Thomas Conn. *Confederate Georgia*. Athens: University of Georgia Press, 1953.

Burnham, Walter Dean. *Presidential Ballots, 1836–1892*. Baltimore: Johns Hopkins University Press, 1955.

Campbell, Jacqueline Glass. *When Sherman Marched North from the Sea: Resistance on the Confederate Home Front*. Chapel Hill: University of North Carolina Press, 2003.

Capers, Gerald Mortimer. *Occupied City: New Orleans under the Federals, 1862–1865*. Lexington: University of Kentucky Press, 1965.

Carey, Anthony Gene. *Parties, Slavery, and the Union in Antebellum Georgia*. Athens: University of Georgia Press, 1997.

Carwardine, Richard. *Lincoln: A Life of Purpose and Power*. New York: Knopf, 2006.

Castel, Albert E. *Decision in the West: The Atlanta Campaign of 1864*. Lawrence: University Press of Kansas, 1992.

Catton, Bruce. *Grant Moves South*. Boston: Little, Brown, 1960.

———. *Grant Takes Command*. Boston: Little, Brown, 1969.

———. *Never Call Retreat*. Garden City, N.Y.: Doubleday, 1965.

Cimprich, John. *Slavery's End in Tennessee, 1861–1865*. University: University of Alabama Press, 1985.

Connelly, Donald B. *John M. Schofield and the Politics of Generalship*. Chapel Hill: University of North Carolina Press, 2006.

Cooper, William J., and Thomas E. Terrill. *The American South: A History*. New York: Knopf, 1990.

Cornish, Dudley Taylor. *The Sable Arm: Negro Troops in the Union Army, 1861–1865*. New York: Longmans, Green, 1956.

Coulter, E. Merton. *The Civil War and Readjustment in Kentucky*. Chapel Hill: University of North Carolina Press, 1926.

Cozzens, Peter. *General John Pope: A Life for the Nation*. Urbana: University of Illinois Press, 2000.

———. *This Terrible Sound: The Battle of Chickamauga*. Urbana: University of Illinois Press, 1996.

Crenshaw, Ollinger. *The Slave States in the Presidential Election of 1860*. Gloucester, Mass.: P. Smith, 1969.

Crofts, Daniel W. *Reluctant Confederates: Upper South Unionists in the Secession Crisis*. Chapel Hill: University of North Carolina Press, 1989.

Cunningham, Edward. *The Port Hudson Campaign, 1862–1863*. Baton Rouge: Louisiana State University Press, 1994.

Current, Richard Nelson. *Lincoln's Loyalists: Union Soldiers from the Confederacy*. Boston: Northeastern University Press, 1992.

Daniel, Larry J. *Days of Glory: The Army of the Cumberland, 1861–1865*. Baton Rouge: Louisiana State University Press, 2006.

Danielson, Joseph Wesley. *War's Desolating Scourge: The Union's Occupation of North Alabama*. Lawrence: University Press of Kansas, 2012.

Donald, David Herbert. *Lincoln*. London: Jonathan Cape, 1995.

Downs, Jim. *Sick from Freedom: African-American Illness and Suffering during the Civil War and Reconstruction*. New York: Oxford University Press, 2012.

Dunkelman, Mark H. *Marching with Sherman: Through Georgia and the Carolinas with the 154th New York*. Baton Rouge: Louisiana State University Press, 2012.

Eicher, David J. *The Civil War in Books: An Analytical Bibliography*. Urbana: University of Illinois Press, 1997.

Einolf, Christopher J. *George Thomas: Virginian for the Union*. Norman: University of Oklahoma Press, 2007.

Engle, Stephen Douglas. *Don Carlos Buell: Most Promising of All*. Chapel Hill: University of North Carolina Press, 1999.

Fellman, Michael. *Citizen Sherman: A Life of William Tecumseh Sherman*. New York: Random House, 1995.
———. *Inside War: The Guerrilla Conflict in Missouri during the American Civil War*. New York: Oxford University Press, 1989.
Foner, Eric. *The Fiery Trial: Abraham Lincoln and American Slavery*. New York: W. W. Norton, 2010.
———. *Reconstruction: America's Unfinished Revolution, 1863–1877*. New York: Harper & Row, 1989.
Fox-Genovese, Elizabeth. *Within the Plantation Household: Black and White Women of the Old South*. Chapel Hill: University of North Carolina Press, 1988.
Franklin, John Hope. *The Emancipation Proclamation*. Wheeling, Ill.: Harlan Davidson, 1995.
———. *Reconstruction: After the Civil War*. Chicago: University of Chicago Press, 1961.
Freehling, William W. *The Road to Disunion: Secessionists Triumphant, 1854–1861*. New York: Oxford University Press, 2007.
Freehling, William W., and Craig M. Simpson, eds. *Secession Debated: Georgia's Showdown in 1860*. New York: Oxford University Press, 1992.
Freemon, Frank R. *Gangrene and Glory: Medical Care during the American Civil War*. Urbana: University of Illinois Press, 2001.
Gallagher, Gary W. *Causes Won, Lost, and Forgotten: How Hollywood & Popular Art Shape What We Know about the Civil War*. Chapel Hill: University of North Carolina Press, 2008.
———. *The Union War*. Cambridge, Mass.: Harvard University Press, 2011.
Gannon, Barbara A. *The Won Cause: Black and White Comradeship in the Grand Army of the Republic*. Chapel Hill: University of North Carolina Press, 2011.
Genovese, Eugene D. *Roll, Jordan, Roll: The World the Slaves Made*. New York: Vintage Books, 1976.
Gerteis, Louis S. *The Civil War in Missouri: A Military History*. Columbia: University of Missouri Press, 2012.
———. *From Contraband to Freedman: Federal Policy toward Southern Blacks, 1861–1865*. Westport, Conn.: Greenwood Press, 1973.
Gillette, William. *Retreat from Reconstruction, 1869–1879*. Baton Rouge: Louisiana State University Press, 1982.
Glatthaar, Joseph T. *Forged in Battle: The Civil War Alliance of Black Soldiers and White Officers*. New York: Meridian, 1990.
———. *The March to the Sea and Beyond: Sherman's Troops in the Savannah and Carolinas Campaigns*. New York: New York University Press, 1985.
Goodwin, Doris Kearns. *Team of Rivals: The Political Genius of Abraham Lincoln*. New York: Simon & Schuster, 2005.
Gould, Benjamin Apthorp. *Investigations in the Military and Anthropological Statistics of American Soldiers*. New York: published for the U.S. Sanitary Commission by Hurd & Houghton, 1869.
Grabau, Warren. *Ninety-Eight Days: A Geographer's View of the Vicksburg Campaign*. Knoxville: University of Tennessee Press, 2000.
Grimsley, Mark. *The Hard Hand of War: Union Military Policy toward Southern Civilians, 1861–1865*. New York: Cambridge University Press, 1995.

Guelzo, Allen C. *Fateful Lightning: A New History of the Civil War & Reconstruction*. New York: Oxford University Press, 2012.

———. *Lincoln's Emancipation Proclamation: The End of Slavery in America*. New York: Simon & Schuster, 2005.

Hahn, Steven. *A Nation under Our Feet: Black Political Struggles in the Rural South, from Slavery to the Great Migration*. Cambridge, Mass.: Belknap Press of Harvard University Press, 2003.

Harris, William C. *Lincoln and the Border States: Preserving the Union*. Lawrence: University Press of Kansas, 2011.

Harrison, Lowell Hayes. *The Civil War in Kentucky*. Lexington: University Press of Kentucky, 1975.

Hearn, Chester G. *When the Devil Came Down to Dixie: Ben Butler in New Orleans*. Baton Rouge: Louisiana State University Press, 1997.

Hess, Earl J. *The Civil War in the West: Victory and Defeat from the Appalachians to the Mississippi*. Chapel Hill: University of North Carolina Press, 2012.

Hewitt, Lawrence L. *Port Hudson, Confederate Bastion on the Mississippi*. Baton Rouge: Louisiana State University Press, 1987.

Hollandsworth, James G. *Pretense of Glory: The Life of General Nathaniel P. Banks*. Baton Rouge: Louisiana State University Press, 1998.

Holzman, Robert S. *Stormy Ben Butler*. New York: Octagon Books, 1978.

Howard, Victor B. *Black Liberation in Kentucky: Emancipation and Freedom, 1862–1884*. Lexington: University Press of Kentucky, 1983.

Hughes, Nathaniel Cheairs, and Gordon D. Whitney. *Jefferson Davis in Blue: The Life of Sherman's Relentless Warrior*. Baton Rouge: Louisiana State University Press, 2002.

Johnson, Michael P. *Toward a Patriarchal Republic: The Secession of Georgia*. Baton Rouge: Louisiana State University Press, 1977.

Josephy, Alvin M. *The Civil War in the American West*. New York: Knopf, 1991.

Kennett, Lee B. *Marching through Georgia: The Story of Soldiers and Civilians during Sherman's Campaign*. New York: HarperCollins, 1995.

Kiper, Richard L. *Major General John Alexander McClernand: Politician in Uniform*. Kent, Ohio: Kent State University Press, 1999.

Kolchin, Peter. *American Slavery: 1619–1877*. New York: Hill and Wang, 1993.

Lamers, William M. *The Edge of Glory: A Biography of General William S. Rosecrans, U. S. A.* New York: Harcourt, Brace, 1961.

Lause, Mark A. *Race and Radicalism in the Union Army*. Urbana: University of Illinois Press, 2009.

Lee, Dan. *Kentuckian in Blue: A Biography of Major General Lovell Harrison Rousseau*. Jefferson, N.C.: McFarland, 2010.

Lewis, Lloyd. *Captain Sam Grant*. Boston: Little, Brown, 1950.

———. *Sherman, Fighting Prophet*. New York: Harcourt, Brace, 1932.

Litwack, Leon F. *North of Slavery: The Negro in the Free States, 1790–1860*. Chicago: University of Chicago Press, 1961.

Long, E. B., and Barbara Long. *The Civil War Day by Day: An Almanac, 1861–1865*. Garden City, N.Y.: Doubleday, 1971.

Manning, Chandra. *What This Cruel War Was Over: Soldiers, Slavery, and the Civil War.* New York: Knopf, 2007.
Marszalek, John F. *Commander of All Lincoln's Armies: A Life of General Henry W. Halleck.* Cambridge, Mass.: Belknap Press of Harvard University Press, 2004.
———. *Sherman: A Soldier's Passion for Order.* New York: Vintage Books, 1994.
Marvel, William. *Burnside.* Chapel Hill: University of North Carolina Press, 1991.
McCormick, Richard Patrick. *The Second American Party System: Party Formation in the Jacksonian Era.* Chapel Hill: University of North Carolina Press, 1966.
McCrary, Peyton. *Abraham Lincoln and Reconstruction: The Louisiana Experiment.* Princeton, N.J.: Princeton University Press, 1978.
McDonough, James L. *Schofield: Union General in the Civil War and Reconstruction.* Tallahassee: Florida State University Press, 1972.
McFeely, William S. *Grant: A Biography.* New York: W. W. Norton, 1981.
McMurry, Richard M. *Atlanta 1864: Last Chance for the Confederacy.* Lincoln: University of Nebraska Press, 2000.
McPherson, James M. *Battle Cry of Freedom: The Civil War Era.* New York: Oxford University Press, 1988.
———. *For Cause and Comrades: Why Men Fought in the Civil War.* New York: Oxford University Press, 1997.
———. *Tried by War: Abraham Lincoln as Commander in Chief.* New York: Penguin, 2008.
Millard, Candice. *The Destiny of the Republic: A Tale of Madness, Medicine and the Murder of a President.* New York: Doubleday, 2011.
Miller, Edward A. *Lincoln's Abolitionist General: The Biography of David Hunter.* Columbia: University of South Carolina Press, 1997.
Mitchell, Reid. *Civil War Soldiers: Their Expectations and Their Experiences.* New York: Viking, 1988.
Mohr, Clarence L. *On the Threshold of Freedom: Masters and Slaves in Civil War Georgia.* Athens: University of Georgia Press, 1986.
Monaghan, Jay. *Civil War on the Western Border, 1854–1865.* Lincoln: University of Nebraska Press, 1985.
Moore, John Hebron. *Agriculture in Ante-bellum Mississippi.* New York: Bookman Associates, 1958.
Newell, Clayton R., and Charles R. Shrader. *Of Duty Well and Faithfully Done: A History of the Regular Army in the Civil War.* Lincoln: University of Nebraska Press, 2011.
Noe, Kenneth W. *Perryville: This Grand Havoc of Battle.* Lexington: University Press of Kentucky, 2001.
Oakes, James. *Freedom National: The Destruction of Slavery in the United States, 1861-1865.* New York: W. W. Norton, 2013.
———. *The Ruling Race: A History of American Slaveholders.* New York: Knopf, 1982.
Phillips, Christopher. *Missouri's Confederate: Claiborne Fox Jackson and the Creation of Southern Identity in the Border West.* Columbia: University of Missouri Press, 2000.
Potter, David Morris, and Don E. Fehrenbacher. *The Impending Crisis, 1848–1861.* New York: Harper & Row, 1976.

Prokopowicz, Gerald J. *All for the Regiment: The Army of the Ohio, 1861–1862*. Chapel Hill: University of North Carolina Press, 2001.

Rable, George C. *God's Almost Chosen Peoples: A Religious History of the American Civil War*. Chapel Hill: University of North Carolina Press, 2010.

Rainwater, Percy Lee. *Mississippi: Storm Center of Secession, 1856–1861*. Baton Rouge, La.: Claitor, 1938.

Ramage, James A., and Andrea S. Watkins. *Kentucky Rising: Democracy, Slavery, and Culture from the Early Republic to the Civil War*. Lexington: University Press of Kentucky, 2011.

Reidy, Joseph P. *From Slavery to Agrarian Capitalism in the Cotton Plantation South: Central Georgia, 1800–1880*. Chapel Hill: University of North Carolina Press, 1992.

Ripley, C. Peter. *Slaves and Freedmen in Civil War Louisiana*. Baton Rouge: Louisiana State University Press, 1976.

Rose, Willie Lee Nichols. *Rehearsal for Reconstruction: The Port Royal Experiment*. London: Oxford University Press, 1976.

Rubin, Anne S. *Through the Heart of Dixie: Sherman's March and American Memory*. Chapel Hill: University of North Carolina Press, 2014.

Scaife, William R. *The Campaign for Atlanta*. Atlanta: W. R. Scaife, 1985.

Schroeder-Lein, Glenna R. *The Encyclopedia of Civil War Medicine*. Armonk, N.Y.: M. E. Sharpe, 2008.

Shaffer, Donald Robert. *After the Glory: The Struggles of Black Civil War Veterans*. Lawrence: University Press of Kansas, 2004.

Shea, William L., and Earl J. Hess. *Pea Ridge: Civil War Campaign in the West*. Chapel Hill: University of North Carolina Press, 1992.

Shea, William L., and Terrence J. Winschel. *Vicksburg Is the Key: The Struggle for the Mississippi River*. Lincoln: University of Nebraska Press, 2003.

Siddali, Silvana R. *From Property to Person: Slavery and the Confiscation Acts, 1861–1862*. Baton Rouge: Louisiana State University Press, 2005.

Simpson, Brooks D. *Ulysses S. Grant: Triumph over Adversity, 1822–1865*. Boston: Houghton Mifflin, 2000.

Smith, Ronald D. *Thomas Ewing Jr.: Frontier Lawyer and Civil War General*. Columbia: University of Missouri Press, 2008.

Smith, Timothy B. *Mississippi in the Civil War: The Home Front*. Jackson: University Press of Mississippi for the Mississippi Historical Society and the Mississippi Dept. of Archives and History, 2010.

Stampp, Kenneth M. *The Era of Reconstruction, 1865–1877*. New York: Vintage Books, 1967.

Starr, Stephen Z. *Jennison's Jayhawkers: A Civil War Cavalry Regiment and Its Commander*. Baton Rouge: Louisiana State University Press, 1974.

Storey, Margaret M. *Loyalty and Loss: Alabama's Unionists in the Civil War and Reconstruction*. Baton Rouge: Louisiana State University Press, 2004.

Striner, Richard. *Father Abraham: Lincoln's Relentless Struggle to End Slavery*. New York: Oxford University Press, 2006.

Symonds, Craig L., and William J. Clipson. *A Battlefield Atlas of the Civil War*. Baltimore: Nautical & Aviation Pub. Co. of America, 1985.

Tap, Bruce. *Over Lincoln's Shoulder: The Committee on the Conduct of the War*. Lawrence: University Press of Kansas, 1998.
Townsend, William H. *Lincoln and the Bluegrass: Slavery and Civil War in Kentucky*. Lexington: University of Kentucky Press, 1955.
Trefousse, Hans L. *Ben Butler: The South Called Him Beast!* New York: Octagon Books, 1974.
Trudeau, Noah Andre. *Southern Storm: Sherman's March to the Sea*. New York: Harper, 2008.
Trulock, Alice Rains. *In the Hands of Providence: Joshua L. Chamberlain and the American Civil War*. Chapel Hill: University of North Carolina Press, 1992.
Voegeli, V. Jacque. *Free but Not Equal: The Midwest and the Negro during the Civil War*. Chicago: University of Chicago Press, 1967.
Wagner, Margaret E., Gary W. Gallagher, and Paul Finkelman, eds. *The Library of Congress Civil War Desk Reference*. New York: Simon & Schuster, 2002.
Warner, Ezra J. *Generals in Blue: Lives of the Union Commanders*. Baton Rouge: Louisiana State University Press, 1964.
———. *Generals in Gray: Lives of the Confederate Commanders*. Baton Rouge: Louisiana State University Press, 1959.
Waugh, Joan. *U. S. Grant: American Hero, American Myth*. Chapel Hill: University of North Carolina Press, 2009.
Weber, Jennifer L. *Copperheads: The Rise and Fall of Lincoln's Opponents in the North*. New York: Oxford University Press, 2006.
Weitz, Mark A. *A Higher Duty: Desertion among Georgia Troops during the Civil War*. Lincoln: University of Nebraska Press, 2000.
Welcher, Frank Johnson. *The Union Army, 1861–1865: Organization and Operations, the Western Theater*. Bloomington: Indiana University Press, 1993.
Wetherington, Mark V. *Plain Folk's Fight: The Civil War and Reconstruction in Piney Woods Georgia*. Chapel Hill: University of North Carolina Press, 2005.
Wiley, Bell Irvin. *The Life of Billy Yank: The Common Soldier of the Union*. Indianapolis: Bobbs-Merrill, 1952.
Winters, John D. *The Civil War in Louisiana*. Baton Rouge: Louisiana State University Press, 1963.
Woodworth, Steven E. *Nothing but Victory: The Army of the Tennessee, 1861–1865*. New York: Knopf, 2005.
———. *Sherman*. New York: Palgrave Macmillan, 2009.
———. *Six Armies in Tennessee: The Chickamauga and Chattanooga Campaigns*. Lincoln: University of Nebraska Press, 1998.

Articles and Essays

Adams, David Wallace. "Illinois Soldiers and the Emancipation Proclamation." *Journal of the Illinois State Historical Society* 67 (September 1974): 406–21.
Atkins, Jonathan M. "Politicians, Parties, and Slavery: The Second Party System and the Decision for Disunion in Tennessee." *Tennessee Historical Quarterly* 55 (Spring 1996): 20–39.
Blair, William Alan. "Friend or Foe: Treason and the Second Confiscation Act." In *Wars within a War: Controversy and Conflict over the American Civil War*, edited by Joan Waugh and Gary W. Gallagher, 27–51. Chapel Hill: University of North Carolina Press, 2009.

Bollier, Sam. "'Our Own Paradise Invaded': Imagining Civil War–Era East Tennessee." *Tennessee Historical Quarterly* 68 (Winter 2009): 391–410.

Bonner, James C. "Sherman at Milledgeville in 1864." *Journal of Southern History* 22 (August 1956): 273–91.

Byrne, William A. "'Uncle Billy' Sherman Comes to Town: The Free Winter of Black Savannah." *Georgia Historical Quarterly* 79 (Spring 1995): 91–116.

Capers, Gerald Mortimer. "Confederates and Yankees in Occupied New Orleans, 1862–1865." *Journal of Southern History* 30 (November 1964): 405–26.

Cockrell, Thomas D. "Patriots or Traitors: Unionists in Civil War Mississippi." In *Of Times and Race: Essays Inspired by John F. Marszalek*, edited by Michael B. Ballard and Mark R. Cheathem, 31–54. Jackson: University Press of Mississippi, 2013.

Copeland, James E. "Where Were the Kentucky Unionists and Secessionists?" *Register of the Kentucky Historical Society* 71 (October 1973): 344–63.

Dossman, Steven Nathaniel. "The 'Stealing Tour': Soldiers and Civilians in Grant's March to Vicksburg." In *The Vicksburg Campaign, March 29–May 18, 1863*, edited by Steven E. Woodworth and Charles D. Grear, 194–213. Carbondale: Southern Illinois University Press, 2013.

Drago, Edmund L. "How Sherman's March through Georgia Affected the Slaves." *Georgia Historical Quarterly* 57 (Fall 1973): 361–75.

Escott, Paul D. "The Context of Freedom: Georgia's Slaves during the Civil War." *Georgia Historical Quarterly* 58 (Spring 1974): 79–104.

Everett, Donald E. "Ben Butler and the Louisiana Native Guards, 1861–1862." *Journal of Southern History* 24 (May 1958): 202–17.

Fliss, William M. "Wisconsin's 'Abolition Regiment': The Twenty-Second Volunteer Infantry in Kentucky, 1862–1863." *Wisconsin Magazine of History* 86 (Winter 2002–3): 2–17.

Frisby, Derek William. "'Homemade Yankees': West Tennessee Unionism in the Civil War Era." PhD diss., University of Alabama, 2004.

Gallagher, Ruth A. "Samuel Ryan Curtis." *Iowa Journal of History and Politics* 25 (1927): 331–58.

Gienapp, William E. "Abraham Lincoln and the Border States." *Journal of the Abraham Lincoln Association* 13 (1992): 13–46.

Harrison, Lowell Hayes. "The Civil War in Kentucky: Some Persistent Questions." *Register of the Kentucky Historical Society* 76 (January 1978): 1–21.

———. "Lincoln, Slavery, and Kentucky." *Register of the Kentucky Historical Society* 106 (Summer/Autumn 2008): 571–604.

Hebert, Keith S. "'The Bottomless Pit of Hell': The Confederate Home Front in Bartow County, Georgia, 1864–1865." In *Breaking the Heartland: The Civil War in Georgia*, edited by John D. Fowler and David B. Parker, 127–49. Macon, Ga.: Mercer University Press, 2011.

Hess, Earl J. "Confiscation and the Northern War Effort: The Army of the Southwest at Helena." *Arkansas Historical Quarterly* 44 (Spring 1985): 56–75.

Horowitz, Murray M. "Ben Butler and the Negro: 'Miracles Are Occurring.'" *Louisiana History* 17 (Spring 1976): 159–86.

Howard, Victor B. "The Civil War in Kentucky: The Slave Claims His Freedom." *Journal of Negro History* 67 (Autumn 1982): 245–56.

Hubbell, John T. "Abraham Lincoln and the Recruitment of Black Soldiers." *Papers of the Abraham Lincoln Association* 2 (1980): 6–21.

Hunter, G. Howard. "The Politics of Resentment: Unionist Regiments and the New Orleans Immigrant Community, 1862–1864." *Louisiana History* 44 (Spring 2003): 185–210.

James, Josef C. "Sherman at Savannah." *Journal of Negro History* 39 (April 1954): 127–37.

Jones, Jacqueline. "Georgia Lowcountry Battlegrounds during the Civil War." In *Breaking the Heartland: The Civil War in Georgia*, edited by John D. Fowler and David B. Parker, 67–93. Macon, Ga.: Mercer University Press, 2011.

McCrary, Peyton, Clark Miller, and Dale Baum. "Class and Party in the Secession Crisis: Voting Behavior in the Deep South, 1856–1861." *Journal of Interdisciplinary History* 8 (Winter 1978): 429–57.

McDonald, Roderick A. "Independent Economic Production by Slaves on Antebellum Louisiana Sugar Plantations." In *The Slavery Reader*, edited by Gad J. Heuman and James Walvin, 486–506. New York: Routledge, 2003.

Mohr, Clarence L. "The Atlanta Campaign and the African American Experience in Civil War Georgia." In *Inside the Confederate Nation: Essays in Honor of Emory M. Thomas*, edited by Lesley J. Gordon and John C. Inscoe, 272–94. Baton Rouge: Louisiana State University Press, 2005.

Penn, James. "The Geographical Variation of Unionism in Louisiana: A Study of the Southern Claims Data." *Louisiana History* 30 (Autumn 1989): 399–418.

Prokopowicz, Gerald J. "Last Chance for a Short War: Don Carlos Buell and the Chattanooga Campaign of 1862." In *Gateway to the Confederacy: New Perspectives on the Chickamauga and Chattanooga Campaigns, 1862–1863*, edited by Evan C. Jones and Wiley Sword, 36–59. Baton Rouge: Louisiana State University Press, 2014.

Roland, Charles P. "Louisiana and Secession." *Louisiana History* 19 (Autumn 1978): 389–99.

Sheeler, J. Reuben. "The Development of Unionism in East Tennessee, 1860–1866." *Journal of Negro History* 29 (April 1944): 166–75.

Tapp, Hambleton. "Incidents in the Life of Frank Wolford, Colonel of the First Kentucky Union Cavalry." *Filson Club History Quarterly* 10 (April 1936): 82–100.

Turner, Martha L. "The Cause of the Union in East Tennessee." *Tennessee Historical Quarterly* 40 (Winter 1981): 366–80.

Turner, Wallace B. "Kentucky Slavery in the Last Ante Bellum Decade." *Register of the Kentucky Historical Society* 58 (October 1960): 291–307.

———. "The Secession Movement in Kentucky." *Register of the Kentucky Historical Society* 66 (July 1968): 259–78.

Vetter, Charles Edmund. "William T. Sherman: The Louisiana Experience." *Louisiana History* 36 (Spring 1995): 133–47.

Westwood, Howard C. "Benjamin Butler's Enlistment of Black Troops in New Orleans in 1862." *Louisiana History* 26 (Winter 1985): 5–22.

———. "Grant's Role in Beginning Black Soldiery." *Illinois Historical Journal* 79 (Autumn 1986): 197–212.

———. "Sherman Marched: And Proclaimed 'Land for the Landless.'" *South Carolina Historical Magazine* 85 (January 1984): 33–50.

Williams, Kenneth H., and James Russell Harris. "Kentucky in 1860: A Statistical Overview." *Register of the Kentucky Historical Society* 103 (Autumn 2005): 743–64.

Wilson, Keith. "Education as a Vehicle of Racial Control: Major General N. P. Banks in Louisiana, 1863–64." *Journal of Negro Education* 50 (Spring 1981): 156–70.

Film

Gettysburg, Blu-ray. Directed by Ronald F. Maxwell. Burbank, Calif.: Warner Bros. Entertainment, 2011.

Online Secondary Sources

Bell, Kelley, and Anne Sarah Rubin. "Sherman's March and America." http://shermansmarch.org (accessed December 14, 2015).

Inscoe, John C. "Unionists." *New Georgia Encyclopedia*. http://www.georgiaencyclopedia.org/articles/history-archaeology/unionists (accessed November 10, 2015).

Tennessee State Library and Archives. "Tennessee Civil War GIS Project." http://tnmap.tn.gov/civilwar/ (accessed June 11, 2015).

Woolley, John T., and Gerhard Peters. "Election of 1860." American Presidency Project. University of California, Santa Barbara. http://www.presidency.ucsb.edu/showelection.php?year=1860 (accessed November 16, 2015)

INDEX

Abbott, Charles, 116–17
Abolitionism: anti-abolitionist sentiments among officers, 63–65, 71–73, 78, 152; pro-abolitionist sentiments among officers, 23, 28–31, 42–43, 61–63, 66–69, 74–75, 78, 88, 102–3, 141, 145, 178n26, 188n49
Abolitionists, 26, 34, 44–45, 58, 74, 110, 121
Adams, Charles, 40
African Americans: citizenship and rights of, 50, 84, 102–5, 156; following Union troops, 46, 53, 133, 141–43, 145, 147, 150; and loyalty to the Union, 98; reaction to emancipation and presence of Union troops, 23, 86, 117, 122, 124, 142; recounting being freed by Union army, 20; seeking refuge in Union camps, 8, 30, 47, 49, 57, 113, 145; viewing Union army as liberators, 4–5, 46, 49, 117, 121–22, 139–42, 147–48, 150, 152, 154, 192n26, 194n51
—as serving Union army, 36, 42, 46–47, 49, 51–53, 86, 92–93, 98, 107–8, 118–19, 124, 129, 143, 149; building fortifications, 44, 47, 51–52, 107–8, 110, 115, 118, 121, 124, 129, 137, 155; building stockades, 51–52; as cooks, 47, 49, 54, 98, 107, 118, 124, 137; digging entrenchments, 44, 115, 136; as laborers, 38, 40, 44, 49, 107, 112, 115, 118–19, 124, 129–30; as nurses, 95, 118; as pioneers, 115, 118, 136–37, 140–41, 148; providing food and water for Union troops, 26, 92–93; providing military intelligence, 11, 20, 22, 24, 32, 38, 52, 92, 110–11, 116–17, 136–37, 142–43, 145, 148–49, 193n43; receiving wages, 44–45, 49, 94–95, 107, 119, 121, 136, 148; as servants, 11, 15, 20, 23–24, 49, 52–54, 83, 91, 94–101, 104, 107, 116, 118, 122–23, 136–37, 141, 148; as soldiers, 43, 78, 81, 115–16, 118, 122–23, 126–27, 130–31, 149; as teamsters, 47, 49–50, 107–8, 110, 118, 123, 136–37, 155; unloading Union cargo ships, 49. *See also* Black enlistment; Servants
Alabama: conflict over confiscation in, 22–24; employment of slaves in, 51–52, 110; political attitudes of people in, 21–22; slavery in, 21
Ames, Lyman, 94, 137
Anthony, Daniel, 26
Antietam, battle of, 127
Antwerp, William van, 72, 74, 110, 138
Arkansas: black enlistment in, 76–77, 95; early confiscation in, 37–39
Atkins, Smith D., 56–57
Atlanta campaign, 96, 99, 134–37, 160
Avery, George, 60–61

Bailey, Joseph, 45, 85, 89–90, 103
Baird, Absalom, 145, 149, 192–93n34
Banks, Nathaniel, 120–24, 173n21, 187 (nn34, 36, 37, 38, 39), 188 (nn39, 40)
Barry, A. C., 32
Baton Rouge, La., 44, 88, 121
Beatty, John, 22, 24, 61, 110
Beckwith, Amos, 140
Bell, John, 9–10, 27–28, 55, 112, 139
Bennitt, John, 87, 134

217

Black Codes, 156
Black enlistment: anti-enlistment attitudes, 27, 29, 43–44, 75–76, 79–81, 103, 136–38; and hostility toward officers of black regiments, 80–81; long-lasting nature of conflict and, 75, 136–38; pro-enlistment attitudes, 42, 43, 75–78, 82, 88, 95, 114–16, 127, 130, 136, 154–55; and recruitment, 29, 76, 114–16, 119–20, 122–23, 126–27, 130–31, 136, 138, 187–88n39, 188n49, 189 (nn60, 61); and slave impressment, 118, 122–23, 130, 189n57
Black suffrage, 50, 102–4, 156
Blair, Frank, 116, 148
Blair, William, 52
Boardman, Frederick, 65
Bolton, John, 24–25
Border South, 3, 10, 153, 195n2
Border states, 5–6, 36, 59, 64, 124
Bosson, Charles, 120–21
Bowler, James Madison, 61, 92
Boyle, Jeremiah, 127–30, 189n53
Brackett, Charles, 61–62, 86–87, 90, 95, 100
Braden, Robert, 119
Bradley, George, 92, 101, 143, 149–50
Bragg, Braxton, 44, 110–11
Bramlette, Thomas, 130–31
Breckinridge, John C., 10, 112, 135, 139
Britton, William, 49, 78, 97–98
Brown, Egbert, 127
Brown, Ephraim, 88, 113
Brown, John, 29
Brown, William, 24, 184n3
Bruner, Jacob, 78
Bryan, James, 119
Buckland, Ralph, 99, 190n4
Buell, Don Carlos, 8–9, 13, 20–21, 23–25, 50–52, 109
Burbridge, Stephen, 56, 130–31, 189n60
Burmeister, George, 70, 87, 90–91, 117
Burnside, Ambrose, 127–30
Burton, Elijah, 87, 150, 154
Butler, Benjamin, 9, 27–32, 34, 41–47
Byers, Samuel, 93

Caldwell, William, 63, 174n30
Cameron, Simon, 15
Campbell, John Quincy Adams, 69
Carlin, William, 16, 143
Carnahan, Robert, 11, 101
Carolinas campaign, 147–51
Chamberlain, Joshua L., 1
Chamberlain, Orville, 67, 99, 184n3
Charleston, S.C., 92, 148–49
Chase, Nathan B., 80–81
Chase, Salmon P., 22, 32, 50, 145–46
Chattanooga, Tenn., 109
Chickamauga and Chattanooga campaign, 109–11
Cincinnati, 58, 84
Clarksville, Tenn., 18–19
Clubb, Henry, 96
Cochran, J. C., 57
Coffin, Levi, 58
Columbia, S.C., 93, 149–50
Confiscation: conflict over, 8–59, 65, 128; as government policy, 36–37, 58–59; limited, 10–11, 18–19, 25, 29–30, 38–39, 50–51; as military necessity, 9, 22, 36–37, 59; in obedience to law/superiors, 9, 14, 45–46, 48; officer opposition to, 12–13, 19–22, 26–31, 33, 41–61 passim; officer support for, 12–16, 20–23, 30, 33, 36–37, 44–46, 55–57, 59, 61; as opposed to emancipation, 48; shift to more, 37–38, 58, 106–11; and slaveholders searching for runaway slaves, 14–15, 54; universal/aggressive, 19–20, 22–23, 26–31, 38, 41–49, 52–53, 56–58, 107–11, 125; in West, 8–9, 34–35, 154. *See also* Military necessity; Union officers
Confiscation Act, First, 8–11, 16, 18–19, 25–27, 35
Confiscation Act, Second, 11, 23, 35–39, 41–43, 45–47, 50, 53, 56, 60–61, 64, 107, 120, 124–26, 154, 188n47; importance of, in changing army policy, 3, 58–59
Congressional act forbidding return of slaves to owners, 18–19, 23, 33–35, 39, 57

Connolly, James, 74, 79, 85–86, 101–2, 141, 144–45, 192n32
Contraband camps, 4, 39, 43, 58, 72, 87, 90, 106, 108, 118, 124, 155
Cook, John, 14
Copperheads (Peace Democrats), 65–67, 177n17
Corden, John, 98
Cowan, Luther, 67, 78, 85, 87, 95
Crawford, John, 68
Crocker, Marcellus, 18, 119
Culver, Joseph, 72–73, 98
Currie, George, 78
Curtenius, Frederick, 33
Curtis, Samuel, 37–38, 41, 47, 125–26

Darr, Francis, 52
Davidson, James, 156
Davis, Jefferson C., 27, 73, 141, 143–46, 192n32
Deitzler, George, 112
Democratic Party, 9, 70, 73. *See also* Peace Democrats
Dickerson, Edward, 93
Dickson, J. Bates, 131
Dinsmore, John, 123–24
Dodge, Grenville, 11, 15, 26–27
Doolittle, Charles, 127
Doolittle, James, 24
Douglas, Stephen, 9, 107
Douglass, Frederick, 121
Dow, John Robert, 70
Duncan, William, 149
Dwight, Henry, 92

Ebenezer Creek, 144, 146, 192 (nn31, 34)
Eckels, Irwin, 78
Edwards, John, 40
Eggleston, Henry, 37–38, 94
Emancipation: division and conflict over, 60, 65, 73, 124; and historians, 4; limited emancipation policy, 113, 133, 137, 139–41; officer indecision about, 69–70; officer opposition to, 2, 12, 47–48, 50, 61, 63–65, 70–73, 79–80, 103, 127, 154; opposition to, during initial stages of war, 154; opposition to, of Northern public, 68–69; and policy in West, 2–4; pragmatic emphasis of, 3–4; and shift to more emancipationist policies, 106–32 passim, 154; support for, during final stages of war, 60–63, 65, 73–75, 106, 154. *See also* Union officers—and emancipation
Emancipation Proclamation, 3, 60, 65, 67, 82, 106, 117, 154
Emory, W. H., 123
Employment certificates, 118
Evans, Samuel, 104, 116

Fairleigh, Thomas, 131
Felker, Charles, 102
Ferree, John, 76
Ferry, William, 65, 71, 80, 90, 103, 155
Fifteenth Amendment, 156
Fitch, Michael, 74, 141
Forman, J. G., 39
Forrest, Nathan Bedford, 52, 78–79
Fort Donelson, 18, 49, 108
Fortier, Polycarpe, 30–31
Fort Monroe, 27
Fort Pickering, 47, 174n30
Fort Pillow, 79
Foster, John, 115
Fouke, Philip, 18
Fourteenth Amendment, 156
Franklin, William, 123
Fredericksburg, battle of, 128
Free papers, 37–39, 41, 47, 125–26
Fremont, John C., 5, 9, 12–13
Frick, Karl Adolph, 69

Gallup, George, 137
Gamble, Hamilton, 125
Garfield, James, 23, 68, 96, 99–100, 108
Garrard, Kenner, 137

General Orders No. 3, 5, 13, 17–18, 24–25; abandonment of, 46; difficulties executing, 14–16, 18–20
Georgia: Confederate desertion among soldiers from, 142, 190n7; emancipation in, 136–46; interviews of slaves from, 146–47; political attitudes of people in, 135, 138–39; and Sea Island order, 147; slave and slave owner evacuation from, 134–35, 191n18; slavery in, 135, 139
Gettysburg (motion picture), 1
Giddings, Joshua R., 65
Gilbert, A. W., 11, 20, 49
Gillmore, Evangelist, 94
Gillmore, Quincy, 55–57
Gilmer, Daniel, 68
Gordon, George, 11
Gorman, Willis, 79
Granger, Gordon, 10–11, 55–56
Grant, Ulysses S.: background of, 14; changing policies of, 169n12, 173n22; and conflict with officers over General Orders No. 3, 14–16, 18–19; defends Gen. Frederick Steele, 39; emancipation policies of, 111–16, 118–20; limited emancipation policy of, 113–14; and policies regarding slavery early in the war, 13–14, 18, 29; pro-emancipation sentiments of, 67–68, 111–12, 114–16, 119–20, 137, 174n30; pro-enlistment sentiments of, 78, 114, 118, 186n18; promotion to commander of Union armies, 134; relationship with black servant, 96; and support of free labor system, 49–50, 114, 118–19, 187n32; and support of Second Confiscation Act, 46–49; utilization of freed slaves, 116, 137; views on black citizenship, 50; views on black suffrage, 50, 156; views on emancipation early in the war, 13–14; views on race, 50; views on Reconstruction, 156; views on slavery later in the war, 118; views on Gen. Lorenzo Thomas's plantation labor system, 114. *See also* General Orders No. 3

Green, Albert, 98
Greene, John, 86
Greusel, Nicholas, 11
Grierson, Benjamin, 79, 88–89, 117
Griffin, Eli, 44, 89, 95
Grigsby, Bennet, 84, 115
Groesbeck, John, 11

Hall, Morris, 127
Halleck, Henry, 5, 8–9, 12–18, 20, 25, 29, 37–38, 113, 146
Hammond, John Henry, 79–80
Harker, Charles, 52, 110–11
Harrington, Jonathan, 84, 177n17
Harris, L. A., 21
Hart, Albert, 102
Hartzell, John, 89, 101
Hayes, Josiah, 40
Haywood, David, 38
Hazen, William, 96, 141, 148, 151
Hedley, Fenwick, 142, 151
Heg, Hans Christian, 19, 63, 73, 94, 98–99
Helena, Ark., 5, 76–77, 85, 95, 186n29
Hepworth, George, 122
Heuston, Benjamin, 58
Hickenlooper, Andrew, 141–43, 193n43
Hinkley, Lucius, 63, 80, 101
Hitchcock, Henry, 140, 144, 192n26
Hoffman, Wickham, 44–45
Hole, Henry, 67
Holloway, Ephraim, 52
Holmes, James, 15
Holt, Joseph, 131
Hood, Humphrey, 89, 96, 100
Howard, Jacob, 33
Howard, Oliver, 96, 143, 147, 150
Howe, Timothy, 33
Howell, Seymour, 102
Hunter, David, 29
Huntsville, Ala., 21, 110
Hurlbut, Stephen, 116
Hurter, Henry, 148

Illinois troops: Ninth infantry, 90, 95; Tenth infantry, 15; Eleventh infantry, 63–64;

Twenty-Fourth infantry, 24, 171n37; Forty-Fifth infantry, 85; Seventy-Seventh infantry, 56; Eighty-Second infantry, 141; Ninety-Second infantry, 56–57, 85; Ninety-Sixth infantry, 94; 104th infantry, 141; 123rd infantry, 141; 126th infantry, 116
Island Number Ten, 19–20

Jackson, Andrew, 44
Jackson, Oscar, 20, 49, 65–66, 95, 102, 143, 151
Jacobson, A., 127
Johnson, Andrew, 155–56
Johnson, W. S., 70
Johnston, Isaac, 93
Jones, Frank, 89
Jones, Samuel, 115

Kalfus, Henry, 70
Kansas troops: Seventh infantry, 26–27; Twelfth infantry, 40
Kellogg, Frank, 129
Kemper, William, 52, 62
Kennedy, Thomas, 40
Kentucky: black enlistment in, 130–31; conflict over confiscation in, 3, 14–15, 53–59, 128–30; decline of slavery in, 127–32; exemption from Emancipation Proclamation, 124; gradual emancipation in, 124, 189–90n61; impressment in, 130–31, 189n57; political attitudes of people in, 54–55; slavery in, 54; and Union army not interfering with slavery in, 12, 59, 127–28, 188n49
Kentucky troops: Third infantry, 90; Fourteenth infantry, 57
Kinsley, Rufus, 43, 79
Kircher, Henry, 95, 103, 186n24
Kirkwood, Samuel, 40

Labor contracts, 119, 121–22
Labor programs, 41, 45–46, 49, 58, 114, 119–20, 124, 147, 155; in Georgia, 147; in Louisiana, 45–46, 121, 173n21; in Mississippi, 114, 119, 124; in South Carolina, 147

Landrum, George, 22–23, 53, 62, 66, 92, 107–8
Lane, James H., 27
Latham, Robert, 66–67
Lawrence, James, 49
Lee, Robert E., 63, 134, 147
Lennard, George, 99
Lexington, Ky.: conflict over confiscation in, 57
Lincoln, Abraham, 8–10, 24, 39, 58, 65, 82, 109, 124–26, 129
Locher, Michael, 141
Logan, John, 77, 116, 149
Louisiana: black enlistment in, 43, 76, 121, 187n38; confiscation in, 9, 28–34, 41–45, 120; conflict over emancipation in, 70, 74; emancipation in, 120–24; impressment in, 122; labor project in, 45–46, 121, 173n21; secession of, 171n46; slavery in, 28, 74, 111
Lovejoy, Owen, 16, 57
Lower South, 6, 153
Lyon, William, 108

Maine troops: Twentieth infantry, 1
Manson, Mahlon, 127
March to the Sea, 138–45
Mason, Margaret Hunter, 20
McCarty, William, 85, 98
McClellan, George, 63
McClernand, John, 15, 18, 112, 115, 117
McCook, Alexander, 12, 23
McCreery, William, 93
McDermott, John, 70–72, 87, 121
McDowell, William, 64–65
McKinstry, Justus, 10–11
McMynn, John, 24, 71–72, 98
McPheeters, Rankin, 116
McPherson, James, 118–20
McQueen, John, 148
Memphis, Tenn.: black enlistment in, 116; labor program in, 47; Sherman in, 174n27
Michigan troops: Sixth infantry, 33–34, 44, 102; Eighth infantry, 136–37; Fourteenth infantry, 155; Eighteenth infantry, 56, 128–29; Nineteenth infantry, 87;

Index

Twenty-Second infantry, 57–58, 128–29; Twenty-Third infantry, 128–29

Midwest: attitudes regarding slavery in, 73, 83–84; soldiers' first impressions of African Americans in, 84–86; political attitudes in, 67, 73

Military necessity argument, 4, 9, 22, 25–26, 29, 36–37, 39, 41–43, 59, 66–67, 77, 106, 126, 194n2

Miller, Charles, 89, 92, 114–15

Miller, Edward, 84

Milliken's Bend, battle of, 75, 78–80

Mississippi: black enlistment in, 76, 78–79, 114–15; decline of slavery in, 119–20, 134; emancipation in, 111–20; labor project in, 114, 119, 124; political attitudes of people in, 112, 185n13; slavery in, 111

Mississippi Valley, 76, 134

Missouri: black enlistment in, 126–27, 188n49; confiscation in, 10–11, 39–41, 125–26; conflict over confiscation in, 3, 14–16, 36, 40, 125–26; decline of slavery in, 127; exemption from Emancipation Proclamation, 124; gradual emancipation, 126, 189n50; political attitudes of people in, 9–10, 40, 125–26; reasons for inclusion in study, 5; slavery in, 10

Missouri troops: Thirteenth infantry, 18–19

Mitchel, Ormsby, 21–23, 26, 51, 53

Mitchell, Robert, 26

Mitchel's division, 21–24, 53

Mix, Elisha, 89

Moore, Orlando, 129

Moore, William, 23–24, 61, 102

Morgan, Thomas, 80

Moulton, Charles Henry, 33–34

Mundy, Marc, 56

Murfreesboro, Tenn., 107–8, 184n3

Murphy, Robert, 16

Nash, Summer, 97

Nashville, Tenn., 20–21, 128–29, 134, 184n3

Nelson, Charles, 95

New Orleans, La.: conflict over confiscation in and near, 28–34; conflict over utilizing escaped slaves in and near, 43–45, 120, 123; political attitudes of people in, 27–28; slavery in and near, 28

Nichols, George, 140

North, Samson, 94

Northern public: attitudes regarding race, 157; attitudes regarding Reconstruction, 155–57; attitudes regarding slavery, 155

Oglesby, Richard, 14

Ohio troops: Second infantry, 23, 53; Third infantry, 22; Thirty-First infantry, 70; Forty-First infantry, 52; Seventy-Eighth infantry, 149

Opdycke, Emerson, 62, 73, 111

Ord, Edward, 117

Osborn, Thomas, 148

Osterhaus, Peter, 115–16

Otto, John Henry, 143, 147

Owen, Henry, 137

Page, Edward, 30

Paine, E. A., 16

Paine, Halbert, 32–34, 44, 80, 85–86, 101, 179n49

Paine, Nathan, 37, 95

Palmer, George, 49

Peace Democrats (Copperheads), 65–67, 177n17

Peck, Frank, 31

Pemberton, John, 116

Pennsylvania troops: Forty-sixth infantry, 137

Phelps, John, 15, 28–32, 42–44, 171 (nn53, 55), 173n17

Pirtle, Alfred, 23, 64, 74, 89, 101, 184n3

Pittenger, William, 143

Pope, John, 16, 19–20

Porter, David, 86, 88, 92

Porter, Horace, 96

Port Gibson, Miss., 78

Port Hudson, battle of, 75, 80, 95, 123, 179n49

Potter, Henry, 76, 90, 138
Preliminary Emancipation Proclamation, 36, 65, 68
Prentiss, Benjamin, 77
Provost marshals: role of, 41, 45, 118, 126–27, 131, 141; examples of, 10–11, 19, 125, 129, 174n30

Quarles, James M., 18

Radical Republicans, 104
Reconstruction, 105, 155–57, 194–95n9
Red River campaign, 87, 90
Reynolds, Joseph, 108
Rice, John, 62
Richards, Channing, 19, 49, 66, 75, 102–3
Richardson, John M., 15
Richmond, Va., 63, 93, 176–77n7
Riddle, Bob, 95–96
Ritner, Jacob, 74–75, 77
Roberts, Cyrus, 148–49
Robertson, George, 58, 175–76n47
Rockwell, Albert, 98–99, 119
Rogers, Samuel, 149
Rolshausen, F. H., 141
Rosecrans, William S., 68, 106–10, 124, 126, 184n5
Rousseau, Lovell, 24, 51, 53, 81, 134, 175n38

Savannah, Ga., 91–92, 101–2, 140–41, 143–46, 192n34
Savannah, Tenn., 18
Schofield, John M., 68, 103–4, 125–27, 188n47
Scribner, Benjamin, 100
Sea Island order, 147, 193n38
Selfridge, James, 137
Servants: officers bringing home, 95, 98–99; negative experiences of officers with, 101; positive experiences of officers with, 94–100; prohibited from using, 39
Seven Days' Battles, 63
Shaffer, George, 88, 98
Shanklin, James, 21
Sheiler, Daniel, 102

Sherman, Francis C., 69
Sherman, Francis T., 69
Sherman, Thomas W., 44
Sherman, William T.: anti-emancipation sentiments of, 12, 47–48, 103, 118–19, 133–34, 139, 151–53, 190n1, 194n51; and approval of confiscation, 12, 47–48; background of, 11–12; emancipation policies of, 136–41, 145–48, 150–52; encounters with African Americans, 140, 192 (nn26, 34); under fire from Washington, 145–47, 191n9, 193 (nn37, 38); March to the Sea, 138–39; military campaigns, 134–35, 147–48, 190 (nn7, 8); opposition to black enlistment, 12, 25–26, 79, 136–38, 191n9; proslavery sentiments of, 11–12, 47–48, 133–34, 169n7; role as liberator, 133, 138, 142, 147–48, 152, 192n26, 194n51; and Sea Island order, 147, 193n38; views on black suffrage, 103; views on contrabands as military burden, 133, 139–40, 143–44, 147–48, 150–51, 193 (nn37, 38); views on race, 48, 87–88, 134, 136, 145–46, 152, 191n9. *See also* March to the Sea
Ship Island, Miss., 28–29
Simms, Phoebe, 137
Sisson, Nelson, 99
Skilton, Alvah, 101
Slavery: in Alabama, 21; decline of, 118–20, 134, 153; distribution of slaves in West, 5–6; in Georgia, 135–39; in Kentucky, 54; in Louisiana, 28, 74, 111; in Mississippi, 111; in Missouri, 10; in South Carolina, 111; in Tennessee, 16–17, 109. *See also* Alabama; Georgia; Kentucky; Louisiana; Mississippi; Missouri; South Carolina; Tennessee
Slayton, Asa, 85
Smalls, Robert, 92
Smith, George, 121–22
Smith, Giles, 141
Smith, Hosea, 79, 88
Smith, Thomas E., 54, 97, 102, 108
Smith, W. S., 51

Snelling, David, 142
Soule, Harrison, 33, 76, 80, 88, 123–24, 179n49
South Carolina: abuse of slaves in, 149; decline of slavery in, 148; emancipation in, 147–50, 152; and Sea Island order, 147; slavery in, 111
Sparks, David, 60, 62, 117
Spaulding, Oliver, 71, 128, 178n26, 189n53
Spiegel, Marcus, 72, 74
Squier, George, 104
Stanfield, Edward, 77–78, 94
Stanley, David, 110
Stanton, Edwin, 22, 31–32, 40, 45, 51, 76, 103, 119, 129, 145–47, 193n37
Steedman, James, 136
Steele, Frederick, 38–39, 77, 114–15, 185n18
Steele, John, 18
Steele Bayou expedition, 88
Stem, Leander, 54
Stevens, Thomas, 70, 76, 84–85, 94, 113, 186n29
Stevens, William, 19–20
Stickney, Clifford, 75
Stillwell, James, 91
Stone, Charles, 123
Stoneman, George, 136
Stones River, battle of, 107

Taylor, Henry Clay, 71
Taylor, Thomas, 88
Tennessee: black enlistment in, 188n49; confiscation in, 46–53, 107–11; conflict over confiscation in, 18–19, 21, 26–27, 34; decline of slavery in, 68, 107, 134; encampment and employment of slaves in, 51–52, 107–8; exemption from Emancipation Proclamation, 107; political attitudes of people in, 17, 109, 170n21, 184n5; slavery in, 16–17, 109
Thomas, George, 137
Thomas, Lorenzo, 29, 76–78, 114, 136, 186n18
Thomas, Peter, 95
Thompson, Heber, 136

Thrall, Seneca, 66, 75–76, 113
Throop, George, 77, 88
Trego, Alfred, 141
Turchin, John Basil, 12

Ullmann, Daniel, 123, 187–88n39
Underhill, Joshua, 77
Underwood, J. R., 20
Union officers: and demographics, 163–64
—and African Americans: assisting, 38, 43, 58, 86–87, 96–97, 125, 137; attitudes toward women and children, 30, 39, 47, 49, 106, 108, 113, 119, 123, 136, 140, 143–44, 147, 150; cruelty to, 89–90, 119, 123–24, 129, 144, 149–50, 155; first impressions of, 84–86; positive impressions and relationships with, 83, 91–100, 137; prejudice toward, 2, 33–34, 42, 45, 83–90, 101–5, 136, 138, 155; sympathy toward, 19–22, 26, 29, 31–32, 50, 52, 58, 61–62, 66, 79, 86–87, 90, 100, 110, 140, 144, 150–51; viewed as military burden, 4, 12, 25–26, 49–51, 53, 55, 106, 113, 122, 133, 139–41, 143–46, 148, 150
—and confiscation: anticonfiscation among, 12–13, 15–16, 20–21, 23, 25–26, 32–33, 38–39, 55–57; arrests over fugitive slave policies, 26–27, 32–33, 56; and conflict over policies regarding fugitive slaves, 2–3, 8–9, 14–16, 18–35, 39–40, 51, 53–58, 128–29; confrontations with civilians, 57–58; criticism over early conservative policies regarding fugitive slaves, 15, 21, 23–27, 31–34; proconfiscation among, 19–22, 26–31, 33, 41, 43–44, 46–50, 52–54, 56–59, 61; refusal to return fugitive slaves, 24–25, 32–33, 51, 57, 128–29; resignations over anticonfiscation policies, 21, 42; resignations over proconfiscation policies, 64–65; returning fugitive slaves, 11–12, 15–21, 24, 26, 32, 39–40, 51, 53, 56, 154. *See also* Confiscation
—and emancipation: examples of abolitionism among, 23, 28–31, 42–43,

224 *Index*

61–63, 66–69, 74–75, 78, 88, 102–3, 141, 145, 178n26, 188n49; opposition to emancipation among, 2, 12–13, 47–48, 50, 53, 60–65, 70–73, 154; resignations over Emancipation Proclamation, 70; shift to more emancipationist policies, 36–37, 58, 65–66, 73, 82, 106–16, 126, 154; support of emancipation for moral reasons, 61–62, 68–69, 74–75; support of emancipation for practical reasons, 2, 4, 41, 66–69, 73–74, 82, 104, 106–7, 114–15, 124, 132, 134, 136–37, 147, 151–52, 154–55; views on racial equality, 102–4. *See also* Abolitionism; Emancipation; Emancipation Proclamation
Upper South, 5–6, 153
Utley, William, 57–58, 176n47

Vanlanigham, C. L., 67
Varian, Alexander, 70
Vaughan, Richard, 40
Vermilion, William, 68–69, 91–92, 112
Vicksburg campaign, 6, 32, 50, 77, 88, 111–20, 185nn12, 13

Wade, Benjamin F., 65
Wallace, Lew, 26
Wallace, W. H. L., 60
Ward, John Hardin, 81
Ward, William, 94
Ward, William T., 81
Waring, George, 15
Warner, Willard, 89
Washburne, Elihu, 46–47
Weitzel, Godfrey, 43–44

Wells, Frank, 42
Wells, James, 137
Wells, Samuel, 88
Western theater, 5–7; as central to emancipation story, 153; and change in army policy, 45; and early success in discouraging pro-emancipation policies, 25
Whig Party, 27, 54–55, 112, 138–39
White, William, 33, 75
White southerners: political attitudes of, 5–6, 9–10, 17
Whiting, John, 115
Widmer, John, 141
Wilcox, Edgar, 94
Wilder, John T., 110
Williams, Alpheus, 137, 145, 149
Williams, Thomas, 32–34
Wills, Charles, 20, 64, 85, 87, 90, 95, 135, 141, 143, 150
Wilson, James, 148–49
Wilson, James H., 88, 104, 111
Wilson, John, 79, 98
Winn, Robert, 80–81
Winston, Thomas, 57, 85, 95–97, 154
Wisconsin troops: First infantry, 37; Fourth infantry, 32–33, 44; Eighth infantry, 78; Tenth infantry, 23–24, 63; Twentieth infantry, 119; Twenty-First infantry, 53; Twenty-Second infantry, 58, 150
Wolford, Frank, 81
Wood, Thomas, 23, 50
Wright, C. J., 18

Ziegler, John, 63–64

www.ingramcontent.com/pod-product-compliance
Lightning Source LLC
Chambersburg PA
CBHW030648230426

43665CB00011B/1009